THE
ROSE
HOTEL

THE

ROSE

HOTEL

THE ROSE HOTEL

A MEMOIR *of* SECRETS, LOSS, *and* LOVE
from IRAN *to* AMERICA

❦

RAHIMEH ANDALIBIAN

■ NATIONAL GEOGRAPHIC

Washington, D.C.

Published by the National Geographic Society
1145 17th Street N.W., Washington, D.C. 20036

978-1-4262-1479-0

The National Geographic Society is one of the world's largest nonprofit scientific and
educational organizations. Its mission is to inspire people to care about the planet.
Founded in 1888, the Society is member supported and offers a community for members to get closer to explorers, connect with other members, and help make a difference.
The Society reaches more than 450 million people worldwide each month through
National Geographic and other magazines; National Geographic Channel; television
documentaries; music; radio; films; books; DVDs; maps; exhibitions; live events; school
publishing programs; interactive media; and merchandise. National Geographic has
funded more than 10,000 scientific research, conservation, and exploration projects and
supports an education program promoting geographic literacy. For more information,
visit www.nationalgeographic.com.

National Geographic Society
1145 17th Street N.W.
Washington, D.C. 20036-4688 U.S.A.

For information about special discounts for bulk purchases, please contact National
Geographic Books Special Sales: ngspecsales@ngs.org

For rights or permissions inquiries, please contact National Geographic Books Subsidi-
ary Rights: ngbookrights@ngs.org

Interior design: Melissa Farris

Printed in the United States of America

14/xxx/1 [Product code, TK from Managing Ed. once printer is awarded]

Author's Note

THIS BOOK WAS BORN OF MY NEED to uncover the truth about my life. This new edition of *The Rose Hotel* has been updated since I self-published it as a "true-life novel" in 2012. I chose that designation to protect the identities of family and friends in America and Iran, but since then, overwhelming support from my parents, brothers, and readers across the country spurred me to publish my story as a memoir.

In remembering and reliving my family's history I have sifted through old correspondence and photos, read contemporary news reports, and spent countless hours interviewing contacts and relatives. To protect the privacy of those who have shared their memories with me I have changed some names and compressed certain events. But in doing so, I've made sure not to compromise the essence of our story.

The water lily grows in a hostile, drowning environment—the water itself—in order to bloom. Once it reaches the sunlight, it rests calmly on the surface, its roots grounded in the murky water below. But the water lily does not drown. Instead, it blooms.

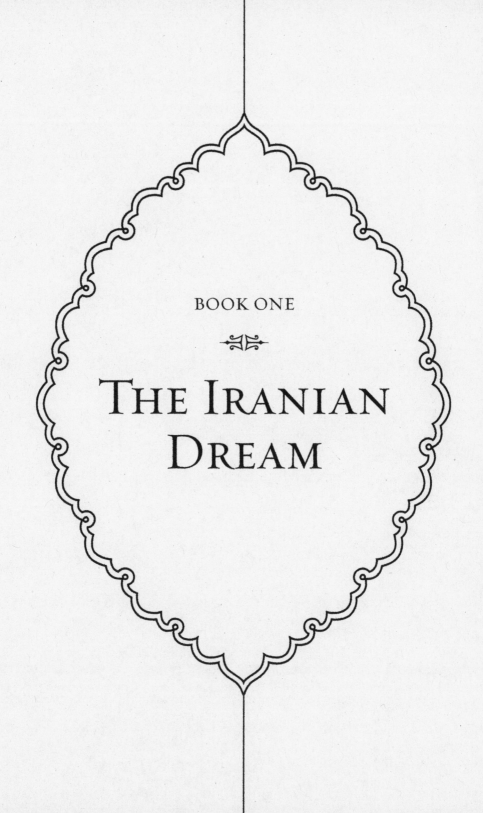

BOOK ONE

THE IRANIAN
DREAM

HIDE AND SEEK

❦

DECEMBER 30, 1978
Mashhad, Iran,

MY FATHER'S HOTEL WAS DESERTED.

I led my baby brother Iman down the long polished marble corridor. No one was watching us. Along with the guests, the staff had vanished—the doorman in his brown jacket with the gold buttons; the maids in their crisp white uniforms. There was no one to shout at us: "*Stop! You are not allowed in there . . .*" What we wished for all the short years of our lives was suddenly granted: The hotel was ours, a private castle playground.

We could slide, run, climb balustrades, and peek into the empty chambers. To a four-year-old girl and a two-year-old boy, the ten-story building had become an infinite indoor labyrinth: guest rooms, public reception areas, secret service nooks—even a banquet hall. We shed our plastic slippers at the entry and, wearing only socks, gathered speed as we slipped and slid on the slick marble floor. Our giggles echoed through the deserted hotel, the single sound.

At the tea and reception room, we paused to filch refreshments. We found the pistachio nougat candies hidden in the pantry, intended as treats for guests. Then, we made the most magnificent discovery of all: The ice cream was still in the freezer. Spooning the stretchy rose water, cardamom, and pistachio *Bastani-e Za'farāni* from the container, we licked our lips like kittens. I made note, for future reference, of a still-wrapped supply of chocolate-covered wafers in the freezer: Kit Kats, my favorite.

High from the sweets, we zoomed down to the basement. In the kitchen freezer, sheep and lamb legs were stored for hotel feasts. Now empty, the cold steel chamber held vapors that smelled faintly of missing meat gone bad. I grabbed the keys dangling from hooks on the wall. There was more to explore upstairs.

We boarded the elevator. Iman's fat little face was reflected in the brass panel, his bright eyes aglow with this new thrill. "Go ahead!" I encouraged. "Press 10."

Soon, we were zooming up to the top floor of the hotel, which we had never seen. We entered a sacred silence: the vast, empty banquet room, sparkling with crystal chandeliers. Heart pounding, I helped Iman drag ten tables together. We placed silverware in lines, creating highways and streets to form a small town. Soon, we were pushing our toy cars in our make-believe city.

Sometimes, Iman felt as much like my baby as my baby brother. My mother had become pregnant with him in the hope of giving me a little sister, buying me and the unborn infant girl-to-be matching tiny golden earrings. I ended up with two sets.

After Iman's birth, my mother had her tubes tied. In secret, I always gloated that he had not been another girl, but my own personal baby boy, sweet and peaceful as a little Buddha. He was always trailing after me, sucking candies and calling out: "Maman Rahimeh!"

We tiptoed past the prayer room, a bit chastened by the portrait of Imam Ali, the son-in-law of the Prophet Mohammad. His stern visage, topped in a black headdress, stared at us as if he could see our misdeeds. He was an animate shadow in our lives, demanding obedience. If we were caught disobeying, what would he do to us? It was too terrible to consider.

Deep in my secret heart, I knew someone would put a stop to this mad ride through the hotel, that we would be apprehended. But no one came. I led the next charge: We road the elevator up to the first floor and ran down the long main hallway, which seemed to extend forever to a vanishing point.

Not far away, men were yelling. From that other place—the great forbidden "Outside"—I heard a faint cacophony, the shrill sound of raised voices and honking car horns. I had no idea that my city, Mashhad—the second largest in Iran—was in the midst of revolt being waged just yards beyond the serene grounds of the hotel. All I knew was the safe cocoon of my family and the palace I inhabited.

As we ran down the hall, Iman and I sensed that something dark, something scary, was happening outside. We ducked behind the heavy tapestry hanging on the main lobby's wall and hid. Just a few seconds later, men stormed past, taking the stairs—their steps pounding all the way to the third floor. Someone paused, stopped. I could feel him—a heaving presence on the other side of the wall hanging.

I held my breath. "Shhh . . ." I whispered to Iman. But it was too late. He let out a baby squeak of fear.

A big hand pushed open the tapestry.

I looked into dark, burning eyes, magnified by black-rimmed eyeglasses—Baba.

Our father scooped up Iman and grabbed my hand. There was no time to scold us for breaking the rules. Baba took us through the side door, set down Iman, and said, "Quick, run . . . into the house!"

And we did.

From the outside, we heard the sounds of chanting and breaking glass. Baba watched us cross the hotel lawn until I pushed open the heavy gate to our home and shooed Iman inside. It shut with a clang, dividing our lives into before and after.

THE LAST
MORNING

❦

DECEMBER 29, 1978
(one day earlier)

THE ROSE HOTEL AND I shared a rare destiny: I was born the day it opened, and our fates were forever linked. Each year, for our birthday celebrations, sheep were sacrificed and fed to the poor; the Qur'an was read, placed upon a mirror.

The hotel had been an immediate success. Its location had been selected for one reason: pilgrimage. Founded to serve visitors to the city of Mashhad, the place of martyrdom, it was built a few minutes from the city's most celebrated holy landmark, the *Haram*. A great mosque with a complex of seven courtyards, 14 minarets and fountains, a museum, a library, and four seminaries under a dazzling golden dome, the Haram is second only to Mecca in the world, and is sacred to Shi'a Muslims. Even as a child, I felt its force field; it exerted a supernatural energy over Mashhad, and an even stronger pull over my family.

The shrine was named for the eighth descendent of the Prophet Mohammed, Imam Reza. Because of its holiness, Muslims from all over Iran and the four corners of the world made pilgrimages there. The most prosperous stayed at the Rose Hotel, known for its religious owner and his impeccable reputation.

As a child, I found the mosque a dazzling place; at almost 700,000 square feet, its crystalline ceiling seemed to soar as high as the sky. To enter, we removed our shoes, which were accepted by rows of men, known as "shoe collectors," who performed this service without pay, as an honor, to serve Allah. Our shoes were stored in shelves with numbers, and we would reclaim them to step back outside into the blazing sun of the ordinary world.

Back then, I didn't know the area was also the setting for an early violent resistance against Reza Shah Pahlavi and his regime's increasing bias toward the West. I also didn't know that my father, my Baba, had struggled to get approval from city officials and secure loans for this "religious tourist hotel."

At four years old, all I knew was the cloistered world of the hotel and the garden of roses for which it was named. The borders of my life were defined by two buildings—home and hotel—edged by trim topiary hedges. A driveway rounded and connected the two, but the house was almost hidden, accessible only from the outside by a separate set of heavy keys.

How often I skipped for joy along that driveway from one pleasure dome to another. In summer, the hotel grounds were aromatic with roses and jasmine; in winter, they were filled with the sweet scent of snow. Our backyard held a small farm and garden. Chickens ran everywhere. In season, the hens lay brown eggs as gifts that we found as if on a treasure hunt. Vegetables—carrots and greens—grew in my mother's—my Maman's—garden. I was not allowed to venture alone beyond the border of the hotel property. But there was no need for me to explore beyond; life was complete within.

Our Rose Hotel stood ten stories high, with its proud sign on the top floor: "Without Music and Alcoholic Beverages." Often, a nightingale would perch on the sign—a good omen, since it is the meaning of our last name.

I can still inhale the perfume of cardamom rising from the samovar as Maman pours tea, the aroma of the fresh baked *Barbari* bread. Maman looks so beautiful. The steam makes her hair curl into wisps that cling to her smooth forehead; her rose-petal lips smile as she regards her children. At 32, she is still young and shapely for a mother of five; even her house chador, soft blue floral cotton, suggests her curves. In the house, she is not hidden under the great heavy black robe and head draping of the outdoor chador.

The steaming tea and baking Barbari bread warm the room. It is a winter breakfast; I remember that well. The corner heater glows with its orange filament fire. We have never been cold, never suffered "the Outside."

The details come back to me in fragments, like pieces of a broken mirror. Gathered around the *sofreh*—the soft plastic tablecloth on which we ate our meals—our family reflected different mixtures of looks and personality: the combinations of Maman and Baba. Three of my four brothers were there: Hadi, ten, Zain, six, and Iman, two. The boys giggled and joked. We were all anticipating the imminent arrival of our brother, Abdollah. At 15, and the eldest, he was the acknowledged star of our family constellation.

We were all the genetic reflections of our parents. Zain and Iman inherited Maman's beauty: her perfect dark eyebrows, those black almond eyes. Hadi and I were a combination that showed more of Baba: wilder dark eyebrows, bigger Iranian noses. Abdollah was the tallest and exuberated the best of both our parents: He had Baba's thick hair and the fine beautiful lips and gentle gaze of Maman. From his brilliant black eyes shone both Baba's authority and Maman's gentleness: the two emotions that dominated our lives.

We were all so eager to see Abdollah that morning. When at last he entered the room, we squealed in delight:

"Dadashi! Dadashi!"

Dadashi, the traditional nickname of big brothers, fit Abdollah so well; he gave off sparks of energy and charm like the name. He appeared in a great rush, and with a dazzle that seemed glamorous to us children. He was so handsome—fresh from the shower, his hair perfectly gelled. He wore Western clothes—a tight-fitting, shiny polyester shirt with a geometric design and large bell-bottom pants. Even though his clothes are modern, he was still within the boundaries of Muslim custom: Unlike the wilder boys who had gone too far, his top shirt button was closed. I will have reason to remember that detail later, afterward. It's so strange, how a life can hinge on something so small: a button. But, as a little girl I could still enjoy Abdollah, rejoice in him.

He bent to kiss us.

The night before, after a pillow fight, Abdollah tucked the four of us into bed, pulling the sheet to our chins. To Iman and me, he whispered, *"Jigar-a-meen"*—"you are so dear to me"—before kissing our foreheads and cleaning up our toys so the maid would have less to do. This was Abdollah's nightly routine after a long day that began before dawn to pray, attend school, then work at the hotel. His job was to greet guests, take orders, oversee the switchboard, act as concierge, do my father's books, and manage our family's car parts shop next door.

At 15, many Iranian boys are considered men, ready to work and to settle down with a family. Many join their fathers in the family business; their opinions and interests reflect this, since young children are often included in adult conversations. Fifteen is also the age when Muslim boys formally become adults in the eyes of Islamic tradition: They are responsible for praying, fasting, and abiding by Islamic rules.

Maman registered a sigh of pleasure at the sight of her children as she fed us bites of Babari bread, spread with sweet, creamery butter. Iman and I held hands as we sat cross-legged with our knees touching at the sofreh; Hadi and Zain played with their toy cars across from us. Hadi, being older, observed us in a paternal way. In the center of the sofreh was a vivid still life—a platter of fresh cut red watermelon, bowls of scarlet pomegranate kernels, ripe peaches, and yellow cherries. Maman rose from the sofreh, and accepted Abdollah's kiss on her cheek.

When Baba returned from the hotel to share breakfast with us, he sat next to Maman on the floor. Baba's presence was immense but kind; his voice deep and reverberating. He was immaculate in his pressed, gray business suit. I knew that even his undershirt was ironed. He smelled vaguely of the laundry starch and all that is clean, like sunshine. He gently kissed Maman's neck.

"*Bas-seh*, not in front of the kids," Maman whispered, tilting her head away and smiling. They were still young and happy. They fell in love when they married—Maman at 14 and Baba at 19—and felt blessed with us five children. While we all pretended to focus on our quince jam and orange slices, we watched and laughed as Baba snuck another kiss, tickling her side.

Baba is as handsome as Maman is lovely. He is a big man, a protector, a leader. He is the source of our wealth and safety; even as little girl, I sensed that Baba was the reason our life was good. We had two drivers, four maids, 25 chickens, a rooster, and daily deliveries of fresh fruit and bread. We led no ordinary life; we took vacations throughout the world, traveling through West Asia and the greater Middle East. We had been to places like Lebanon, Syria, Iraq, Kuwait, Turkey, and the holiest of places, Mecca and Medina.

At the sofreh, Baba turned to Abdollah as they began to talk of the day's business. He offered Abdollah the freshest bites of feta cheese and the crispiest *sangak* flatbread. Then, as he always did, he wrapped his arm around Abdollah's neck and kissed his forehead.

We waved to Abdollah and Baba as they stopped at the front door to put on their shoes and walk, side by side, to the Rose Hotel. Abdollah carried Baba's briefcase.

Then the phone rang. It was the Grand Ayatollah.

That night, I was awakened from a strange and uneasy sleep by the sound of voices on the other side of the bedroom wall. I sat up in bed, my heart hammering. First, Maman's low murmur: "Not here, not in our hotel. We have a daughter! And the woman they took was older than I am!" Then Baba's voice: "Hush, woman! No more talk, the children might wake up." More urgent whispering. The only other phrase I could make out were the words "Room 314."

The Naked Woman in the Snow

❦

Kilometers away, while we were finishing our breakfast, an elderly woman regained consciousness, shocked by her incomprehensible condition. Her skin was dark with frostbite and bruises. She could taste blood in her mouth, feel the jagged edges where her lips were torn, her teeth broken. And from deep within her, the worst pain of all.

She stared at the hunks of hair and bloodied scalp that rested near her head, then recognized them as her own. She could not stand; her ankle twisted under her. Naked and numb, she began to crawl toward a distant light. Around her, the snow fell, whispering as if in pity—or complicity.

The snow had nearly covered the misdeed, and her body. Yet some willpower remained, and slowly, she continued toward the distant doorway, where the light and curlicue wrought-iron gate offered a possible sanctuary. Her only thought was the prayer that she would live to see her husband and children once more. To her, the world had already ended; she could not have known that it was also ending for many thousands of others. She had only been one of the first.

Bit by bit, the previous evening came back. After spending six hours in an Islamic religious ceremony at a friend's home, the woman had welcomed the cool wind as she walked out onto the street. A rose-violet light filtered through the falling snow.

The heavy fabric of her black chador was now damp as she walked in the quiet night, accompanied only by the moonlight, faint as a shred of gauze. Passing between bare trees, branches now outlined in white, the woman left a trail of footprints in the snow. Her eyes began to water from the wind, and she clutched her chador to keep it closed. Through the blur of snow, she could see the glow of lamplight only half a block ahead. She relished the thought of her warm home; there would be hot food, the embraces of her family, kisses on her cheeks.

Then she heard the engine behind her. She pulled the chador even tighter; in the past six months, there had been so much unrest. Lootings and assaults had become more common.

"*Ya Allah* . . ." she whispered, her prayer rising up as vapor in the cold night air. God would keep her safe. This was, after all, her childhood neighborhood. Suddenly, she heard the sound of the car's tires braking. Startled, she slipped on the icy pavement; when she tried to stand, her ankle buckled under her, broken or sprained.

When she didn't hear the car doors close—only the sound of the engine and footsteps behind her—she turned, hoping a neighbor was stopping to help her. But silhouetted in the headlights of a Paykan car, two teenage boys were coming toward her. The taller one pulled a whiskey bottle from behind him and slammed it on the wall near her head, shattering the bottleneck. As they approached, a scream rose in her throat, but somehow she could not make a sound.

"What are you afraid of, sexy lady?" asked one of the boys. He couldn't have been more than 17.

"*Salaam.* I have a grandson your age," she said, a survival reflex. "Perhaps you know him? Ali? He is a good boy, as I'm sure you both are." The stench of alcohol on the boys' breath reached her nostrils and her throat burned.

"Don't be afraid of us," the smaller boy said. He came close. She could smell his hair: unwashed, long, and stringy with grease. He offered her the broken whiskey bottle, as if encouraging her to drink. She pulled the chador tighter around her, exposing only a sliver of one eye.

"You don't want to have fun with us? Come on, we just want to talk to you about God!"

She tried to stand, but collapsed, her newly twisted ankle anchoring her in place.

Taking a drink from a whiskey bottle in his other hand and waving the broken bottle in the air, the boy put his foot in front of her, blocking any move, and pushed her. She was on the ground—trapped.

"Where are you going? You too good for us? Too godly?" he asked.

He raised the heavy glass bottle and slammed it against the back of her head. She felt her mouth force shut with the impact, involuntarily biting her tongue. Blood surged in her mouth.

"We're inviting you to a party. I said, take a drink!" the other boy hissed, pinning her arms to the icy ground.

She struggled to push the boys away. As the taller of the two pushed the broken bottle against her mouth, she began to retch. Her resistance and his drunkenness made his first attempts unsuccessful, but he did not stop until he was able to force the strong brown liquid down her throat. The force of the bottle's impact broke her jaw; she heard her teeth crack, and screamed as the jagged edges of the glass tore her lips.

They dragged her, gagging and choking, and threw her into the trunk of the car. As she fell, through the red blur of pain, she caught a glimpse of her house—the white-decorated gate, the glow of light reflecting on the snow. In front, a stray dog gazed at her, the only witness.

After a cold, bumpy car ride, in which she drifted in and out of consciousness, the boys hauled the woman out of the trunk and dumped her on the ground. She landed on her back, hard against the snow-packed road. She tried to scream, but the boys crammed her chador in her mouth. They pulled at her clothes; she could feel her bare skin against the cold earth. She tried to cover her nakedness, the boys kicking and punching her body as if she were already dead.

At last, when she was almost unconscious, they held down her legs, and parted them wide. Then, one after the other, the boys shoved themselves inside her. They panted like animals; she felt their hot breath in her face.

The woman closed her eyes, picturing the smiles of her husband and grandchildren. She had never known any man but her husband, in the sacredness of their long marriage. At last, the boys—hot and bloodied—were finished with her.

When she heard the car speed away, her body began to shiver and convulse. She thought she was dying. But then, the convulsions stopped. For a moment, she turned to her side and opened her eyes, trying to focus on the moon, now half covered. Then everything went black.

Dawn broke; the woman had managed to crawl, inch by bloodied inch, toward the dim lights ahead that promised a possible sanctuary. When she reached the doorstep of the first house, she rang the doorbell before she fell into a fetal position, curling her knees to her chest to cover herself.

The woman who answered the door screamed, and at once removed her own chador to cover the stranger's nakedness. With gentle hands, she pulled the wounded woman inside her house and began to clean her, murmuring that she would be all right.

The woman, almost unconscious, flinched when her protector brought the warm washcloth toward her ripped mouth. "Time and God will heal you," she whispered. Wrapping her in a cashmere blanket, she rushed to the black rotary phone and dialed the number of someone important: the Grand Ayatollah.

BABA

Two nights earlier, Baba had witnessed a confrontation in front of the Rose Hotel that he dismissed as "an incident." He imagined that he had headed off the conflict, not comprehending the larger implications.

Hostilities had been building with the government ever since Baba had openly denied the shah's political cronies access to the Rose Hotel. His reason was that they refused to observe his strict religious codes of conduct: no alcohol, no music, no women who weren't covered in a chador, and no unrelated men and women together.

After that perceived insult, the shah's officials would pull up in the driveway of the hotel in armored cars, jeering out the window. This most recent time, they had pantomimed shooting at the hotel, aiming with their fingers as if poised on their automatic rifle's release. The guns they wore at their hips were real enough. Baba was not intimidated. "Get out. You are not welcome here," he told them.

As owner of one of the biggest hotels in the city, Baba took his orders from God, not the monarchy. It did not take long for the story to get around.

Unrest had been building for a year. Rumors were that the exiled Ayatollah Khomeini's son had been assassinated while being interrogated by the *Savak*, the shah's feared and hated secret intelligence organization established with the help of the CIA. The first antigovernment protests had begun, and the Shah's attempt to stifle public dissent had resulted in many civilian deaths. Iran was thrown into political turmoil, which was fast becoming a national movement to end the shah's rule.

The United States and Britain were seen as the powers behind the Pahlavi regime. A long history of resentment had been festering against the two countries since 1953, when both nations led the military coup d'état against democratically elected Prime Minister Mohammad Mossadegh.

By the winter of 1978, Mashhad was in the throes of massive unrest. Baba was sympathetic to the growing Islamic movement, as were the majority of Iran's people. The shah, with Western and U.S. support, had full authoritative control in Iran, leaving no room for involvement of average citizens. The people could not yet foresee what dangers lie ahead; all they knew at that time was that they preferred the religious leader, Ayatollah Ruhollah Khomeini, to the shah. The shah was viewed as a corrupt and irreligious monarch who was fueling his own lavish lifestyle with Iranian oil, while average citizens suffered and income disparity worsened.

The daily protests were beginning to affect every aspect of daily life. Mistrust filled the air, and unrelenting strikes by transportation and oil industry workers, as well as street demonstrations, paralyzed the country.

As we innocently enjoyed our last peaceful breakfast, the revolution had begun. During this turmoil, two decisions tore apart my family: the first, my father's, and the second, my brother Abdollah's.

What followed was inexorable.

The phone call might as well have been a draft notice for our father: Grand Ayatollah Shahami's call to Baba would enlist our family in the forthcoming regime destined to become the Islamic Republic of Iran.

Ayatollah Shahami, an important member of the clergy, had asked Baba to marshal the hotel staff to search for the two boys accused of raping the woman and apprehend them. It was easy for Ayatollah Shahami to draft Baba for the job. "Only a man with your courage and sense of duty to God could do this," he told him.

Baba gathered a search party of his hotel employees who each headed in different directions, combing the streets of Mashhad. For 11 hours, they hunted for the two teenage boys.

The victim had provided few details: a white Paykan car with a broken back window, a taller teenager with arrogance in his voice, and his meek and shorter accomplice who was thinner and had longer, tangled hair. Everything else had been a blur. Baba had little to go on, but he was determined to find the attackers.

The team had been searching since morning. Now the moonlight was brighter, the wind cooler. From a distance, he spotted the Paykan. Pigeons scattered as he sped down the dimly lit alley toward the muddy car. The headlights reflected the edge of the broken back window as he began to inspect the bumper, then the scraped, dented trunk. When he saw the dried blood, he knew he had found the perpetrators. Anger rose in his chest. He went up to the house where the car was parked and pounded on the door with both fists.

The door opened, only a crack, and a teenage boy with long tussled hair peered out, meeting Baba's glare.

The smell of alcohol was strong. "Come outside! Now!" Baba demanded.

The boy squinted. "Who are you?" he asked, lacking the usual politeness that was customary between strangers.

Baba slapped a hand on the door frame. "I said come now, or I'll wake up your entire family. Where were you last night?"

"Nowhere. I wasn't anywhere."

Pushing the door open and grabbing the boy's arm, Baba pulled him down the alley to the Paykan, and pointed to the brown stains smearing the trunk. "You want to tell me how this blood got here?"

The boy's lower lip quivered.

"Is your father home?"

"No."

Baba squeezed the boy's arm again, twisting it. "Open the trunk."

Drenched in the stench of liquor, the bloodied chador and the victim's ripped blouse and skirt sat in a tangled heap. When Baba saw a chunk of gray-streaked hair, he slammed the trunk and shoved the boy against the car.

"You were 'nowhere'?"

The boy began to cry. "I want to call my parents."

"What, you want to call your *Savaki* father?"

The boy shifted from foot to foot. Everyone knew that members of the *Savak* would be hunted down and executed by the new regime for the crimes they committed against opponents of the shah's regime.

"He's not a *Savaki*. He left the shah a long time ago. I want to call him."

"Get in and shut up," Baba ordered as he pushed the boy into the backseat of his car. Livid, he didn't notice that the boy hadn't yet pulled his foot in the car before he slammed the door. The boy let out a yelp. Shattering the winter quiet, Baba hit the accelerator and sped down the street, scattering the pigeons again.

Baba cursed the boy under his breath as he weaved through the dark street; he did not slow down, even when the car tires hit potholes. Instead, he sped up.

"It wasn't my idea," the boy mumbled from the backseat. "I can't even remember what happened."

Baba reached the main street. He hit the brakes and turned to face the boy behind him. "Where does your friend live? Direct me!" He accelerated, then slammed on the brakes; the boy's chest hit the seat in front of him. Baba pointed his finger at the boy's eye. "Right or left?" Baba didn't bother asking him for his name, it didn't matter. The boy's crime was what identified him.

"It was his idea, I swear to God." But he lifted his arm and pointed to the right.

As they approached the home of the co-conspirator, Baba kept his hand gripped tightly around the boy's arm, preventing him from escaping. When they reached the front of the house, the boy knocked on the door, asked for his friend, and took a step back when his accomplice came out. Baba grabbed the new boy by his shirt collar, and, paying no attention to his flailing arms or shouts, pulled him toward the car. The first boy tore at his hair and wept; head down, he got into the backseat and didn't look up when Baba threw his friend in next to him.

The second boy stared out the window, avoiding eye contact with Baba in the rearview mirror. His body was wobbling, his eyes almost shut by the swell of a hangover as his head bounced on the headrest.

Baba broke numerous speed limits crossing town to the Grand Ayatollah Shahami's home. He wasn't worried about getting pulled over by the police. He was on a mission, above and beyond the law.

Because of the widespread turmoil on the streets, the boys were unlikely to be arrested or even put on trial for rape, so Baba knew that getting them to Ayatollah Shahami was imperative. The ayatollah had told Baba that until order had been restored, he would lock them in his son's bathroom. This was the best plan for the time being.

Baba was confident that these two boys would be properly dealt with. After an 18-hour ordeal, having done his duty for his community, he headed home.

ABDOLLAH

January 1979

Baba and Abdollah pushed through the crowd of protesters chanting "Death to the Shah!" Posters of the stern Ayatollah Khomeini were stapled to sticks. Graffiti slogans were painted on walls on every street. My father and brother made their way, not joining in, careful not to be jostled into the drainage ditch near the screaming crowds. Burning placards of the shah curled at the edges; pieces of ash floated in the air. Baba ducked to avoid being hit by a poster depicting a bloody fist smashing the shah's face. The Islamic revolution was in full flame.

It struck Abdollah as odd when Baba turned down a side street and stopped at the large double glass front doors of an anonymous-looking building. He hurried to catch up. "Where're we going?"

As Baba touched the door handle, two men rushed across the cream-colored marble floor to pull it open, and a third man ran to meet Baba. He clasped his hand and began kissing Baba's cheeks before reaching out to embrace him.

The shouts of the protesters grew fainter as the doors slid shut. Placing his arm around Abdollah's shoulder, Baba kissed his cheek.

"This is my son, Abdollah. He's the *noor*, the light of my eyes, and has made me very proud." Baba gently guided Abdollah into the one-car showroom, and then pulled out the heavy wooden chair at the manager's desk. "Let's talk price and make this finally happen."

Abdollah was shocked—buying a new car in the midst of a revolution? It didn't make sense. Nonetheless, he was 15, and his heart pounded with joy at the thought.

He stared at the sleek black 240-horsepower Camaro parked in the center of the marble floor. He was accustomed to receiving lavish

European and Kuwaiti gifts from Baba, but this was extreme. No one in Mashhad had such a car, and certainly no boy his age. He looked at Baba, "This is too much, Baba jaan."

Baba winked at him and turned back to leafing through papers. Abdollah stepped closer to the Camaro and placed his palm on the gleaming hood. "But I can't drive yet."

That my 15-year-old brother would not be eligible for a driver's license for another three years was of no concern to Baba; he had let Abdollah regularly practice with the hotel vehicles in the parking lot. Baba was determined to buy his firstborn son this imported foreign car even if, in part, it symbolized the excess of the Western world—the same West whose influence Baba feared and fought. He didn't see the contradiction.

While the salesmen refreshed Baba's tea for the fifth time, Abdollah circled the shiny, two-door sports coupe, studying each detail and curve: its brushed aluminum panels, the shiny leather interior, and the responsive six-cylinder engine. Since the age of six, when he first saw a Camaro in a magazine, he had dreamed that one day he would drive one of these powerful machines. He had even imagined driving one all the way to Mecca or through the streets of Paris.

In response to Baba's bargaining, the dealer suggested a less expensive car. "No, no. It's got to be this car, this make, and this model. Nothing else. My son has been talking about this car for some time. Make the price work."

After Baba walked out several times and the dealer begged him to come back, the two men put down their teacups and embraced.

"Let's go home, son." Baba handed Abdollah the keys. "We'll take the back roads."

Abdollah, dazed at his good fortune, hopped behind the wheel, "This is the best day of my life," he said. He turned the ignition and drove off, into the revolution.

Abdollah had owned the Camaro for only a week when Baba summoned him to the office with the news that they had to drive to a house on the other side of Mashhad. He ordered the porters to fill the Camaro's trunk with enormous packages of food and supplies. Baba insisted they go after midnight and observe the speed limit. "We can't be pulled over. We can't risk anyone finding out who lives there."

When they arrived at the distant house, it was dark inside and the curtains were drawn. It appeared to be deserted. Baba knocked twice, and then paused. He knocked a third time, offering a signal to those on the other side of the door. The man who answered grasped Baba's hand; his eyes were moist. "We're forever indebted to you. For the first time in weeks, we're wearing clean clothes and having a fresh meal."

Abdollah blinked. He recognized Ayatollah Khabazi from the newspapers. An intimate from Khomeini's circle, Khabazi had been arrested and tortured for treason when he had openly challenged the shah for executing anyone who opposed the monarchy. He was rearrested for the fourth time when he spoke out against the *Savak,* accusing them of more terrible acts than those of the KGB. The shah had ordered Ayatollah Khabazi's execution, but the holy man had disappeared. The truth was that he was right here, in Mashhad, under Baba's protection.

Now Abdollah learned that Baba had been hiding Khabazi and his family for months in the home he had bought for his own aging aunt, supplying them with everything they needed from clothes to appliances. The family never left the house, except when Khabazi went to the Haram in disguise to pray. They had not registered their children in school.

Abdollah shook Khabazi's hand and kissed his cheek. He noted the cleric's tightly buttoned white-collar shirt and his long black cloak, which was wrinkled and worn. While the men spoke, Abdollah gave the bags of food to a woman whose face was almost entirely covered by her black chador. Abdollah recognized her by the shape of the tip of her nose. From that point on, he would bring groceries to Khabazi's family after dark, and then secretly drive him to the mosque for prayer.

It was official: Abdollah was a man. And now he had a greater purpose: He would use the Camaro to commute across secret lines— lines that would soon be redrawn between factions of the Islamic revolution. They were lines that would impact his own life, writing an ending he never could have foreseen.

He was 15. Abdollah, the "servant of God," drove forth on dangerous missions, glad for the car and the thrill of the forbidden.

RAHIMEH

After Baba brought Iman and me back from our illicit afternoon at the Rose Hotel, the number "314" was whispered often. We were not allowed to leave our house, and the hotel was forbidden—even the lobby. And especially the third floor.

"If they ever go anywhere near there . . ." Maman said, late at night to Baba. I had not meant to eavesdrop, but the intensity of their exchange had traveled like electricity through the wall.

Hadi, older and more adventurous, was also curious. Over the past few days and nights, he had reported mysterious activities. Why did strange men enter the hotel at regular intervals? Why was there a sudden flurry of motion on Sunday night? Why did we continue to see one light on the third floor when the rest of the hotel was dark?

Before Hadi could find out more, Maman discovered the truth.

We were sitting in the kitchen, eating oranges and waiting for Maman to create tiny human shapes from the peels—one of our favorite treats. Suddenly she slammed the receiver onto the phone's cradle several times before hanging up. I had never seen her so angry. In fact, I had never even seen her angry. It frightened me, and I felt inexplicably guilty.

"What's happened that you had me run home so fast?" Baba was out of breath.

"What are you doing, Haji?" Maman called Baba by a nickname earned by Muslims after their pilgrimage to Mecca. "My brother just called," she said, standing over him as he took off his shoes at the door. "I know what you have done!"

He stopped and looked up at her. "And what did Mohsen have to say?"

Maman, always so adoring, glared at my father. "I don't care if the Grand Ayatollah Shahami says there's no police force to take them, Haji. They're rapists. They may be boys but they raped a woman my mother's age. We have a little girl. Haji, are you blind? Why isn't your instinct to take care of yourself and your family first? For God's sake, Abdollah works there. How could you keep this a secret from me?"

Baba looked down, averting his eyes.

"You are behaving like your father!" Maman yelled. Baba's father had lived a secret life for years, hiding an affair from his wife. The pain forever damaged Baba's mother. Of course, Baba was keeping secrets; he knew no other way. But what he was hiding was far more dangerous than a mistress.

Maman closed her eyes and took a deep breath. "It's not enough that we're in the middle of a revolution—riots, fires, flying bullets. Now we have rapists staying in our hotel? How can you possibly believe this is a good idea?"

Baba fell into a chair. "I know it's chaos out there. I know this doesn't feel good, but it's the right thing to do. There's no choice, *azizam*. These boys would be walking scot-free, sweetheart. At least we know where they are. I promise you, it'll just be a few more weeks, just until Ayatollah Shahami has an official position and they have a handle on the government's new police force."

Maman was livid. "If it's only a short time, why doesn't Shahami keep them in his house? I'll tell you why! Because he doesn't want to risk exposing his wife and kids to criminals. And yet he asks us to do it!" Maman began to pace, hugging herself. "He's using you. Do you think about that? They all use you. You don't need to help everybody, and you don't need to be a big shot." She put her hands by her side and let her voice soften. "Please don't do this for them."

Baba explained that Khomeini's ad hoc security forces were jockeying for power over the shah's police, the *Kalantari*, and neither police force was willing to apprehend the boys. Under these circumstances, Ayatollah Shahami requested that Baba confine and guard the two boys in the hotel.

"Just for a short time—until things settle down," Baba explained. "Do you want them to run free? Isn't that even more risky?"

I put down the orange slice and looked toward the window. What was going on?

Pulling a chair toward him, Baba motioned to Maman. "Sit with me."

She didn't sit, but let her body slacken. "What about Abdollah?"

"Trust me. The manager and I will be guarding the room; we'll feed them. A revolution is coming. We have no tourists; no one is coming to stay at the hotel right now. And no one will, until the boys are gone and sent to a proper jail. I promise you."

Maman straightened her shoulders, sighed, and dropped into a chair. "Listen to me. Our little children aren't to put one foot in the hotel until those thugs are gone. I don't care if the rooms are locked. Not one foot. And it's only a few weeks, right? You promise?"

Baba kissed Maman's cheek. "You have my word."

I stared in the direction of the hotel. *How will I get the Kit Kats out of the hotel freezer now?*

A week later, Baba burst into the house. "Khomeini's in Iran," he declared with a smile. "Everything's going to change. It's going to be all right." Unable to contain his enthusiasm, he piled us into the car to drive down to the celebration where thousands, including some of the shah's former police, poured onto the streets to welcome Ayatollah Khomeini back from his 14-year exile in Iraq and France.

From the car window, I watched as people threw candy, lollipops, and bubble gum into other open car windows. Men were riding each other's shoulders chanting, *"Esteghlal, azadi, jomhouri-ye Eslami."* They wholeheartedly believed in independence, freedom, and the Islamic Republic of Iran.

People danced, and joy erupted from the crowds that pushed into every corner of the street. I recognized that something significant, something hopeful, was taking place. I could read it on people's faces. I saw it on Baba's face.

The shah had fled Iran; the 54 years of the "modern" Pahlavi dynasty was over. For the first time, a religious leader, a Shi'a Muslim, an ayatollah—the Ayatollah Ruhollah Khomeini—would also be the "Supreme Leader," or head of government. There would no longer be a shah. Power would be delegated to a range of clerics—including religious leaders akin to archbishops. At that moment, no one seemed to consider how dangerous that absolute power might be. No one foresaw that the end of one bloodbath would only be the beginning of another.

Maman was happy, too. And shortsighted: To her, this would be the end of the two boys imprisoned in Room 314. Law, order, and religious principles would be restored.

Across the courtyard, at the Rose Hotel, the boys' short-term stay had stretched to 65 days. With Khomeini officially in power, there were now ad hoc tribunals and revolutionary courts in place, and Baba was ready for justice to be properly served. It was time for the two boys to check out.

I saw Maman relax at last as Baba made the final call. "I can no longer keep the boys in my hotel," he told the Ayatollah Shahami.

"It is not a prison." Shahami agreed to turn them over to the new authorities.

As a way of thanking Maman for her patience, Baba took our family on a ten-day pilgrimage to Mecca. He left the manager and Abdollah in charge of the hotel and released the boys into Shahami's custody. As the revolution calmed down and the new regime established itself, the two boys were held in a real jail cell, without a bathroom or the service of a hotel. At last, Baba believed, they'd receive justice. And they were no longer his problem.

He was wrong on both counts.

If only Baba had never allowed the ayatollah to turn his hotel into a prison. If only Maman had not relented . . .

❧

Holding the door open with one hand, and flipping through the prayer beads of his *tasbeeh,* the hotel manager was waiting for Baba the day we returned from Mecca. "I need to report something." He didn't meet Baba's eyes.

"What?"

"Haji, the government has released the two boys."

"When?" Baba looked out the hotel entrance's glass doors.

The manager followed Baba's gaze. "Three days after you left."

"You didn't inform me?"

"I tried to get a message to your hotel in Mecca. International calls were impossible to make with all the turmoil here." The manager twirled his beads. "Haji, they've been here, at the hotel."

"What?"

"I warned everyone to keep their distance. They were talking to the staff, especially the cook."

"That can't be possible." Baba slammed his hand on the reception counter.

"They're claiming they are innocent and that's why they were freed, and that you wrongfully imprisoned them. They blame you for their inability to find work."

"This is not happening."

"They've told everyone you ruined their reputations."

"Reputations? What reputations? But why are they free? I must talk to Ayatollah Shahami." Baba turned and entered his office, slamming the door behind him. At first, he spoke loudly to the ayatollah; slowly, his voice quieted. He opened the door and called out to the manager.

"The next time you see those boys, bring them to me."

The manager looked at Baba and then at the floor.

Baba hit his hand on the table. "What now?"

"It's probably nothing, but I've seen them talking to Abdollah."

That night before dinner, Baba asked Abdollah to join him in the garden. We watched as Baba trailed behind him, raising his hands and yelling.

"It was nothing, Baba. They came to me asking for a job. I felt sorry for them. They say they're innocent, and their families threatened to disown them."

"Sorry for them? I told you never to talk to them. Never!"

As Baba dropped his arms to his sides and came to a halt, raindrops spattered his glasses. "Listen to me. This is important. You need to promise me that you will stay away from those boys. You don't know who they are or what they've done."

"Well then, tell me about them, Baba."

"You don't need to know anything more. Just promise me, if you see them, don't talk to them. Can you promise me?"

Rain was streaming down Abdollah's cheeks as he faced Baba. "How would I see them? They won't come around now that you're back."

"Just do as I say. Nothing. Not even a conversation."

Abdollah lowered his head. "Yes, Baba."

Walking through puddles, they headed back to the house to dry off and join the rest of us for a dinner of *Khoresht-e Karafs*, Abdollah's favorite celery lamb stew with cilantro, parsley, and saffron. During dinner, no one spoke of the boys. Baba felt confident that his son had grasped the gravity of the situation—and that he could count on Abdollah to heed his warning.

Baba paced back and forth in his office. The ayatollah had told him that the boys had repented. Could it be true? The memory of the crime scene—the bloodied clothes, the poor woman's wounds—was still vivid. Can anyone repent from such viciousness? Though Baba's mind said no, his faith in God decreed that anyone—especially young boys—could repent and begin again.

Hours later, the two boys stood with their hands folded in front of them, their heads bowed. Adjusting his glasses and taking a sip of water, Baba took in their bouffant hair and gold chains. "Ayatollah Shahami tells me you've repented."

"Yes sir, we have. We've learned a new way to be." The taller boy toyed with his long fluffy hair, trying to flatten it with the palm of his hand.

The other boy nodded. "We've learned our lesson. Grand Ayatollah Shahami has been teaching us, and we want to change our lives."

"How often are you praying?"

The tall boy with extra medallions hanging from his neck spoke for both: "We've been making all five prayers, every day, three times a day, sir. We want to live a good life and make something of ourselves, *sir*."

"Are you ready to abide by God's laws and give up everything else?"

Both boys nodded.

Baba stood. "Prayer starts at 5:00 a.m. Arrive on time, cut your hair, throw out your medallions, and button up your shirts." Baba waved his arm toward the mosque. "You're to pray three times a day and meet with Ayatollah Shahami regularly. For now, you'll work here five hours a day. The manager is your direct supervisor. I'll fire you if you're caught glancing at a woman, even if her entire face is covered in a *neghab*. And you're only to work in the restaurant—nowhere else. You are forbidden to go near the lobby or towers of the hotel. You don't cross the parking lot. And you keep away from my family."

⚜

When Baba got home, Maman was waiting for him. "Are you crazy? You've hired those thugs to work in our hotel? We just got rid of them!"

Maman was incredulous—and furious. She dismissed all of Baba's rationales that "this way" he could be sure the boys were not around Abdollah or loose on the streets of Mashhad.

"What are you thinking? They will be around Abdollah all the time!"

Baba protested. "Their religious studies can pave a new path for them. And maybe I can do my part to make them change."

Maman took a step back and shook her head.

"You can't make anybody change. Why are you putting us all at risk again, Haji? You're going to regret this."

"It's not me, it's God. They will follow the right path; we will make sure of it." The decision required Baba to reaffirm his basic faith: that everyone could repent.

Maman would have none of it. "I want those boys out of here. The children haven't been able to go to the hotel for the two months they've been there. Now they're free and we're in prison? You don't see how crazy this is? Is Shahami pressuring you?"

Then Maman did something she never did. She walked away. The door to the kitchen slammed.

My brother Zain, who was watching this, began to bounce his leg rapidly against the table.

By the next morning, Maman was letting Baba sweeten her tea for her. And the last part of Baba's decision was set into action: The boys began working at the hotel. But Maman's predictions were to be proven terribly correct.

FROZEN SNAKES

※

As Abdollah walked into the living room a few weeks later, I felt a strange shiver at the back of my neck. Something had changed, and I felt a premonition of trouble.

How strange that a single button could signal oncoming catastrophe. But to Baba, good Muslim men and boys do not leave their shirts unbuttoned—not even one.

Abdollah was wearing one of his tight polyester shirts. The top button was open, exposing a gold chain on a few dark chest hairs. He carried a pair of black three-inch platform boots that resembled the ones we had seen in his Western magazines.

The evidence, which had not seemed serious until now, added up: Abdollah was acting more and more like other teenagers in Mashhad, boys who didn't follow the strict traditions observed inside our family's walls. Before, he had only a few contraband magazines hidden under his rug. But now I heard Elvis songs coming from Abdollah's room. Vinyl records and stacks of *Newsweek* and *Life* magazines had found their way to his closet, buried under his navy blue suit and work clothes.

When we heard the rattle of the front door handle, my eyes darted toward Abdollah. It was Baba, returning to surprise us with fresh bread from the hotel.

I knew what must follow. I would save my big brother from Baba's wrath and Baba from Abdollah's rebellion. If I got on a chair and reached around Abdollah's neck, I could button the shirt from behind. No one would notice. I glanced at Abdollah. The door was open; he could still get out. But he didn't. Instead, we sat still and silent. The piece of buttered *sangak* I was about to give Iman grew cold in my hand.

Baba frowned and adjusted his glasses. "Abdollah, what're you wearing? You're not going to work like that."

Abdollah lowered his head; he didn't answer. I set the spoon I was holding back on the plate, trying not to clink the metal against the china.

"Button that collar," Baba said. He brushed past Abdollah's shoulder and moved toward the sofreh, where we were sitting cross-legged eating breakfast. He dropped the fresh *sangak* flatbread onto the dishes of quince jam; the impact sent splatters onto the sofreh.

"No man of respect dresses like this. You're not an entertainer. You're the son of a businessman." Baba pointed his index finger at Abdollah. "Your name means 'servant of God.'"

Abdollah adjusted his shirt collar to hide the gold chain. "But Baba, this is the style everyone is wearing. It's only a button."

"What did you say?" Baba cocked his head at Abdollah.

Maman rose and waved Baba back. "Be patient, *azizam*. He just got out of the shower. Give him a few minutes."

Turning his finger to Maman, Baba's voice grew hoarse. "Time? This is the time to protect him. Just because all these young boys have been following the shah and his Western shenanigans—men with their shirts open and girls with bare legs—doesn't mean I'm going to let my son disgrace himself. If we don't protect him now, then when? When it's too late?"

The new regime promised to forbid theater, music, dating, drinking alcohol, and dressing inappropriately. Ayatollah Khomeini would ensure the implementation of Islamic law. My father had always observed the traditions, and although he was a modern man in many ways, he knew which rules were too important to bend. To disobey essential teachings would bar one from heaven. Enforcing the rules was Baba's way of protecting us and securing our afterlife.

Maman tilted her head—a sign to Baba that she was going to stand up for her children over him, just as her mother had done with her father. Her voice was soft. "I'm sure he'll button it before he leaves home." She nodded at Abdollah.

Baba's face grew red with anger, overwhelming the pink birthmark on his left cheek.

"Can't you see what's happening? Your son is strutting like a gigolo with his chest showing. I will not tolerate this in my family." He was talking to Maman, but his eyes never left Abdollah's.

The sunlight was beginning its climb up the living room wall and, out in the hall, a jangling of keys indicated that the maid had arrived. The morning routines of the Rose Hotel were beginning.

Abdollah broke eye contact with Baba and glanced toward the kitchen. "I'm late. I'll be leaving now, Baba."

The slap of Baba's palm on Abdollah's cheek was fast and sharp. Abdollah dropped his boots with a thump on the carpet. I knocked over a teacup with my knee. As the brown puddle spread across the sofreh, I covered Iman's eyes with my hand. Baba had never struck any of us before. Abdollah quickly collected his shoes and bag and kissed Maman on both cheeks.

"With your permission, Maman, I'll be back soon." Then his eyes traveled over us one by one before he pressed his palm to his chest, bowed to Baba, and said his customary goodbye. "*Gorbanetoon*—as always, I would sacrifice myself for you." Abdollah walked out as I tried to wipe the spilled tea with my hands.

Baba's voice shook as he called after his eldest son: "Don't forget the meeting today. I've rehired most of the staff and I need you there. And change your clothes." Not meeting our eyes, Baba put on his shoes and closed the door on his way out.

What appeared minor—an unbuttoned shirt, a slap on the face— was in fact, the sign of an outright war. I felt the danger. But I could do nothing to avert the future catastrophe.

BABA

Urgent business matters were at hand. Although the two boys had checked out of Room 314, the Rose Hotel's most famous guest was about to check in.

That afternoon, Baba placed his palms on the reception counter and welcomed back the staff he had laid off for months during the revolution. "We're a top-notch hotel. Everything I've trained you for will be put to the test in the coming weeks. We'll be dedicating the two top floors to a secret guest and her family."

He glanced at Abdollah. They hadn't spoken since the morning, but the top button of his son's white shirt was fastened.

"Their privacy is critical. Anyone who leaks the information will be fired on the spot. We won't be using our regular waiters and bellboys. Abdollah, you and the manager will be in charge of making sure all her needs are met, and that no one knows they are staying here. There will be no bills or other charges to their rooms. They're my guests."

As the staff dispersed, Baba motioned Abdollah to remain behind. "You're my son. I need you to make me proud and focus on your work. And remember: Keep away from those boys."

Abdollah kissed Baba on the cheeks. "Yes, Baba, I know."

That afternoon, Baba, the manager, and Abdollah greeted the wife of Ayatollah Khomeini and her daughters, grandchildren, and staff. On the top floors, Baba segregated Mrs. Khomeini and her family from the public and the paparazzi, who would pursue the Khomeinis like movie stars if they knew they were in Mashhad. The Supreme Leader's wife and daughters had come on pilgrimage to the Haram of Imam Reza, where they would be secretly taken each day to pray in private.

Every morning before Abdollah escorted the nine women into town, Baba whispered to him, "Treat Mrs. Khomeini like your mother."

For the next three weeks, Maman cooked for Mrs. Khomeini and her party: elaborate Persian stews and rice dishes; *doogh*—a yogurt soda; *mast-o khiar*—cucumber and mint yogurt mixed with dill and rose petal; and *sabzi*—fresh garden-cut mixed greens of parsley, cilantro, mint, and radishes. Sitting on the Persian rug around the sofreh, Mrs. Khomeini shared with Maman a new vision of Iran and a belief that prosperity, security, freedom, and faith would come to our country.

"Your son is fine example of what we hope for our youth. I can see he is a smart, family-oriented, man of God. A truly unique young man—*Binazir*. He will make a great husband someday," Mrs. Khomeini told Maman over tea.

This was exactly Baba's idea.

❦

"Baba, I'm too young, please!"

The noise of Zain's toy cars came to a standstill, and Iman stopped sucking on his pacifier. We all looked up at the table where Baba and Abdollah were sitting.

"The greatest gift my parents gave me was finding your mother. She's an angel. I only want the same for you."

Less than a month after the day he had seen Abdollah's unbuttoned shirt, Baba had found his 15-year-old son a wife. Bringing trays of imported bananas, local pomegranates, blood oranges, persimmons, *zulbia bamie*—sugared bread sticks—and *ghotab*—almond pastry—to the homes of several high-profile clerics, my parents had handpicked the daughter of an ayatollah for their son. He would be married before he committed a sin. In the week since the announcement, Abdollah had been making excuses not to visit her.

Abdollah's voice was calm. "I'm not ready, Baba. Please. I want to study English and travel to Kuwait and live in Dubai and Lebanon. I want to see Rome and Madrid and London."

Baba pushed aside his teacup and stood.

Maman, who was bringing in a platter of fresh cut watermelon, stopped short in the doorway. A slice slid to the floor.

Baba shoved back from the table and moved to stand over his son, his index finger stabbing the air. "Only after you're married. Only *then*." Baba believed that a boy traveling abroad alone would become westernized, would sin, and go to hell. He had seen it happen to his nephews; he would not let it happen to his son.

Baba motioned for Maman to join them at the table. "We love you. We have more experience than you."

Without looking at either of them, Maman placed the fruit on the table between them.

"I want you to build on my experiences, son. I want you to trust me the way I trusted my parents." Baba placed a hand on Maman's shoulders. "They only wanted the best for me when I married at 19. And we want that for you." He placed a slice of watermelon on Abdollah's plate. "I want to see you grow with someone, settled."

Abdollah stared at the watermelon slice and slowly stabbed his fork into its rosy flesh.

⚜

Two weeks later, at the *aghd* ceremony, I caught an image of Abdollah and his bride sitting at the white silk wedding sofreh facing the symbolic mirror. It was meant to reflect back to them the joy and happiness they were to remember in their marriage. Neither Abdollah nor his bride looked in the mirror or at one another. They didn't smile. I looked at Maman; she was looking down. Abdollah's eyes caught mine, and I began to gnaw on my index finger. I wanted to take him to a place I'd heard about, Paris. We would go in his Camaro.

Even though they were married, Abdollah didn't touch or kiss his wife. In fact, he refused to be alone with her. The day after the wedding, on behalf of his absent son, Baba sent his driver to the bride's house, where she continued to live with her parents, to deliver several trays of fruits and sweets. Shaped like pyramids, each was four feet high, topped with yards of decorative ribbons and tied in giant bows.

The following day, Maman made an excuse as Abdollah sneaked away before Baba's driver brought his new bride for a visit at our house. The bride was dark-haired and soft-featured, reserved, with downcast eyes. I invited her to play with me. Placing a box of matches on the floor, she gave me a sweet smile as she taught me how to gently pluck each stick away from the pile without disturbing the others. When she thought I wasn't paying attention, she would look up at Abdollah's empty room. Once, when the doorknob turned, she knocked over the stacked matches. I let her start over.

＊＊＊

As he hurried across the courtyard, Baba's mind was spinning with yet another plan to force Abdollah to spend time with his new bride. That morning, he had received a call that another special guest was waiting for him in the hotel lobby. Mr. Gaffari was the principal investor and architect of the Rose Hotel, and now his closest friend. This must be urgent. He did not often arrive without notice.

Ten years earlier, when he was 25, Baba had entered the office of the famous Mr. Gaffari. He'd never been so nervous—not even on his wedding day. Although Baba had surpassed others his age in business, securing the city's approval for a third luxury hotel in Mashhad that catered to the needs of the religious community during the antireligious climate of the shah's reign, it had been a significant and risky venture. All Baba could think of was his debt: 95,000 tomans. How could he ask this man to help him fund his hotel when he himself had no money to invest?

Mr. Gaffari motioned for Baba to sit. "You know, I met you one night a few months ago. I heard you give a sermon at your father's home. I know what you do for your community. I respect your faith and your purpose."

Mr. Gaffari had done his homework. Baba had trouble swallowing.

"I will help you build your hotel." The checkbook was large; it covered half the table when Mr. Gaffari flipped it open. Baba's eyes froze at the sight of the check: 100,000 tomans made out to Baba.

"Pay off all your debts. With the remaining money, get ten men to start breaking ground." Mr. Gaffari rose, kissed Baba on the cheek, and shook his hand tight. "I'll be on-site in five days."

On the sidewalk outside Mr. Gaffari's office, the pounding of Baba's heart had calmed. Falling to the pavement, his forehead on the cement, he kissed the ground and cried out, "Thank you, God. Thank you."

Now, at the Rose Hotel's reception desk, the look of worry on Mr. Gaffari's face alarmed Baba. They retired to his office, where Baba poured him a cup of tea. "Someone told me one of the boys you hired was serving tea at a Rose Hotel ceremony," he said.

"I know from the outside it doesn't seem like a good idea, but they've been here two months and they're attending mosque and praying every day. They show up for work, and when they serve women, their eyes never leave the floor. I'm keeping a close eye on them. I can reform them."

"Haji, listen to me. To temporarily imprison these criminals to protect the community, that's one thing. But hiring them is another. Even with your faith and your skill, you don't have the power to reform them. Regardless of your good intentions, you are making a big mistake. There are some creatures beyond the reach even of God. They are not just young and misguided; they have committed evil."

"No one is beyond redemption."

Mr. Gaffari put his teacup in the saucer without drinking. "Don't be blind Haji. These thugs are like frozen snakes. The moment they thaw out, they'll strike you first."

Baba had been raised to believe that everyone deserved a second chance. Couldn't a new way of life reverse even the worst of human choices? Baba desperately wanted this belief to be true.

Mr. Gaffari leaned forward. "Get them out of there today, or you'll forever regret this. Your wife is a good woman. Don't upset her anymore by ignoring her concerns. She's right: Your faith is blind, and this is not something you can ignore anymore. It's getting serious."

Mr. Gaffari put his hand on Baba's shoulder.

"And get them away from your son immediately," he commanded.

Baba cocked his head, frowning. "Are you saying something about Abdollah?"

"You have to know." Mr. Gaffari squeezed Baba's shoulder.

"What?" Baba stepped back.

"I think they are friends, Haji."

Baba looked out the window. "I told him to stay away."

"The manager said he's seen the boys going into the car parts shop.

They are just a few years apart, Haji, and they see each other every day at work. Like it or not, they are going to influence your son."

Baba kissed Mr. Gaffari on both cheeks as they rose. "You're more than a brother to me. This will end here. I'll get rid of them today."

꧁꧂

Hadi and I had gone to visit Abdollah in the shop that afternoon. We found him leaning back in his chair, twirling the beads of his *tasbeeh* without saying any prayers. He looked miserable.

When he saw us, his eyes lit up, and he gathered us together in a hug. "*Jigaretoono beram.* Seeing you delights me," he said smiling.

As I wrapped my arms around his neck and kissed his cheek, two strange boys, one taller with slicked-back hair and a gold medallion around his neck, appeared in the doorway. "Take a look at that— you're smiling! Well, you should be; you're a married man," one of the boys said, his voice too loud.

Abdollah lowered us to the floor and told us, "Go to the other side of the shop."

"You've got it all, Abdollah: a business, a hotel, a hot Camaro, and now a wife. The only thing your father can't get for you is friends."

The second boy, who called Abdollah his buddy, "*Rafigh,*" cocked his head toward the parking lot. "Come on, Abdollah. Everyone's waiting. Send these little kids home and let's go play some soccer." The other boy was balancing a soccer ball in his palm.

I squinted up at Abdollah. "Who are they, *Dadashi?*"

I didn't like them.

"Don't worry honey, they're friends." Abdollah kissed my cheek. His hand, which I was holding, began to sweat. Finally, he spoke to the boys. "I have the kids here. I can't go."

One of the boys smirked. "There'll be girls at the soccer match. The one that likes your car is coming."

Hadi stepped in front of Abdollah. "Let's you and me go for a ride in the Camaro, *Dadashi*."

The other boy put his arm around Hadi's shoulder and pulled him to the door. "Not today, kid. Your brother needs a break. You guys run along." He waved us toward the door.

Hadi grabbed the boy's leg and said, "Get away from us." Then he bit him.

The boy jumped and swatted at us as we ran away, ducking under Abdollah's desk.

Was it a minute? Suddenly, Baba stood in the doorway, "Didn't I tell you never to talk to these thugs?" he said, clenching his fists and turning toward the boys. "Get off the property and never come back!"

The manager and three hotel employees were right behind Baba. The boys backed away.

Baba went nose to nose with the taller boy. "I said get out! And don't come back."

The boys scattered fast—like bugs.

Abdollah stepped around the desk, his movements cautious. "Baba, *Salaam*." He pulled out a chair. "Sit. Can I get you some water?" His voice shook.

"Abdollah, tell me this isn't true. You're a married man now."

Abdollah's tone changed. His voice rose. "I might be married, but that wasn't my choice, was it? And I still need friends even if I'm married."

"Tell me you're not friends with those thugs? Just tell me you kept your promise."

"I hardly know them, Baba. We've just talked a few times."

"What else?"

"It was nothing. They begged me for a ride and I drove them to a soccer game once. I swear to God, Baba, nothing else."

Baba was shaking. "You took them in the car? You've been giving them rides?" With the tip of his finger, Baba pushed Abdollah back behind the desk and into his chair. "I trusted you, son."

He looked down and saw Hadi and me under the counter, cross-legged on the floor. Hadi smiled up at him. "Baba, I bit that *thug*."

"The kids are here? Those criminals were here with the kids?" The look he gave Abdollah could have lit the shop on fire. "We need to take your sister home. Now!"

Hadi pulled me to my feet, and we waited in the doorway.

"This is the end of it. You're married now. You've got to start taking responsibility and acting like a man. Finish work and come home." He left, slamming the door.

Abdollah snatched his beads and rocked slowly in his desk chair, his eye trained on the open window. He had a look on his face that I had never seen before. When I think back, it was as if he was already gone, taken from us.

Was that the moment he made the decision that would cost him everything?

I followed his gaze to the polished Camaro. I knew what he was thinking: How long would it take to drive far, far away?

That night, Hadi saw Abdollah sneak out his window. All night, he lay in bed with his fists balled and his eyes squeezed shut, waiting for the scraping noise that would indicate Abdollah sneaking back into the house. The night passed; light seeped into the room. By the time morning prayers had passed, there was still no sign of Abdollah.

"Rahimeh, have you seen *Dadashi?*" Hadi woke me up, looking worried.

"No, why?"

"Nothing, nothing." Hadi walked out, Zain trailing behind. Before going to school, Hadi had recruited Zain to help him find Abdollah. After hours of searching the yard, the hotel parking lot, and the car parts shop, they gave up. He sat in the living room, wondering. Should he have told our parents that he had heard the motor late at night, or that he'd seen Abdollah sneaking out the window? In truth, Hadi had seen this happen twice before, but his brother always returned by dawn.

The next morning, Baba awoke to his son's defiant disappearance. He pushed past Maman, who held out his breakfast, grabbed his jacket, and headed out of the house to look for Abdollah. "Haji!" Maman called after him, "I'm sure he has a good reason. Something must have happened and he is probably with my parents. He is . . . just a boy!" Her voice trailed. Baba had not heard her.

The school called: Abdollah had not shown up for the second day in a row. Baba rushed to the hotel to call our relatives. Maman sank down on the floor and rocked Iman on her lap. She stared at the door to Abdollah's room as if she could will him to reappear.

As the day went on, there was no sign of either my brother or his Camaro. My parents tried to maintain the routine for us children. That afternoon, I went with Baba to pick up Hadi from school.

On the way home, without warning, Baba made a sudden turn that sent us toppling onto each other in the backseat. Baba sped across traffic, cut ahead of a rickety truck carrying rocks, and passed a motorcycle carrying a whole family. Ignoring the truck driver honking and yelling out of his window, Baba closed in, chasing the car ahead.

When I peeked through my hands, I saw the taillights of a black Camaro. There was only one Camaro in all of Mashhad. I could see my brother, and riding next to him was a girl—a girl who was not wearing a head scarf. Her long black hair whipped in the wind.

Baba pressed his foot to the gas pedal and swerved in and out of traffic to try to catch up to the Camaro as it roared down a back street.

Abdollah saw Baba over his shoulder and accelerated. I could feel the wind and warp of the speed. My brother jerked the Camaro around another corner.

That turn of the wheel, to evade Baba—was that when Abdollah made his fateful decision to not come home? Was it the wild impulse of an adolescent boy, in the first fire of rebellion against his authoritarian father? Or was it just a reflex that had the same terrible effect?

If only, if only . . . Abdollah had no car, *if* . . . he had not left the house in secret; *if* . . . he had not been seen with the girl without a head scarf. *If only* . . . he had not reacted. *If only Abdollah had stopped then . . . the rest might not have happened.*

In the rearview mirror, I could see Baba's face, distorted by rage; the veins in his temples throbbed. We could hear the shrieks of car horns in our wake. *If only* Baba had not lost control of his own temper, and had just driven home and waited.

"Hold onto your sister," my father called back to Hadi, executing another high-speed turn. Even as a child, I could see his driving was reckless.

When the Camaro finally disappeared around the last corner, Baba's car limped back to the main road, where the car horns still blared. When one driver got out and tried to undo the knot by directing traffic, Baba pulled to the side and banged his fist on the wheel. The rage in his voice made me shiver. "*Khodaya komak kon.*" He repeated his prayer, "*God please help me.*" Then the tension left his body. He jerked the stick shift into gear and drove the car in the direction of home.

THE LESSON

❧❦

1979–80

Mashhad

BABA

It was growing dark as two police cars, their lights off, pulled over the curb. Baba was in the first car with the head officer of Khomeini's newly formed Mashhad police force. After several hours of interrogating the cook at the Rose Hotel, Baba had what he needed: the address where the two boys were staying.

As they stepped out of the police cars, Baba's face flushed. He was breathing hard. When a girl with long black hair and without a head scarf opened the door, Baba rocked back on his heels. It was the girl he had seen riding in Abdollah's Camaro. Love songs from Googoosh, the celebrated Iranian pop singer, blared in the background.

As Baba and the head officer questioned the girl, the police searched the house, which smelled of cooked rice and body odor. The only furnishings were a few stained mattresses spread on the floor; strewn between the bedding were half-eaten plates of food and empty beer bottles.

The officer questioned the girl but she refused to speak. He resorted to threats and raised his voice, "I'm going to tell your parents that you sell yourself. You'll be disowned and your family will be shamed!"

The girl was still silent. The officer walked closer to her, almost nose to nose, and slammed her against the wall. "You want to be disowned? Is that what you want?"

The girl looked at the ground and tried to back up, but he pinned her against the wall.

"Now answer my questions before I arrest you!"

"I don't sell myself, and this isn't my house." She told them that ten people lived there: two boys in their 20s who had rented the house, the rest runaway teenagers who periodically stayed there. She began sobbing and begged the police not to call her parents, finally admitting that the people in the house regularly had parties, consumed drugs, and engaged in sex. She didn't mention Abdollah.

After several hours of searching, the officers found no drugs or alcohol. But as they were about to leave empty-handed, an officer stopped and unrolled a bamboo shade. A handgun fell to the floor.

⫘

An hour later, shattering the silence of a starless dawn, the squeal of tires on our gravel driveway awoke the roosters. The thump of a soldier's rifle butt on the heavy metal gate scattered the chickens; their startled cries rose with the slam of each car door.

Maman rushed down the path and tripped over the squawking birds at her ankles. She hung onto her head scarf to shield her face, pushing against the gate latch to keep it closed. "*Kieh?* Who's there?"

"*Komiteh.*" Morality Police: Islamic revolutionaries recruited to monitor people's "moral" behavior.

Another car door slammed. "Open up!"

Maman fumbled with her chador, to cover her bare legs. What was Khomeini's police force doing here? And where were her husband and son?

"Open up now!" another revolutionary yelled. Behind him were more soldiers. They pounded their rifle butts on the gate, rattling its hinges. Maman pressed a palm against the door. "My husband is not at home. I must call him first."

"*Khafesho!*"—Shut up!—Open it or we'll break down the door." She could hear the thud of more heavy boots coming down the driveway.

Arranging her chador over her face, Maman pulled open the heavy metal gate and tucked herself behind it. Twenty bearded men with semiautomatic rifles pushed through the front door. They stormed inside and kicked aside the frantic chickens as they moved through the yard. Some of the soldiers couldn't have been more than 15 years old—Abdollah's age.

One guard tossed the squawking rooster into the air with the tip of his rifle. The soldiers' footsteps shook the deck, herded like sheep by their superiors in a game they didn't fully understand. They pushed into each other as they pressed themselves through the doorway. Bypassing our neatly organized shoes at the entryway, they trampled on the living room rug with their muddy boots.

Maman stumbled up the steps after them. "I beg you. My children are asleep!" The living room was now crowded with armed guards.

The commander, an older man, walked two steps toward Maman and pushed against her. He searched for her eyes beneath the fold of her chador. "*Khafeh, zanikeh!*"—Shut the hell up, bitch!" he barked.

Staggering for a minute, she sank against the door frame. She had never been spoken to like this, never been called *zanikeh*. No stranger had ever stood this close.

One soldier bumped a vase off the mantel and sent it shattering to the floor. The smell of rotten flower water spread over the rug. The commotion immediately woke up Iman and me, and I helped my baby brother from his crib. Scared by the noise, he clutched his zebra-striped blanket. Even though he seemed on the verge of bursting into tears, he held his thumb in his mouth. Hadi and Zain shook themselves from sleep and followed Iman and me into the living room.

We gathered around Maman. At the sight of the armed soldiers, Iman began to cry. Maman begged, "Sir, please, you're frightening my children."

The man ran a flashlight beam across our faces, making us blink, and then focused on Maman. "Where's that son of yours who runs the hotel?"

"Abdollah?" Maman braced herself against the wall.

The man strutted into Abdollah's room. "Where is he, I said?" He flipped over a couch cushion with the toe of his boot. "I know you're hiding him!"

Chewing on my lower lip, I glanced at Hadi. Why would the police be looking for Abdollah? This must be a mistake.

Iman, who was buried in his blanket under the corner of Maman's chador, began to sniffle and whimper.

The commander shined the flashlight back at Maman. "*Khafeshoon kon!*—Don't breathe or I'll arrest you. Now shut your kids up."

I could feel Zain's shoulders trembling as we moved closer to Maman. I placed the pacifier in Iman's mouth.

When they realized Abdollah wasn't home, the commander waved the white flashlight beam and yelled at the others: "Look for heroin, guns, bullets, alcohol, money. Anything. Go."

As the guards stomped past us, a teenage soldier with soft eyes leaned down, moving his rifle aside, and whispered to Maman, "It's orders from the Revolutionary Guard. I'm sorry. We're only doing what we've been told."

For hours we sat in the corner, listening as the soldiers opened and closed drawers, removing and throwing clothes, papers, and other objects at the floor. The sound of doors banging, the rise and fall of the soldiers' voices, and rifles pounding against the walls made us more frightened. As we cowered in the corner, we watched books, cushions, prayer rugs, bed sheets, silverware, and toys fly and then land in the middle of each room. The guards flipped over the heavy Persian rugs and sent swirls of dust into the air that made us cough.

Maman seemed to be in a trance, unaware that the heel of her foot was exposed. Since the day after her wedding, she had never been seen without thick black knee-high socks. As I covered her foot, I stared at a tiny yellow feather caught in the fold of her chador.

Finally, an excited shout followed the opening of the basement door, and one of the guards reentered the living room with a soccer ball, a roll of fabric, and a stack of Abdollah's European magazines.

The leader nodded. *"Berim!"* Kicking aside the toys and prayer rugs, the soldiers left as suddenly as they had appeared. The house was silent except for the ticking of the clock in the living room.

Why were they taking our soccer ball? Where was Baba? Where was our brother?

Later, we learned that Baba was out searching for Abdollah. The *komiteh* found him first.

⁂

Three weeks later, on a windy September day, my parents pushed their way through the bottleneck of family members, reporters, and the public to get into the courthouse. They waited in the dark hallway of the courtroom for the final day of Abdollah's two-week trial. The charge was murder.

After interrogating the girl from the house, the police had ultimately picked up everyone connected to the hotel, including the two boys from Room 314. They were accused of bank robbery and a murder connected to the hidden gun. After fabricating, then recanting a story that Baba had masterminded the crime, the two boys claimed that Abdollah had driven them to the bank where they stole a total of 2,000 tomans—the equivalent of $300—and shot the bank security guard who attempted to stop them.

To our family, the idea that Abdollah had done such a thing was as ludicrous as the charge that Baba had been involved. Baba and Maman believed that they knew their son and the limits of his adolescent rebellion. Would he drive off? Resent an arranged marriage?

Would he leave the top button of his shirt undone? Yes. Rob a bank, kill someone? Impossible.

Abdollah was caught in the momentum of the ayatollah's machine. In the bloody chaos that followed the revolution, there was no justice—only blind vengeance.

The headline of that morning's paper read: "More *Mofsede-fel arz*—offenders of the moral order—to be brought to justice and executed." In the article, Abdollah's name appeared first. Under the new Islamic Republic, Ayatollah Khomeini established a judicial system run by clerics that carried out heavy punishment for even the smallest crimes that were believed to be "spreading corruption" through Iranian society. In these new religious courts, boys like Abdollah were judged as men, even at the age of 15.

Baba was a man of faith, but what he saw had nothing to do with faith. Thugs ran amok, as they had in our home, wreaking destruction. In the U.S. media, "ayatollah" came to mean that one man, Khomeini. But in Iran, several ayatollahs held positions similar to those of archbishops. Each ayatollah held his own views. And even at the launch of the new regime, many ayatollahs dissented; this was not the way of Islam.

Baba underestimated the significance of Abdollah's trial, which was covered extensively in the newspapers and on the radio. And although ayatollahs were now asking for peaceful demonstrations and a new system where religious jurists would serve only as advisers to elected rulers, their pleas were silenced. In effect, a dictatorship in the name of religion usurped law and order in Iran. Anyone could be sentenced to death on any charge—without proof in court.

Abdollah's case was one of the first tried in the new courts: a test of Ayatollah Khomeini's power and that of his newly appointed judges.

One of these was Sheikh Ferdus, a disciple of Khomeini who would use this case to establish a name for himself. Abdollah's claim that he had no knowledge of the robbery was irrelevant.

In the courtroom, among the buzz of conversation, Baba overheard a man ask, "This is what our country has become?" He looked at Baba. "Shepherds with a few religious classes under their belt and no legal experience will decide our fate? This is not what we wanted from our revolution."

Baba, however, remained confident that this new system was in the hands of men who believed in God and that Abdollah would soon be vindicated. To reassure Maman, he whispered in her ear, "It will be over soon, he will be coming home. I promise."

In the windowless courtroom, Baba stared at the empty chair where Abdollah's lawyer would have sat. Recognizing that the verdict was already decided, the celebrity lawyer Baba had flown in from Tehran had quit mid-trial.

"It's the Islamic Republic of Iran now," he told Baba before leaving. "This is a losing battle. They're going to make an example of your son. You are too much in the public eye. I'm against this and their regime, and my dissent will only hurt you. This is becoming personal, and I want nothing to do with these courts." He knew what Baba didn't—or rather, what Baba chose not to believe.

In those panicked moments when Baba found himself without a lawyer for his son and saw the court was about to adjourn, he made a request to address the court himself. He had spent most of the previous night pacing the hallway as he prepared his speech.

In the back of the courtroom, Maman closed her eyes, thanking God that this was the last day of the trial, the last day she would be sitting far away from her son as he stood trial. She opened her eyes only when Abdollah entered and walked past the judge to his chair.

Weeks before Abdollah's trial, a bigger picture of his accusers had emerged. Earlier on the night of the rape, the two boys had also robbed and murdered a jewelry store owner. How could anyone believe these criminals as they accused my brother, who had barely known them?

There was a hush as Baba rose from the seat where his lawyer once sat. Squaring his shoulders, he walked to the center and faced the courtroom full of people, looking directly into their eyes as he spoke. "To all the parents in this room, I say this: We were brought up believing that we had to watch over our daughters with extreme care and caution. But today, I have news for you all: We have to watch over our sons.

"My son is a good boy. And he was exploited—*Ighfal shod*. He's honest and hardworking. He's only 15. He's married. These two thugs lied to him and manipulated him. He didn't need money; he makes four times the amount they stole in one week. He's no robber, no murderer."

Maman didn't take her eyes off Baba as he addressed the courtroom, talking about his son, his family, his business, and his commitment to the community. When he finished speaking, many women dabbed their eyes with tissues or with the corner of their chador. Almost everyone in the courtroom, including the 40 hotel employees present, stood at the close of his speech.

Judge Ferdus sneered at Baba and demanded everyone take their seats. He refused to give the verdict in court and declared that it would be reported in the coming days.

In the morning, Baba sat by the sofreh. He rubbed his eyes that burned red from lack of sleep. Kneeling, he pressed his forehead against the ground as sunlight began to spread over the floor. "God, thank you for letting this nightmare end. I know my son will be safe soon."

As Baba rose and folded his prayer rug, the hotel manager came running toward him, sweat on his forehead. "Haji, look," he said, holding up the newspaper.

Baba's knees buckled when he read the words: "Abdollah, *Mofsede-fel-arz*—moral sinner—Found Guilty."

When Maman woke that morning, she collapsed when she heard the news of her son's fate. The sentence was death or life in prison. That morning, there was no breakfast, no hand-fed bites of Barbari bread. On the deck, under the blue sky where she could reach out to God as she wept, Maman unrolled her prayer rug and raised her arms, palms open, as she recited Arabic verses. Tears poured down her face during prostration, and her shoulders were racked with sobs. Afraid that she couldn't stop crying, I sat at her feet, keeping guard.

Baba reassured her that although the two boys had been ordered to death, Abdollah would remain in prison, awaiting a review of the judge's decision by the newly organized high court of Grand Ayatollahs in Qom.

The rest of the day, when Maman wasn't on the deck wailing, she lay on the couch. When I brought her two cucumbers to fix with salt the way we liked—one for me and one for Iman—she looked at me with her soft eyes, a tear inching behind her ear. I slid one of the cucumbers behind my back and held out the other, but she closed her eyes and turned away.

Two days later, Maman was still tearful, but off the couch and busy cooking pots of stew and rice. The maids and driver made deliveries of radishes, mint, and parsley mixed for *sabzi*, as well as a large assortment of vegetables. The sizzle of the green beans frying in the pan told me Maman was also preparing *lubia polo*—Zain's favorite beef and bean rice dish.

Was food being prepared for some kind of celebration? A party perhaps?

Careful about interrupting, Zain tugged on Baba's pant leg. "Baba, where're you going?"

Baba was bent over, packing the car trunk with watermelons, cantaloupes, and boxes of canned fruits. "I'm not going anywhere, son. We're all going together to see Abdollah. Go check with your mother and let me know when the food's ready."

In the kitchen, Maman pushed away a box she had received days ago. It was filled with photos from Abdollah's wedding; the bride and her family had been scissored out of them. Maman did not hear from the girl she had welcomed into her heart as her daughter-in-law. After Abdollah was arrested, there were no calls, no notes, no conversations. Maman heard rumors that because the marriage was never consummated, the young bride was promised to another family, to an ayatollah's son.

In the car, Maman barely met our eyes as she leaned over the backseat to hand us single orange and apple slices, and *ajeel*—the perfect mixture of walnuts, raisins, pistachios, dried mulberries, and almonds. As we bumped down the dirt road, clouds of dust blew into our noses and mouths through a small opening in the window. Small rocks slammed against the undercarriage of the car, but Baba did not slow down. I could see Maman's shoulders tense as the truck in front of us accelerated over the potholes and an explosion of exhaust sounded off like a gunshot. Baba continued reciting Qur'anic verses in a soft whisper as Maman stared out the car window.

When we finally pulled into a field of dying patches of grass, Maman held her black chador tight, only one eye and the tip of her nose showing. Under the hot summer sun were hundreds of women. Fighting for shade, they crowded together under a weeping willow tree whose yellowish, feather-veined leaves hung over a gray cement building and the field.

The women fanned themselves as they poured basmati rice onto serving dishes placed on sofrehs laid on the uneven ground. The smells of stews and *lavash* bread filtered through the air around us, but all the faces were blank.

Baba chose a spot closest to the cement prison building and placed our blanket on the muddy ground where a few patches of grass were still exposed. Through the afternoon, as the sun began its downward climb, family after family shuffled their belongings into bags and flowed toward the entrance.

Finally, we were herded into a hot room that smelled of wet mud and body odor, facing the reception area. A five-inch-thick glass panel smeared with fingerprints separated two chairs, two tables, and two telephones. But on one side, a heavyset guard wearing a holster and badge watched as prisoners approached the glass to speak to their families.

Each prisoner picked up the telephone receiver. A line of dark-haired, dark-eyed, unshaven men came forward; they all looked grim. In the back I could see Abdollah's smile shine through the group of men, but his face wasn't as I remembered. Although his hair was combed with care and parted from the left, it was unstyled, and he looked exhausted. His luminous eyes, so like Maman's, were shadowed; his color was ashen. I stared at a purple bruise on his temple. My eyes moved to the floor and, out of instinct, I grabbed Iman's hand.

Baba snatched the black phone's cracked handle and whispered across the glass partition.

"*Pesaram.*" My son.

"Baba, I'm fine."

When Abdollah saw me sneaking a look at him, I quickly shifted my gaze to the dried mud on my new red shoes, which I had worn for the occasion. There was no ventilation in the room; I coughed as it became more difficult to breathe. Although I was afraid to talk on the phone, I wanted to ask Abdollah how we would have a pillow fight through the glass. When I finally pressed my palm against his, the glass between our hands felt slippery and thick, like lamp oil on my fingertips. I smiled as I left my sticky handprint.

Hadi shook his head from side to side as Maman tried to hand him the phone.

Baba had anticipated our discomfort. He pulled a roll of money from his pocket and reached to shake hands with the large bearded guard.

"Just one of them and only for a minute," the guard answered, accepting the handclasp and concealed cash. He motioned to us.

I followed as Baba pushed Hadi into a room with metal bars. When Baba put his hands on Hadi's shoulders and walked him toward his brother, Abdollah whispered, "Hadi, come here. Let me hold you. I miss you all so much."

Slowly, Hadi approached, his arms open to Abdollah who was kneeling on the floor, his orange prison suit now dirty at the knees. I remained at the entrance, mute. Around us, we could hear the clang of slamming metal doors and women crying. I wanted my Maman.

Hadi was quiet as Abdollah spoke. "How's school, Hadi? How's Maman? Are you helping her around the house?" When they finally embraced through the bars, Hadi dug his fingers in Abdollah's orange jumpsuit, squeezed his eyes shut, and placed his head on the bar closest to his brother's shoulder. Soon, Abdollah would be marking his 16th birthday in prison.

Abdollah touched Hadi's shoulders and gently pulled him closer. Staring in his eyes, he began to whisper. Slowly, Hadi nodded and shook his brother's hand through the bars. As he walked away, he looked back twice and waved. Hadi appeared changed, more troubled then than before the conversation.

Back in the muddy yard where families waited, we helped my parents hand out the stews and rice dishes to those still waiting on the patchy grass for visits with their loved ones. When we piled back into our car, a heavy silence prevailed.

We children understood that the hot, gray building where Abdollah sat behind greasy glass was a bad place and that he couldn't leave any time soon. But none of us really knew the reason he was there. Our parents didn't tell us, and we knew not to ask.

We didn't know about the calls to Grand Ayatollah Shahami, who said he could do nothing to help Abdollah, or the attempts to reach Ayatollah Khabazi, the revolutionary cleric whom Baba and Abdollah had hidden for a year and who was now at the center of the newly established government. Khabazi never returned Baba's calls. We didn't know about the meeting with Maman's brother Mohsen, a city official who served as the right-hand man of Mashhad's Mayor Tabasi.

When my parents tried to meet with Mohsen, he shaded his eyes from the sun and bowed his head, refusing to meet Baba's eyes.

"Let it be handled in Qom," he told Baba. "It's the new Islamic court, Haji. The new clerics will review the judge's decisions. I have no authority. The decision is in their hands."

Baba waved his arms in frustration. "Surely you can see that this is a terrible mistake? The judge must be made to understand that this sentence is unjust."

"Each one of these clerics, these new mullahs, are fighting for power. And, Haji, the judge doesn't like you. You've been talking about this too much." Mohsen stopped walking and faced Baba. "He's not going to let Abdollah go after he's already ruled and have the community accuse him of accepting a bribe. You have to know who you are dealing with."

"Mohsen jaan," Maman said, as she placed a hand on her brother's arm.

Mohsen didn't look at her. "It's out of my hands. I can't do anything. It's a new regime. Even my boss has no power here in Mashhad. And for my own family's sake, I cannot risk any involvement."

For the next six months, except for once a week when we drove to the prison with a trunk filled with watermelons, canned beans, pineapple, and peaches for Abdollah and the other prisoners, Maman spent her days making bargains with God and Imam Reza. Although Baba hated the Islamic state run by men who had hijacked his beloved religion for power, he had no choice but to appeal to those clerics, the "men of God," for his son's release.

Nothing more could be done in Mashhad. Baba's goodwill and community service were no match for the ambition and fear inspired by the men of this new regime. People who had been intimate friends and had borrowed money from Baba, stayed at his hotel, and even traveled with him for free, were now distancing themselves. After the revolution, everything was fraught with uncertainty; no one wanted to risk their rank or connection in the new government or put their families in jeopardy.

It was a dangerous time and, although I was too young to realize what was really going on, I felt Maman's uneasiness and sensed that we were all at risk.

THE
POMEGRANATE
FARM

——❧——

WITHOUT TELLING US WHERE we were going, Maman and Baba crowded my three brothers and me into the backseat of the car and drove 16 hours west to Rasht, where the Salamats, our close family friends, owned a pomegranate farm. This was the first time we were to be away from our parents, and our distress was palpable. After the Salamats greeted us and our parents had left, Iman wouldn't let go of my hand; we both kept our heads down and our eyes focused on the ground. As they ushered us through the pomegranate trees and fruit fields, we barely noticed the bright flowers that stretched like an endless line of ballerinas, or the heavy scent of lemon blossoms. We didn't stop, as we normally would have, to taste the cherries and mulberries—the *toot*—that the Salamats picked in an attempt to distract us and make us feel comfortable.

Hadi, restless and agitated, finally took his eyes off the ground and climbed a tree, then jumped down to climb another. Like a monkey, he clawed his way up and down the trunks, trying to settle himself. When he finally came down, Mr. Salamat reached for his hand and put his arm around his shoulder. Hadi shrugged it away and ran ahead.

Zain was the only one who ate that night. He shoved bread, rice, and fresh whitefish in his mouth, and then complained when the tiny fish bones pricked at his mouth and throat.

Iman and I slept on a mattress on the floor, our bodies tangled in an embrace, while Hadi stayed awake watching the door. I couldn't hear Zain crying himself to sleep, but I woke up a few times and saw the vibration of his sobs beneath his blanket. And for the first time since I was in diapers, I wet the bed every night. After changing my pajamas, I eased my sleeping little brother to the dry corner of the mattress and curled my arms around him again. Avoiding the wetness of the mattress would become our nightly routine as we counted the days until Maman and Baba would return for us.

MAMAN

In Tehran, across the mountains and hours away, Maman's hands and legs still trembled as she adjusted her chador and underwear after the strip search at the entrance to the Khomeini compound.

"I'm so deeply sorry for their behavior," Mrs. Khomeini whispered. "They're overprotective of my husband. They had specific instructions not to search you. Please forgive me."

Embracing Maman, Mrs. Khomeini kissed her on both cheeks. "I told them you're like a sister. I will never forget your great hospitality and all the wonderful meals you prepared for us when we stayed at your hotel in Mashhad."

"I'm here about my son, Abdollah," Maman answered, trying to be businesslike though she couldn't disguise the pleading tone of her voice. "A great injustice has been committed and I came to speak to Ayatollah Khomeini, to tell him what people are doing in his name and in the name of religion, and to beg him to intercede. My son is just 16." Maman, who was squeezing Mrs. Khomeini's hand, said this all in one breath, then gulped for air, trying to control her tears.

One of Mrs. Khomeini's three daughters offered Maman tea and sweets, and the women gathered around her, touching her hands and shoulders and listening as she told her son's story. Taking Maman's hands again, Mrs. Khomeini reassured her that Abdollah would be exonerated.

When the eldest daughter returned from speaking to her father, she reported that illness prevented him from receiving visitors, but that he had promised to intercede in Abdollah's case. Later, in fact, he arranged a meeting between Baba and a lead judge who was to reroute Abdollah's file from the court in Qom to Tehran. There, under Khomeini's oversight, the judge was to "personally review the case and correct it."

However, my parents had heard of so many innocent deaths in the midst of the postrevolution chaos that they worried Abdollah's file would not be handled as planned. They decided to drive to Qom to intervene with the newly formed religious high court, which would ultimately decide Abdollah's case.

The son-in-law of Maman's sister, a cleric with the new court, was the next person to take Maman's hand. "I know his case well. I know it's on its way here to Qom. I'm to receive it and personally take it to my superior. Rest assured." He added, "My mother is inviting you all to her house for a feast after Abdollah's release. Go home and rest. Your nightmare will be over soon."

Even with reassurance from Mrs. Khomeini and now Maman's family, my parents decided to seek the support of one last person. Although Ayatollah Khabazi had received many urgent messages that Abdollah was in trouble, he had not returned Baba's calls in the months since the verdict. Now a key figure in the Qom leadership, it appeared that Ayatollah Khabazi had forgotten the risks Baba had taken for the Khabazi family when he hid them from the shah back in Mashhad.

At his home they found only Mrs. Khabazi, who invited them in, offered tea and dinner, and insisted they spend the night. Again and again, Mrs. Khabazi thanked Baba for saving their lives during their year in hiding, and said that if it hadn't been for him, her family would not have this chance for a new life in Iran. Although she reported her husband was traveling, she promised that he would take care of the matter.

"They're back. They're back!" Zain screamed as he jumped down the stairs, having caught a glimpse of our parents' car pulling up the long driveway. It had been three days since we had seen them.

I ran to the window, and as I watched Maman step out from the car, my shoulders relaxed. Iman, Hadi, and I ran down to greet her. She was overjoyed to see us. Baba, looking deflated and exhausted, gathered us up in his big arms. Refusing an offer of dinner, my parents stayed at the pomegranate farm only long enough to perform the ritual cleansings—*wudu*—before their evening prayers, and then herded us into the car for the journey back to Mashhad.

With promises from the highest authorities in Iran, including the deputy to the Supreme Leader himself, our parents' hopeful mood filled the car for the long ride home. Holding Iman with one arm on her lap, Maman reached with the other to massage Baba's neck. "*Khaste nabashi.*" She whispered endearments for the first time since this ordeal began. Baba reached behind his neck to touch her hand. "I did my duty. This has been a hard burden for you, but I promise our family will be whole again soon."

Eventually Maman sent Iman to me in the backseat so she could feed Baba slices of peeled tangerines to keep him alert for the 18-hour drive home. Looking at her, he began singing the only song lyrics he knew: the song he always sang when we traveled in the car. "*Baroon barooneh*— it's raining, it's raining and the ground is getting wet. Don't worry my flower, everything will be set. We'll survive the storm, we'll survive the pain." One by one, we all joined in, humming in unison as we arranged ourselves on two blankets that kept us warm over the course of the cold drive east. Iman's head was on my lap, and he held tight to my index finger with both his hands as I rested my head on Hadi's shoulder, which had now pressed against Zain's. I worked hard to keep my eyes open, but finally began to dream as Maman continued to hum to us.

When we finally arrived home, my parents each carried a limp child into the house. Afterward, Baba dropped to the couch. Still wearing his glasses, he fell fast asleep. He had been driving for three days.

As I finally began to drift off, I felt Maman's loving eyes pass over each one of us. She left our bedroom door open and paced through the quiet hallway, the rustle of her nightgown the last whisper of fear.

When Maman finally fell asleep with her black stockings still on her feet, I could faintly hear the sound of her moans. The promises from people in high positions had not left her at peace. At one point, I heard her gasping for breath and saw Zain leap from the bed to check on her. We all woke in unison and stood by our door and saw Baba cradling Maman's head in his hands. She clutched at her throat and gestured toward Baba to help her. Pounding on her chest, she whispered, "*Khoda*, please help me, my heart is closing."

Half asleep, her palms clammy and wet, she mumbled the content of her dreams to Baba. She seemed unaware of her children listening nearby. She told Baba of the shadows of young men, standing hunched next to each other in a line like trees in a forest, screaming as bullets rained on them. Blood splattered everywhere and she, a witness to this carnage, could do nothing. "When I moved closer to the trees, I saw him: It was Abdollah and his lips were moving. He was reciting his final prayer. He had a light around him. Bullets flew at him but bounced off," Maman choked through her tears.

MAMAN

Mashhad, 1980

Days later, Maman walked around our house at the Rose Hotel before dawn, waiting for the dim light that signaled prayer time. The visit to see Abdollah was drawing closer. Hearing sounds from the outer walls, she walked toward the open front door. Dozens of women entered the courtyard, their faces pale. Maman's breath suddenly caught, and she pressed her hand over her heart.

The voices of my grandmother, three of Maman's sisters, and dozens of other female relatives and friends woke us as they flooded into the house. My aunts entered, slapping their cheeks with their hands as they cried out. Maman's fingernails dug in as she gripped her chest. She couldn't breathe or speak; she dropped to the couch. The women encircled her, fanning her as they recited Qur'anic lyrics.

The sound of shoes on the brick walkway shook the deck, and angry caws filled the yard as the chatter of men's voices talking over one another woke the crows. Through the window we watched dozens of ayatollahs, many of whom we had never seen before, rip off their turbans and dash them to the deck, crying out "foul play," and chanting in unison "*Chera?*"—asking each other why this had happened and praying for God's help.

Maman started to tremble. "What's happened? Tell me the truth." She fell to the floor and then tried to stand, pounding her chest, but her legs gave out again and she fainted. Minutes later, she opened her heavy eyes, seeing a glimpse of her gentle older sister, our favorite aunt—Khaleh—holding a glass of rose water with sugar crystals. As her eyes shut again, her fingers loosened her blouse, exposing her chest.

At the window, still in our pajamas, we watched the sweat drip down the foreheads of the clerics whose head wraps were piled on the cement deck. At first no one seemed to notice my brothers and me.

When Khaleh brought us to kiss Maman, she whispered, "Say goodbye to your mother. We'll come back home in a few days." Maman's breathing was labored. Zain started to cry, and Hadi scrambled away.

"I won't leave Maman!" Hadi yelled as Khaleh pulled him toward the door.

"Mamani," I whispered as we stumbled down the walk, the strange ayatollahs on the deck wailing, "God, please forgive us."

I repeated my mother's desperate pleas although I knew no one could hear me: "What's happened? Tell me the truth."

The air in my grandparents' home felt thick in my throat as I hurried past the open cellar door to bring some water for my grandfather, Iman, and Khaleh. We were finally together again after a disorganized exit—Hadi and Zain had climbed out the bedroom window and run when Khaleh explained that we would be leaving home for a while. But where was Abdollah? Still in that dark gray building? How would he know how to find us?

The house had been quiet all day, and everyone appeared changed. Grandpa's eyes were heavy, lined with dark circles. A sadness had settled over us.

Every corner of the house felt scary, but the staircase down to the cellar terrified me. It yawned open, dark and gaping as a tomb. But that night a light coming from the bottom of the stairs caught my eye. Someone was down there. I called out: "Iman? Khaleh? Zain?" No answer. I froze. The light glowed brighter, and warmth traveled up my spine as the shape of a figure emerged: a fleeting image, his hand waving.

I put my foot on the first step, shaking. "Dadashi?" I gasped. He'd found me.

His smile broadened as he waved me toward him. I tried to go down another step but my knees buckled and the light disappeared. "Come back, Dadashi. Come back," I said to the empty darkness. Suddenly hopeful, I ran down the dark steps so fast I almost stumbled. I opened the storage room doors, searched in the adjacent bathroom.

I never saw Abdollah again.

❦

A few weeks later, we trudged up the walk, home at last. I stared at our yard, dirty and overgrown with weeds. I pushed open our front door, and the sound of burning *esfand*—rue seeds—popping on the stove startled me.

It was not Maman who greeted us, but Khaleh, who had left us with our grandparents so she could return to caring for our parents. She kissed us and shook the tray of esfand seeds over our heads, saying, "This is to protect you little angels from the evil eye." The incense left a thick trail of smoke. Khaleh recited a prayer in Arabic, mixing the religious with the superstitious, just in case.

The door to Abdollah's room opened as my grandmother leaned out. "Quiet, my dears. Your Mamani is resting." Iman squeezed my index finger. Zain, now six, began sucking his thumb—something he hadn't done since he was a baby—and hung on to Hadi's pants. Hadi pushed into the room, Zain stumbling behind. Iman and I stopped at the doorway.

Buried deep in blankets, Maman's eyes were fixed on a place no one else could see. An untouched cup of lentil soup and a glass of rose water and dissolving sugar crystals sat on the bedside table. Quiet filled the room.

Hadi elbowed past my aunts and ran out, Zain trailing behind him. Minutes later Zain's cries broke the silence, piercing through the open window. "Maman, come quick."

Khaleh went instead. We couldn't understand that our Maman was deep in a Valium-induced sleep.

Outside, Hadi sent crows flying as he climbed the final rung of a rickety wooden ladder and stepped onto the roof. He turned and sat with his legs dangling over the edge.

Khaleh waved her arms. "Hadi jaan, come down. You're going to get killed."

"I'm staying here until Maman comes out. Don't try to talk me out of it. I'm going to stay here forever if I have to."

The hotel personnel milling in the yard whispered to each other as they watched Hadi. One worker started up the flimsy ladder, but his weight splintered the first step in half.

Khaleh turned to the crowd and waved them away. "Leave us alone. He doesn't need an audience. He just wants his mother." She went to the ladder and put her right foot on the second rung. It too cracked.

Hadi put his hand up, "Stop climbing, Khaleh. Just stop!" He began to back down the ladder. "I'm coming down."

Hadi sat cross-legged in the middle of Abdollah's room, his back to Maman. She knelt down next to him. In the dimness, her movements were heavy and slow, as if she was underwater, but she leaned down and kissed his shoulder. "What are you doing Hadi *jaan*?"

It was the first kiss anyone had received since we had returned home. Hadi wrapped ropes around the pile of broken toy car parts at his feet. He had gutted all of our high-end Kuwaiti toys, and was now engrossed in putting the mismatched parts back together.

"Do you want some help?" Maman reached for a toy.

"I don't want anything from you."

Maman flipped on the light switch and caught her breath. For a moment, she seemed to truly waken—in horror. Red blotches and streaks covered the walls. She looked down at Hadi and saw that he had painted a red moustache above his mouth, his weapon now abandoned on the floor beside him: a tube of lipstick. Crushed Pomegranate.

"Oh, Hadi!"

Hadi turned away from Maman and faced the window. "If you don't like it, paint over it."

Maman's heavy eyelids began to close. It was too much. She stumbled over the broken toys and drifted back to Abdollah's room, falling onto his bed under the hanging cloud of *esfand* smoke.

We all fell under the cloud's spell. Zain slept all day, blanket up to his chin, face to the wall. Iman stared at the ceiling, sucking on multiple lollipops at once, his toys at the other end of the room. And I wet my bed, every night.

Maman was faring no better. When my grandmother helped her sit up in bed, plucked her overgrown eyebrows, and dressed her in a clean blouse, she didn't seem to recognize her. When she force-fed her broth from meat stews, Maman vomited. For weeks, she consumed nothing but spoon-fed rose water, flavored with Valium. Without sedation, she hit herself, as was the custom in distress, banging her head against the walls and shuddering with wracking sobs that left her unconscious. Every day, doctors and natural healers visited, trying to cure her of what was—to us—an as yet unnamed sorrow.

After a few weeks, Maman could walk with assistance. She would leave Abdollah's room only to use the bathroom, where she would stay for long stretches of time. One day when I went to check on her, I found her with the metal chain from the water tank around her neck. My mind spun. When she saw me, Maman quickly untangled the chain and walked back to her room. From then on, whenever she went into another room, I waited in the doorway, keeping guard.

For months, while Maman slumbered in a drugged sleep, Baba was away, negotiating to sell the hotel. We lived in a false winter, not feeling the sun on our skin although, outside in the world, it was spring, then summer. The garden, which once rang with laughter, fell silent. Our playhouse sat empty in the backyard, leaves and rainwater collecting on its roof. Our bikes slumped against the side wall, pedals rusting in the rain. The vegetable garden grew high and wild with weeds.

Stillness settled over us. My brothers and I didn't know what had happened to Abdollah, but we knew this much: Not only was our eldest brother missing, but we had lost our mother, too.

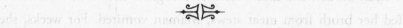

When change came, it would bring another blow: Maman's father, who had gone into the hospital for a routine surgery on his shoulder, fell suddenly ill.

The four of us were in the backseat of the car with Maman when the hotel manager, who was driving us, slammed on the brakes.

"Bismillah! What in the name of God is this?"

The manager lowered the window to face the barrel of a semiautomatic rifle.

"Where do you go in the middle of the night?" a young revolutionary guard demanded.

"I'm driving this woman to see her ill father."

Maman gripped the door handle and pulled her *chador* closer.

The guard pointed to the side of the road with the nose of his gun. "Pull over here."

Three other young guards, all armed, lined up beside him.

The manager got out of the car, and the first guard led him away, into the darkness.

Iman began to whimper.

When they didn't return, Maman rolled down her window and called to the other guards. "*Khasteh nabasheen*—Good evening and I hope you aren't working too hard." Her voice was calm. "Please call my husband at the Rose Hotel. Our manager is driving us to see my father who's very ill. I must go to him now."

This was the longest sentence she had uttered in weeks.

"We don't have phones in the middle of the streets, *zanikeh*. Bitch." The guard tapped the tip of his gun against her car door. "Your husband can't do anything for you. This is an Islamic state. *Mifahmi?* Do you get it now?"

Maman's breathing became shallow; her body began to tremble.

Then it happened; I didn't even have time to flinch. Maman opened the car door and flew at the guard, her *chador* flaring like bat wings. She walked straight at the gun barrels and screamed: "My father is sick. He might be dying. Let me go!" she screamed.

"Get back in the car, *zanikeh*."

"You think I'm scared of your gun? You're hiding behind the guns you don't even know how to use!"

Maman moved closer; the guard stood, too stunned to move away. "You're my son's age, but my son had more honor in his little finger than you'll ever have in your entire life." Her voice rose to a scream, "It was you that took my son. It's you who destroyed our lives."

Hadi bolted out of the car, and ran toward Maman. The moment she heard his footsteps, she turned and caught him. At ten, he was tall for his age—almost as tall as the guard. Hadi shouted "*Pedarsaga*—you bastards." The three other guards and the manager came running.

"Please, return to the car," Hadi whispered to Maman.

"Have mercy." The manager pleaded with the first armed man. "This woman is not of sound mind. You can see that she's not well." He offered his hand and, in his palm, I caught a glimpse of the wadded pink. Motioning to Maman to get in the car, the manager passed a roll of money to the leader with a handshake and placed his other hand on the lead soldier's gun. I had never seen so many pink bills. A small fortune.

The men lowered their guns.

As the manager slipped back into his seat and shifted the car into gear, his voice shook. "Thanks be to Allah."

That night, Zain sobbed for our Grandpa Rahim, who never awakened from his surgery. Maman moved back to her bedroom, and pulled Zain into bed with her. When my nightmares woke me before dawn, I ran into my parents' room. But neither Maman, who was in Valium slumber, nor Zain, who was tucked under her arm, was awakened by my sobbing. Zain and Maman were glued to each other on one side, far from Baba.

I looked at my Baba lying at the edge of the bed, awake. His feet dangled, and something in this struck me as wrong. Baba and Maman always slept entwined—even their feet.

"I'm scared," I told Baba.

Tapping the space between him and them, he said, "Come, *azizam*." I climbed in, pulling the sheet over me. As we lay awake, I wondered about the missing—and the dead. Baba and I looked up at the ceiling, side by side, in silence.

BABA

The Rose Hotel sign—the sign that had taken three years to design and install, the sign that symbolized the business that, for ten years, had consumed Baba's life—stared down at him. He had spent the past three months trying to find a buyer for the place that had been home, his other family, and his life's dream.

The trees were bare, and the cold wind signaled the arrival of a new winter. The sounds of the trucks, motorcycles, and the honks of drivers were fading as Baba lifted his head, looking into the dark sky, his eyes filled with tears. Even now, he could hear the sounds of the shovel he used to break ground all those years ago. Baba turned when he heard footsteps behind him.

Mr. Gaffari put his hand on Baba's shoulder. His voice was soft.

"The doors of the hotel are locked. It's time to go, Haji," he said gently.

"I'm indebted to you for all my life," Baba told his dearest friend. "I don't know how I will manage without you."

As Baba climbed into the driver's seat of the car where we waited, Mr. Gaffari said a final goodbye to Maman, who kept her head turned away from the house. As we drove away, I looked back, just as the lights of the Rose Hotel sign blinked off and went dark.

Rahimeh

The hotel and I were five years old. We had been "born" together. When I saw it go dark, a shiver ran through me.

Our journey began uneasily. Zain was sullen, biting his nails. He had to be dragged, screaming, away from his toys: "I don't want to leave!" Hadi was working the door handle, trying to remove it. And Iman, sucking his thumb, sat in Maman's lap.

"But we'll come home someday," I said, afraid to phrase this as a question.

No one said anything.

As Baba drove, the image of Mr. Gaffari and the nightingale, which perched on top of the hotel roof, faded and vanished. I squinted and kept waving even after they were out of view.

Through the back window, I could see the glistening golden dome of the Haram reflected in the sunlight. The third time I saw the dome come in and out of view, I asked, "Why do we keep circling the Haram, Baba?"

"We are saying goodbye to Imam Reza, *azizam*. Repeat after me." Baba began to recite the Arabic prayer.

Goodbye? We never circled the Haram unless we were going on a trip. Maybe we were going very far this time. *Maybe we were finally going to visit Abdollah, wherever he was.*

Maman's palm never left the window as she looked back at the golden dome.

Now, of course, it is obvious that something terrible had happened. But we did not want to know. The most extreme conclusion I ever considered was that Abdollah had been convicted and sentenced to life in the bleak prison where we had visited him. Again, I asked where he was. Baba's voice went high with strain. "He went away to study," he told us. Maman was silent.

We didn't want to know the real answer and, intuitively, we understood that to question this version would cause our parents more pain. For the next three months, we four siblings lived with an invented story about our brother and our family. *Perhaps Abdollah had gone on another humanitarian mission, as he had at 13 when he went with Baba to help earthquake victims in central Iran. Maybe he was in America. Could we drive there?*

MAMAN

Every night since Abdollah's disappearance, after the Valium-induced drinks wore off, Maman prayed for hours. She inhabited a world where the living and the dead were both present; her gaze turned inward and her spirit was gone.

As the weeks passed, it became clear that Maman could not engage fully with us, her remaining children, until she found the will to live again. One morning, she woke from a dream so vivid it seemed real. In it, Abdollah appeared, telling her that he was in a beautiful place and that he was free. Releasing her from her grief, he begged her to return to her other children. That day, we welcomed our mother back to life. We needed her, and, she needed to care for us.

BURYING
THE SECRET

❦

1981
Tehran

SUNLIGHT BOUNCED OFF the orange cherries hanging on the tree outside. I wanted to reach across Maman's windowsill and touch one. Pushing a pillow under my knees, Maman knelt beside me, and we watched the chickens scurrying beneath the fallen persimmon and plum blossoms. The chicks were like fuzzy yellow billiard balls, changing direction and bumping into one another. Bursts of laughter drifted up through the flowering forsythia bushes as my cousins taught Iman, now almost five, to ride a bike. Careful not to disturb us, seven-year-old Zain entered and pressed his head on Maman's back. A warm breeze tugged at his hair.

A beam of sunshine lit Maman's face, brightening the pink in her cheeks. She smiled—something I hadn't seen for over a year. I saw myself, a little girl, in the reflection in Maman's eyes for the first time in almost a year. I rested the heaviness I'd felt on her shoulder.

In that instant, we were perfect. I wanted to stay that way forever.

Perhaps Baba's plan to help our family go on was working. The hope was that we could move through the days without Abdollah and believe somehow that he hadn't left us; then, perhaps life would return to some semblance of normal. Our father must have hoped for this when, six months before, he moved us from our home in Mashhad to the cloistered, 21-room estate in Tehran. Here, far from the turmoil of the Iran-Iraq war that began shortly after the revolution, our traumatized family might find a way to come back to life.

Baba had worked tirelessly for months to sell the Rose Hotel to the right buyer. Even though some so-called "men of God" had politicized his religion and destroyed his life—and even though they were confiscating property, falsely arresting religious minorities, and committing mass murders—our father's faith in God or belief in his beloved true Islam was not shaken. Besides Khomeini, who is well known for his writings on theocratic political rule, there were other *Marja:* men of emulation, who like Baba, believed religious leaders should act as advisers and guides to elected officials. When the hotel was sold, Baba donated the majority of his equity to a religious school that shared his view. With the remainder of the proceeds, he paid his investors, including his debt to his best friend Mr. Gaffari. Finally, he paid off his bank loans and bought an estate in the finest neighborhood in Tehran.

The Mansion With The Green Door

⁂

LATER IN MY LIFE, I came to appreciate the boldness of my father's actions: the way he reinvented himself and did what he could to heal his family. But being uprooted and transplanted to Tehran without warning was another sort of shock. As usual, he had chosen a valuable property, somehow gotten "a deal" on a newish mansion in one of the loveliest parts of Tehran. The area, known for its lush greenery, was mixed in with the embassy residences near the end of Parvaneh—Butterfly—Street. The estate, nearly nine hundred kilometers from Mashhad, was beautiful.

We began to set down new roots—but would they take? All of us were fragile, and an unspoken tension threatened to shatter us at any moment.

The estate was so large that it felt like a posh sanatorium—which was, in effect, what it became for us. The grounds were especially soothing to behold and to cultivate; the garden in particular had an impressive array of lush red, yellow, orange, and white rose bushes.

The mansion was someone else's grandiose dream: a bleached stucco and tile exterior, shaded by birch trees and a fertile fruit orchard. The trees were bright with cherries, peaches, and apples. Inside, the house was 21,000 square feet, with two ballrooms, ten bedrooms, and white marble staircases. Outside, there was a greenhouse, a pool, and a lawn that took ten minutes to cross.

While he searched for work, Baba began remodeling one of the house's ballrooms, so that he could hold religious gatherings for over a hundred guests on Thursday nights and Friday mornings. The ballroom was the one place we children weren't allowed to enter, and the project gave Baba a positive focus. Artists spent more than a month covering the walls with hand-painted domes framed in gold-plated Qur'anic writing. Decorative cabinets held copies of the Qur'an, and an enormous Persian rug with large red flowers kept the cold cement floors insulated. The only thing that made this space different from an actual mosque was a real dome, which Baba would have built on the top of every room if he could have. Though my parents were devastated and disillusioned with the Islamic Republic, they could separate their devotion to their faith from the politics of the painful land in which they lived. They cherished the Qur'an and turned to it. Often, they fell prostrating on the prayer rugs.

Although my brothers and I each were assigned enormous individual bedrooms upstairs, we continued the arrangement of our house in Mashhad, sleeping all together in one of the downstairs rooms closer to our parents. We continued to play the same games we had in Mashhad; when we weren't outside in the garden, we would spend hours inside, creating make-believe cities. Hadi was always the real estate agent—buying and selling buildings and negotiating the corner lots. Zain liked being the police officer and sometimes the lawyer; I held multiple roles as the banker-florist-teacher. And little Iman always wanted to run the car dealerships.

This play engaged us for hours until we were interrupted by the sound of Maman calling us to come and eat a snack of fresh fruit. She had to work hard to pry us loose from our pretend city; for days on end, we left and entered it together, consumed by the pretend lives we constructed. In our playroom, we felt powerful, safe, and in control.

Leaving Mashhad had been good for Maman. She began to eat, and then sleep. She'd stopped taking the pills her mother and sister gave her. She spent long hours in the garden, watering her new plants and trees; slowly, she found more energy to engage with us. The joy and whimsy she once possessed—as when she would cut orange and apple peels into little human figures—did not return. But every day, it seemed as if the light in each room grew a little brighter.

Maman had yet to regularly regain the full pink color of her cheeks or put on her lipstick. But slowly, the color was returning to our lives. Almost every morning, she rose from the prayer rug where she now slept and made her way to my bedside, where she changed the wet sheets before I could try to do it myself, or hide them. She seemed to understand my body's reaction to the trauma we'd experienced, and never shamed or scolded me. In our silence, I felt Maman's full presence and affection were returning.

I imagined how pleasing the acre of blossoming sour cherry and fig trees would be to Abdollah. I told myself that when he came home from his studies, we would be able to crack open a giant pomegranate. But when I looked at the empty fifth bedroom, I couldn't help wondering why Abdollah didn't write or call from abroad. So I cultivated the same limbo as my brothers: not asking, not wanting to know, but filled with longing for missing *Dadashi*.

But soon, Hadi and Zain began to act out.

One morning, I heard shouts and looked outside: Baba was yelling and chasing Hadi with a menacing pair of battery-operated hair clippers, intent on recapturing his son with his half-shaven head.

Maman heard the commotion, too; her body went stiff at the sound of Baba's shouts. Looking sad and old in her black clothing, she rose and stepped outside. She seemed angry and irritated with Baba—routine since she had stopped sleeping in their room.

Hadi dashed past us into the ceremony room, "I don't want my head shaved, Baba!" he yelled.

Baba gripped the door frame with one hand. "I said stop!"

Hadi kicked the Qur'an cabinet hard, shattering glass. "I don't want to wear a uniform for that stupid school. I don't want to go there at all."

Baba had bought Hadi an expensive Samsonite briefcase and spent hours explaining every good thing about his new, private religious school. It was going well until he gave Hadi a tour of the place. During the visit, Hadi had watched his soon-to-be classmates line up with precision, all in crisp uniforms, and with the prescribed appearance: polished, close-shaven heads. They stood, hands folded in front of them, reciting morning prayers.

Hadi had backed away. After that day, he had come home and smashed his toys.

Maman caught up to Hadi and placed a hand on his shoulder. He stopped running. "Haji, is this really necessary? The school is an hour away, and he doesn't like it."

"I've made my decision. He'll start there tomorrow." Baba left the room and returned with a sofreh and a chair to finish the haircut.

Hadi dropped into a crouch, his fists balled up. "I won't go! I don't want to go to that stupid school."

"Haji, listen," Maman began.

But before she could finish her sentence, Hadi's shrill voice interrupted her. "You didn't do this to *Dadashi!*"

A heavy silence fell. We were shocked—that he had defied Baba, and that he had mentioned our brother.

Baba relaxed his finger on the clippers' "on" button; the buzzing stopped.

Before anyone could react, Iman climbed into the chair. He knew the unspoken rules: Don't mention Abdollah, don't upset Maman, and listen to Baba. To disobey would be to shatter this delicate peace. After Maman lifted Iman from the chair and kissed his cheek, we waited to see who would sit in the makeshift barber's seat. When Hadi didn't move from the corner of the room, Zain settled himself in the chair. "Baba, you can shave my head first. I'll like a buzz cut." Unlike Hadi, Zain was looking forward to a new beginning, glad to be away from the third graders in Mashhad who had teased him when, after seeing Abdollah in prison, he showed up at school sucking on a pacifier. In his new school, he hoped he would make friends and learn to read and concentrate better. That was what Baba believed anyway, and Zain was happy to show his support for the new plan.

Even though I did not show it, I was excited, too. Baba had chosen a rather strict, all-girls Islamic school for me. I was determined to be the most pious student at the school. At six years old—a full three years before I was legally or religiously mandated to wear a head scarf in public—I was determined to attend the first day of school in a chador. I would be the youngest girl in my extended family—and as it turned out, in my school—to wear one. After I begged her for weeks, Maman bought the material, and together we sewed a black chador that covered everything but my face. So I wouldn't have to hold it at my chin with one hand, we made a seam in the middle and added sleeves that allowed both my arms and hands to remain free. Maman always wore a chador outside the house, and so did most women that Baba knew and respected.

If I ever doubted that I might wear a head scarf, those misgivings died when I saw Abdollah in the company of a girl without one. He never came home again.

The boys submitted to their haircuts, to Baba's will. When Hadi finally dropped into the chair, his stiff posture betrayed his feelings. The buzzing clippers cut the heavy silence.

As Maman watched, anger crackled around her like electricity. "There you go again—making a decision for all of us without including me. Remember the last time you ignored my advice?"

I began to shake and clenched my thighs to control myself: I might wet the rug. *What had Baba done? What advice had he ignored?*

When I went to bed that night, I tried to lull myself with the image of Maman's shining smile. Instead, I dreamed about my handprint on the oily glass window, Abdollah on the other side.

While the sun was out, we would keep busy in the yard. But when dark descended, Iman rarely spoke, Zain woke up screaming with nightmares, and I wet the bed almost every night.

Tension built, as before an electric storm. One morning, the family's unspent emotion exploded with actual thunder and lightning. A hard rain beat on the windowpanes, and thunder growled as we ate our bread and jam and drank tea in silence. Zain pushed the saucer around in circles. When Baba finally looked at him disapprovingly, he said the unthinkable.

"Where is Abdollah, *really?*"

I stopped chewing. Zain's face was backlit for a second by a flash of lightning.

When no one answered, Zain lifted and then slammed his teacup down on the saucer, chipping a piece of the flowery pattern. "*Pesaram,*" Baba took in a breath, thinking over his answer, not looking at Zain. "Son, your brother is far away, in school. In America. Studying."

Without excusing himself, Hadi ran upstairs and slammed the door of the room behind him.

Maman's gaze was fixed on a spot in the air, far away.

Zain frowned from across the table. "What's America? You let him go there?" His right foot, hammering nervously against the table leg, was causing the breakfast dishes to rattle.

"Yes, *pesaram,* eat your breakfast now," Baba said.

"OK, then." Zain excused himself. Without saying a word, I followed behind him.

As I made my way up the stairs toward my room, beads of rain rapidly moved down the windows. I stopped at Hadi's door, and caught my breath. Hadi stood before his full-length mirror, wearing Abdollah's favorite navy blue suit jacket; he was turning side to side in the mirror, buttoning the jacket then opening it again, adjusting his shoulders. The sleeves dangled over his hands, the shoulder seams sagged, and the jacket hem hung close to his knees. When he raised his arm, I caught a glint of gold on his wrist: the Kuwaiti gold watch, Abdollah's prized possession.

Hadi bent his head to the crease in the inner elbow folds and inhaled the scent of the material. When a thunderclap shook the momentary quiet, he startled and caught my eye in the mirror. Stepping behind the door, he pushed it closed. He knew I would never mention what I had seen.

That night, lying in bed, I tried to picture Abdollah sitting at a school desk in America, his eyebrows knit in concentration over a book. All I could manage was an image of my brother lost in a big building, holding a bag filled with school supplies and weighed down by heavy books he couldn't carry. I pictured him wearing his navy blue suit. Then I didn't want to imagine Abdollah at all.

After a year of attendance, it turned out that Hadi's new school didn't want him and his shaved head any more than he wanted the school. Tangled in suspension, disciplinary actions, and meetings with my parents, he came home from school one day looking pleased with himself. "I'm not ever going back," he declared. A teacher had slapped him hard in the face.

Hadi had been expelled for being disruptive and confrontational. As the months passed, he always found a way to get even with any teacher who struck or humiliated a student. After one shamed several classmates by making them stand in the corner, Hadi took the leg off the teacher's chair and put it back together with gum, smiling when the teacher sat down and crashed to the floor.

Maman inspected the pink mark on Hadi's cheek again. "Kids have to love where they go to school. They have to like and respect their teachers. This will serve no one."

My father interrupted. "It's the best of the best private schools. It was nearly impossible to get him in there in the first place."

"Haji, they hit him. Do you understand that?"

"Yes, I know. Let me think this through."

Hadi put down his fork.

"They tell us not to hit. They say parents are the only ones allowed to punish their children. What gives a teacher the right to hit me and other kids? They're hypocrites, Baba. All of them."

He had Baba, and he knew it. In his fantasies of the hereafter, Baba reserved a special place in hell for hypocrites. Baba swore to change Hadi's teacher.

I knew more trouble would follow.

teacher who struck or humiliated a student. After one slapped several classmates by making them stand in the corner, Hadi took the leg off the teacher's chair and put it back together with gum, smiling when the teacher sat down and crashed to the floor.

Maman inspected the pink mark on Hadi's cheek again. "Kids have to love where they go to school. They have to like and respect their teachers. This will serve no one."

My father interrupted. "It's the best of the best private school. It was nearly impossible to get him in there in the first place."

"Baji, they hit him. Do you understand that?"

"Yes, I know. Let me think this through."

Hadi put down his fork.

"They tell us not to hit. They say parents are the only ones allowed to punish their children. What gives a teacher the right to hit me and other kids? They're hypocrites, Baba. All of them."

This had Baba, and he knew it. In his fantasies of the hereafter Baba reserved a special place in hell for hypocrites. Baba swore to change Hadi's teacher.

I knew more trouble would follow.

ANOTHER CAR RACE

❧

1984

EVER SINCE BABA'S CRAZY CAR CHASE after Abdollah, I didn't like to be in cars—especially when they accelerated without warning. So one quiet Sunday morning, when Hadi led me to the family station wagon with the offer of a ride, I balked. It did not seem like a good idea. But even at 12, Hadi had developed the bold black stare that would later control us all for so long. So I obeyed. After he started the engine, I saw his head disappear as he slumped down in the driver's seat to reach the gas pedal.

"You don't even know how to drive," I said, confused. It was bright out and, as usual, the street was empty of cars and people.

"Don't worry, Sis. *Dadashi* taught me." He seemed entirely too confident. "This will be fun."

I looked through the back window at the house, anxious.

"Sit in the middle, slide forward, and hold on to the front seats," he yelled, gesturing to the middle of the seat behind him. Before I could

~ 107 ~

position myself, I felt the car jerk forward. Hadi pressed his foot hard on the accelerator.

"Here we go," he said. "Hold on tight."

The sudden lurch of the car caused me to lose my grip, and my head snapped hard against the backseat. Hadi tried to keep his foot on the accelerator and his hands on the wheel. We weaved down the road and then, without warning, were suspended in air. The car had rammed into one of the large trees that shaded Parvaneh Street. The front half was squeezed together: My body was thrown against the seat again, and I could see Hadi's face, full of surprise, turning back to look for me. As smoke and steam escaped from the hood, we poked our heads up to see the front-end suspension start to bow.

Hadi pulled himself together, climbed in the backseat, and held my hand as we escaped the car, which was tilted halfway into the air. When the radiator burst and sent steam up the tree, we looked at each other, still holding hands, and ran for home.

I found Maman on her knees on her prayer rug. She was wailing and sobbing. A small photo was on the floor next to her; I sensed it was Abdollah. She didn't see me come in. I sat cross-legged on the rug nearby and folded my hands in my lap.

After slamming the front door closed, Baba stomped through the house. "Maman? Maman?" he called out. "Maman?" His voice boomed down the hall toward the living room. "Where's Hadi? How did he get the car?"

When Baba stormed into the room, Maman sat back on her heels and raised her eyebrows. "He took the car? Oh my God, is he OK?"

"I don't know, but the car is totaled, crushed up against a tree."

Baba moved closer to me and lowered his voice. "Do you know where he is?" he asked, eyes piercing.

"He didn't mean to crash the car, Baba . . . we're OK."

"You were in the car?" he said in an even louder voice. Both my parents stared at me. "Yes," I said, obediently. "But I'm fine."

Maman got up from the prayer rug and began to search the house. She found Hadi sitting in the upstairs hallway. She sat down next to him and placed her arm on his shoulder. "You could have hurt yourself or your sister, *azizam*. You know I wouldn't survive if anything happened to any of you. Promise me you'll never do anything like that again."

Hadi sighed, "Yes, Maman. I'm sorry."

When Maman returned to the dining room, Baba was pacing back and forth, seething. "This has to stop right away. We're losing control of that boy."

"Hadi's sorry, Haji. He won't do it again. Let him think things through. He knows he's done wrong."

"But they could have been killed! He needs to understand that! This time we have to punish him."

"Your punishments lead to no good. That isn't what the boy needs." Maman slammed the lid on a pot, and I let out a squeak.

"Rahimeh? What are you doing?" she said. I had been hiding behind a plant, my back against the wall. "Go, honey. Go find Iman." Maman commanded.

MAMAN AND BABA

"I will never forgive him," Maman swore, lifting a metal spoon and banging the edge of a pot. "I will not!" She turned on the water and began to scrub at one of the pans. "I can't believe you want to do this. After everything, you're still willing to forgive that damn ayatollah!"

After Abdollah's trial, his judge had moved up the ranks and was among the 72 men involved in a bomb explosion during an assassination attempt on Ayatollah Khamenei, Khomeini's second in command. Expected to be in a vegetative state, the judge was hospitalized. When his family sought forgiveness before he died, Maman had refused.

Baba had finally agreed to a visit from Khabazi, the man he had hidden from the *Savak* for more than a year in Mashhad. As Khabazi was now one of the key players in Khomeini's government, he traveled with an entourage, and today, Maman was reluctantly cooking for him and his staff of 17 people.

"I will never forget how he was so conveniently 'out of town' when we needed his help—and how he never got any of our messages," she said, fuming.

Baba leaned toward her. "I put two sofrehs down. OK? Khabazi's security guards can eat in the yard."

Maman stabbed the frying greens with a wooden spoon and didn't say a word as she stirred the meat stew with *gheymeh* lentils. After a few minutes, as Baba turned to leave the kitchen, she stopped him.

"Do you remember when Abdollah used to drive food over to Khabazi's house and hide in the dark waiting for him to open the door? Do you remember when Khabazi was a nobody and we sheltered his family from death, Haji? We risked our lives to save his. Now, after he did nothing to help us in our worst hour, he wants to see us and clear his conscience." Maman was yelling. She poked at the fried lentils again and oil splattered on her hand. "How can he work for Khomeini? How can he be pretending to be a big shot in this government and destroy so many people's lives?"

"He'll be here for an hour, and then we'll make them go. After this, they will stop bothering us and we can get on with our lives." Baba's voice was soft. "Plus, I have a few things I want to say to him face-to-face."

Without responding, Maman turned off the fire under the pan and moved toward the sink.

After the meal, during which Khabazi's wife spent an hour begging Maman to see her husband, she finally relented, and he joined them at the sofreh spread out on the floor. During the 20 minutes Khabazi spent begging her for forgiveness, Maman cried uncontrollably, her head down, her chador hiding her face.

Khabazi pulled out a pocket Qur'an and put his hand on it. "I swear to you, his file never came to Qom." He bowed his head. "I would have done anything for you. I owe you and your husband my life. I will never forget Abdollah's kindness to me and my children. I never saw the file; I swear on this holy book."

His fingernails dug into the pocket Qur'an. "No one can truly be absolved, and nothing will ease your pain, I know this. We were forming a new government, and many mistakes were made. Please forgive . . . and understand. I'm so deeply sorry."

Maman didn't look up. She said nothing, but tears continued to roll down her cheeks.

Watching Maman's sadness vibrate under her chador, Baba stood and turned the doorknob. He could feel Maman's face flare. He knew her head movements, her heavy breathing, and could tell by the slightest change around her eyes what she was feeling. It was time for the Khabazis to go.

Baba opened the door and looked straight at Khabazi. "You were a man of God, not politics. Maybe you could have done more, maybe not. But when it happened, your silence was your greatest sin. You needed to speak up against injustice, especially when it was done in the name of Islam. Your hands are bloodied, too. My son is gone, and that hole will never be filled." Baba's voice was soft and sad. "Only God can forgive now."

After the door shut behind them, Maman's face grew pale, and she began hyperventilating. I hated the ayatollahs for making Maman cry. When Baba came into the kitchen, he saw her distress as she threw the dishes into the sink without regard for their fragility. He took a dish from Maman's hand. "I'll do them. You go rest."

I had never in my life seen Baba offer to do the dishes.

"*Nakhastam*. You've done enough," she answered sharply.

Baba moved to the table, pulled out a chair, and sat.

"And you were going to become an ayatollah? It's hard to tell a good one from the bad." Maman's voice began to rise. "If you had continued your religious studies, I would be divorced from you right now. Not that I wouldn't have better reasons."

Baba shushed her from the table. "*Azizam*, please. The kids are around."

Maman dropped a bowl, splashing sink water all over herself and the counter. Walking to the table, she slammed her fist on it. "You trusted those bastards, those child-killing 'men of God.'"

Baba met her gaze.

"Your faith makes you blind. I tried to warn you, but of course, you didn't listen. And here you are forgiving again."

Baba took in a deep breath. He was preparing for what was about to come.

"You married him off before he was ready. You forced your excessive rules on him. You brought those snakes into our hotel!" She was yelling now. "You took him from me!" She flattened a palm on her chest. "It wasn't just the government. You did this, Haji. You did it!"

I felt the warm liquid on the inside of my pant leg. I didn't understand, but I knew something was deeply wrong. *What did she mean? What had Baba done?*

Baba's jaw tightened and clenched, but he remained at the table as Maman went back to the sink, finished cleaning the dishes, wiped the counters, and put the food away. When she washed her hands for the final time and started to make her way toward the door, Baba rose to say his prayers and spend another night alone. As he left the room, Maman slammed both hands on the table and screamed loud enough for the whole house to hear, "Don't ever bring an ayatollah into my house again. I hate them." She pounded her fists again. "And I hate you!"

When I heard the water turn off in the kitchen, I headed to the yard, where I knew I would find her. As I watched from behind the shrubs, Maman fell to her knees, muddying her skirt as she dug into the grass with her fingers. Her pain was bigger than ever—nothing, not even the earth, could contain it. I closed my eyes and tried to remember her smile, but couldn't.

After Maman finally went back inside, I stayed in the yard. That was when I saw the dandelion. I felt hope filling up inside me. My cousin had always told me that when you make a wish with a dandelion, it will always come true. I bent over and picked it. I chose one that had gone to seed—its golden petals turned to white silver fluff, easily dispersed by a breeze. I shut my eyes, and prayed: *God please help my Mamani find her smile again, and please bring us together again, oh and please end the fighting.* Then, I blew as hard as I could. The flower head disintegrated into the air, sending my message with its seeds.

I feared my effort, my prayer, was hopeless. The only force that could stop the fighting was my parents' concern over Hadi's latest school suspension and Zain's failing grades. My straight A's, study of Arabic, and ability to inspire a dozen little girls to piety by my example of donning a chador in first grade wasn't going to give them a reason to unite again. Only my brothers seemed able to do that.

The next morning, Maman found Zain sitting by the front door, finger in his mouth, pajama shirt damp from tears, and staring straight ahead.

"What's wrong, *azizam?*" Maman asked.

"I'm never leaving this house to go to school alone unless you come with me." He put his head on her shoulder.

This campaign worked for a while. Maman sat at a little wooden table in the back of the classroom, Zain glancing over his shoulder every few minutes to make sure she was there. She was.

Zain clung to Maman's chador as they walked home from school. He ate all the fruit in the bowl and all the bread on the sofreh most mornings. Iman kept sucking on candy forced down by his pacifier. Hadi left our toy cars and planes untouched, but snapped my paint-brushes in half and ripped the wires out of Zain's radio.

We were all questioning whether Abdollah was really "studying abroad." Was he in prison for life? Or was he . . . ? No one could finish a thought so dangerous. We had all tiptoed around the secret; it felt shameful to even speak of it.

✦

The moment arrived during a visit from Mr. Gaffari. Hadi was about to turn 15—the age Abdollah had been when we'd seen him last. For a long time, he hadn't believed the thin story Baba had told, and as the eldest son, he felt that he had a right to know what really happened. Baba did not want to discuss it, but Hadi knew one person who might tell him the truth.

Tugging on his pajama top to unwrinkle it, Hadi hurried out the front door, ripping a leaf as he passed a plant. Squeezing between Baba and Mr. Gaffari as they walked toward the greenhouse in the middle of the yard, Hadi said hello and didn't waste another minute.

"I have wanted to ask you a question for a long time. I need to know before you go back to Mashhad! I trust you, Mr. Gaffari. You're an honest man, and I know you'll tell me the truth."

Baba looked at Hadi as he took a deep breath.

"Mr. Gaffari, Baba told me a few years ago that Abdollah was studying abroad. Now he says he's in America. But *Dadashi* doesn't call; he doesn't write; he doesn't visit. Every time I ask anyone, they give me a different story."

The two men stopped walking. Hadi took another breath and continued. "My aunt tells me that he's never coming back to us. I don't ask Maman. Baba avoids the answer every time. Where is my brother? What happened to *Dadashi?* Please. I need an answer, and this might be the only time I can ask you." Hadi looked at Baba now without apology or approval. "I'm sorry, Baba, but I have to know."

Baba was still, staring at the willow tree, lost in memory.

Hadi wasn't finished. "You see, I'm now the oldest one here, and I told Zain and Rahimeh that he was studying in America. They know something is wrong, but like me, they don't know anything for sure. No one tells us. I've lied to them, too. I've turned into a liar. You see? A big liar."

Mr. Gaffari put his hand on Hadi's shoulder and began to walk with him. "You know you're like my son, Hadi jaan. So was Abdollah." He rubbed Hadi's back. "I'm glad you're telling me this. And I'm sure if you give me some time to talk to your father, I can help you figure this out. Can you do that, son? Can you give me some time to talk with your dad and make sure he talks this over with you?"

Baba was still looking at the ground.

Hadi stopped walking. "Can't *you* tell me, please?"

"I'll talk to your father, *pesaram*. I will. I promise you I'll do that right now." Mr. Gaffari put his hand gently on the back of Hadi's shaved head and let his fingers stroke his neck.

Mr. Gaffari's hand curled around Baba's shoulder as they walked away, their backs to Hadi as he stood silently. His look was as pleading as his words.

For days Hadi waited, but the conversation never took place. He assumed Baba forgot. But he was not about to let his troubles be forgotten.

It was just before 8:00 p.m. the following Friday night. Hadi knew that the anti-aircraft warning shots, which had been lighting up the skies since the Iran-Iraq war had escalated, were about to go off. He had a plan, and it involved his own, personal war games.

The real war—the eight-year Iran-Iraq war—had begun when Saddam Hussein, fearing a Shi'a insurgency and looking to gain the upper hand in long-festering border disputes, launched an air and land invasion into Iranian territory. Saddam worried that Iraq's long-suppressed Shi'a majority would be influenced by Iran's Islamic revolution. By 1984, the conflict had resulted in hundreds of thousands of deaths. By now, we were all too familiar with the nightly anti-aircraft shots.

Zain and my cousin, ten-year-old Mahnaz, were searching for Hadi on the roof, where we often went to play since we weren't allowed outside. Suddenly, a warning crack of a gunshot shattered the air. Hadi, hiding behind an air-conditioning unit, disguised his voice and yelled, "Hands up. Empty your pockets and give me everything you've got!"

Cousin Mahnaz screamed, "Zain, run!" But Zain froze, staring into space.

"I said, give me everything you got!" Hadi yelled again in his thick false voice.

"Zain, let's go!" Mahnaz grabbed Zain's hand and began to run. Pulling him behind her, they moved toward the ladder, but in their panic, they leaped from the roof and fell to the lower story. Zain landed halfway on my cousin, who broke both her legs in multiple places.

Hadi ran out after them, shocked to see the blood. Screams filled the air as he ran for help. After my cousin was taken to the hospital and Zain was bandaged, Baba walked around the yard and the house; he was looking for Hadi who was now missing. "Has he lost his mind? You don't play pranks like that on the roof. He could have killed them."

Five hours later, Hadi was curled in a ball, hiding inside a kitchen cabinet. I kept guard, until it was safe for him to come out. My parents talked to him, but he didn't need the lecture. He knew how badly things had turned out. He had caused our cousin Mahnaz to suffer severely. If she had struck her neck or spine . . .

Later that night, I found Hadi lying in the hallway. He was listening under the doorway to the room where my cousin and Khaleh were now staying full-time during her recovery.

"What're you doing?" I whispered.

Hadi nodded toward the door. "When she wakes up crying, I run and get Maman to bring her pills." I dropped down next to him and we lay face-to-face, our cheeks against the floor, our noses touching, keeping guard.

Even though I was only eight, I understood that Hadi was truly sorry and wished the whole thing had never happened—wished that he, and not Mahnaz, was the one who fell from the roof.

For the next several months, Hadi was on his best behavior: He woke up earlier than usual for school, he asked Baba to buzz his hair as soon as it grew, and he didn't kick his soccer ball in the house anymore.

The good behavior would only last so long.

A few weeks later, the sweet smell of jasmine and cardamom filled the room as my grandmother prepared four cups of tea: two for my parents, one for herself, and the fourth cup, out of habit, for my grandfather. They were sitting cross-legged around the sof-reh, the *samovar* between them, when an orange Ping-Pong ball smashed above their heads into a window. Hadi dashed into the room after it.

"Hadi, stop that right now!" Maman cried, trying to grab him. Hadi snatched the now rolling ball from the rug and used his racquet to smack it hard against the wall in the very spot where our grandfather would have been sitting if he were alive.

The small ball ricocheted into my grandmother's chest and she reactively hit the samovar with the back of her hand, flipping the teapot from the top and pouring steaming tea onto her leg. Her screams sent Hadi running out of the room. When he looked back, Maman was busy trying to take off her mother's scalding black stockings and blowing on her legs to bring some relief.

When Maman found Hadi leaning against the wall in our room, she sat down beside him. "I know you're a sweet and smart boy. I also think that you know the rules about balls and Ping-Pong in the house. So, that leads me to believe that you've either forgotten completely or you got so excited about having an orange Ping-Pong ball that you just couldn't wait to show it to us. Am I right?"

"I didn't mean it, Maman." Hadi's eyes focused on the ground. "Is she OK?"

"She'll be fine, *azizam*. Please, never again. I have your word?" Maman kissed his cheek.

"I'm sorry, Mamani."

Maman rose and held her hand out for Hadi. "Let's take Grandma some fruit."

Hadi was forgiven, again. Although he was getting expelled from school, had wrecked the family car, broken his cousin's legs, and, most recently, had inadvertently burned his grandmother, he was forgiven.

Baba was waiting for Maman in the kitchen. "Don't you see what's happening here? And don't tell me that time will mature him. He's 15. Time to be responsible. At this age . . . ."

Maman met Baba's gaze. "At this age Abdollah was married and running a business? We both know what comes from your control, your way. Hadi needs time." Maman took a step toward the door. "You've ruined my life, but you're not ruining his," she said quietly as she exited the room.

Standing out of sight, listening, my eyes welled up. Why did Maman think Baba ruined her life? Again, I prayed for the fighting to stop, forever.

And then, one day, it did.

Maman stayed at her prayer rug for over two hours, reciting her invocations at twice her normal speed. The sunlight was gone, the house was getting colder, and, as we gathered in our communal bedroom, Baba turned on the radiator. He appeared distracted as he folded and refolded our bedsheets, making sure the pillows were fluffed. This had always been Maman's job.

Later, as I lay in bed, I heard the murmur of their voices, low and urgent, just outside our room. There were no raised voices, no interrupting. The next day, Maman began to let Baba put sugar in her tea like he used to, and Baba didn't yell at Hadi.

Zain, Hadi, and I exchanged looks: What had happened?

❧❧❧

Our hands were sweaty in a tight grip as Iman and I followed Maman and Baba across the outer yard of the busy Tehran airport. The smell of fuel floated around the large crowds of travelers, and the summer sun beamed down on my head, making my chador feel heavier.

I kissed Iman's fat little cheeks over and over. But after two hours of embraces, we had to say goodbye. The reason for the 12-day trip, they told us, was that Maman needed to see a "special doctor," and Iman was going too because he was too young to be without his parents. The reality, however, was that Baba couldn't get visas for us all to travel to England. Because of the Iran-Iraq war, obtaining visas for an entire family—or for adolescent boys that could serve in the war—was impossible.

Although it was hard to let Iman go, we were excited about going to Khaleh's house, just a few hours north of the airport. Our mother's older sister—the one who had nursed her with Valium after Abdollah's disappearance—had also left Mashhad soon after we did. She visited us every few weeks, and we loved our visits with her family in Karaj. There, we would play with our cousins, swim in the streams, and eat Kit Kats every day.

I looked for Hadi among the throng of people. He was by himself, leaning on the empty cart that had held my parents' luggage. Shoulders upright, he was looking around, his gaze shifting.

As my parents and Iman disappeared into the crowd of passengers waiting to depart, Hadi dashed into the restricted area, rolling the cart past the guards and crashing through the crowd. "Maman, wait!"

As the soldiers grabbed him, Hadi shouted, "*Pedarsag,* leave me alone, you bastards."

"What did you say?" a guard growled. He ran after Hadi, grabbed him, lifted him off the ground, and took him to the other side of the barrier.

"Someone take this kid before I beat him," a second guard shouted.

As Maman screamed, "Please don't hurt him!" Baba dropped his bag and began to run toward Hadi. But an airport official blocked him. Baba pushed against the guard's chest.

"He's my son. Let me go talk to him."

"Turn around and go back or don't fly out today." The guard placed a hand on his gun.

Khaleh pulled Hadi away from the guards and wrapped her arms around him, holding him back. "He's OK. I've got him." She called to my parents, "Go ahead. He's going to be all right. Don't worry."

Baba grabbed Iman's hand and guided Maman away from us. "We will be back in 12 days. I promise," he called over his shoulder. Elbowing us, the crowd kicked up dust that blew into my eyes; when I opened them, my parents and brother were gone. I felt my stomach churn. *How would I survive without Iman, my best friend?*

LITTLE RED SUITCASE

THAT NIGHT, KHALEH EMPTIED THE POT of celery stew into a decorative bowl next to the crispy jasmine rice: the glistening *tahdeeg*. "Abdollah loved celery stew. God rest his soul." She coughed.

Zain, who had been busy eating, froze, rice falling from the corner of his mouth. He stared at her, his spoon halfway to his mouth. *God rest his soul.*

Hadi stared at my aunt and squinted his eyebrows as if he were communicating a secret message with her. Then he ducked his head and continued to eat without looking up.

Khaleh stared at Hadi, dropping the pot on the counter. "You're joking? Are you saying they don't know?"

Khaleh had hoped that by now, two years later, my parents would have told us the truth.

I felt my belly clench. Khaleh looked straight at me. "Rahimeh!" She took a breath. "You know he's dead, right?"

Now I was floating, suspended in the corner of the room. The only thing at the table was my shell, my body. Zain took another bite of rice.

"I don't know what you're saying Khaleh," I said, my eyes on my plate. "He's not dead." Even as I said this, I didn't know if it was a question or a statement.

Hadi stabbed the lamb with his fork. "No, he's not. He is studying in America like I told them." He shoved his plate and fled, slamming the front door so hard it shook the windows.

I felt bile rise and fill my mouth. I pushed back the chair and ran to the bathroom. *I would never speak to Khaleh again.*

When Hadi returned to the house, he found me in my cousin's room, brushing her doll's hair. "Do you wish you could have a doll, too?" He didn't wait for the answer. "I'll get you one someday soon," he said. He brought his hand from behind his back. "For now, you can have these."

"Kit Kats. So many Kit Kats!" I screamed in joy. I had never been allowed to have more than one a week. I opened one of the candy bars and offered Hadi two sticks.

"No, no. It's all yours, little sis."

I ate the first stick slowly, licking my fingers.

"Don't worry about what Khaleh said. She's wrong." He gave me a quick wink and as the door closed behind him, I tugged at the brush. *Khaleh doesn't lie, does she?* I gave another sharp pull. Melted chocolate tangled the doll's hair.

That night Zain came to sleep next to me in my room with my cousin. Even though I felt safer, my body spoke for me around midnight, and I began to wet the bed again.

As the 12 days stretched into three months, and my eighth birthday came and went, our parents still had not returned. But we *were* with our favorite aunt Khaleh, who had Maman's gentle voice and soft skin. Her eyes were full, less slanted; her coloring was lighter, almost pale white, while Maman's skin was more olive, smooth and golden. Even with these differences, at night, when she whispered to us, Khaleh sounded enough like Maman to reassure us. We continued to live in our parallel universes, our days filled with cousins, sunshine, fresh fruit, and Kit Kats.

But soon, summer waned and the nights grew cool; fall was coming, and it was time for school again. Located in Tehran, our schools were an hour apart, and this meant splitting us up. Khaleh broke the news in person, so that our parents wouldn't have to tell us over the phone. Her voice cracked a few times. "It will be a little longer before your parents are back. Rahimeh, you'll be close to Butterfly Street, and the boys will be together an hour south near their school. But we will come and visit you every Friday and take you to your house, where we will all stay together every weekend. Soon, your Maman will be home to make you breakfast again, and Baba will take you to school."

Khaleh sounded confident. *And she would never lie to us, right?* And she was right about Baba coming back.

Every few weeks, Baba would fly home and visit for a few days. Khaleh and our cousins would join us at the estate on Parvaneh Street on our days off: Fridays. Saturday through Thursday, the school week meant separation from my brothers.

Those days I stayed at the home of some family friends, the Jahanis. I slept on a hand-stuffed foldable mattress on the floor, my belongings in a plastic bag under the beds upon which the two teenage girls, Mansoureh, 16, and Monir, 14, slept.

The cold from the marble floor rose up fast through the thin mattress and shook me fully awake each night. I snuck from bed and, hand over hand along the wall, guided myself toward the bathroom. The Jahanis would not be waking for morning prayers for a few hours; I had time. Once inside, I eased the door closed without making a sound and turned on the light. I took off my clothes and began the ritual of washing my underwear, pants, and shirt with soap and ringing them dry. Maman always encouraged us to use the nice towels. But here, I didn't dare use the decorative hand towels in the bathroom.

Naked and cold, I stood there for a few minutes as I shook the wet clothes in the air. When I put them back on, my teeth chattered and I clenched my shivering shoulders. *Where was my Maman?*

The route back from the bathroom was always more difficult, going from the light and into the dark. Six doors and one hallway later, I was finally back at the bedroom, where I could see the shadow of the two beds. I made my way over to my mattress in the corner. It had been a lucky night. A nightmare had woken me before the entire mattress and blanket were soaked through, and I could go back to sleep on the dry half. Most nights I wasn't so lucky. Then, darkness would become my friend. I would sit curled in a ball, waiting for the air to dry it all: me, my wet clothes, the blanket, and the mattress.

Far from our ballrooms, rose gardens, and imported bananas, I pulled the dry side of the blanket over my shoulders and felt for the sweater under my pillow. The sweater was my favorite gift from Maman—she had sent it to me from London—a sweet, little, soft pink cashmere sweater that smelled of her jasmine perfume. I took the sweater with me everywhere in my red suitcase. But I would never wear it, no matter how wet and cold I was.

As usual, I barely slept, and I rose a few minutes before Mansoureh and Monir so I could hide my mattress and fold the blankets in such a way that they wouldn't see the yellow stains.

Maman and Baba's promise of a few weeks had become three, and now five months. I had been staying with the Jahanis for two months.

Across town, an hour away, Hadi and Zain were staring at the celery stew in front of them. It was green. Even though Hadi kept nudging Zain to eat and spooned out rice for him, Zain refused to eat any stew that wasn't red, the way Maman made it. Although he couldn't leave the sofreh before everyone was done, he sat toying with the rice and waiting to be excused. He hoped to find refuge in the room he shared with Hadi at the home of their school's vice principal. With a look of distaste and confusion, Zain kept swirling the stew on his plate with his fork, mixing it with the rice, but not taking a bite. *How could the principal's wife not know that tomato paste was the secret ingredient to celery stew?*

Hadi nibbled on the soft *sangak* bread, wishing it was toasted crisp, the way Baba liked.

Once in their room alone, they pulled out their schoolbooks and doodled in silence. There were no toy cars or board games. The only sounds were the growls of their stomachs.

I was found out. One morning while I was at the dining room table doing my homework, Mrs. Jahani entered, screaming, "She's been peeing on this mattress!"

Her two daughters came running from the kitchen.

As their mother unfolded the mattress, my damp pajamas fell out. "*Ey Khoda.* What a stench! How could she sleep in this?" She pointed to the two dozen yellow circles on the blanket she held, pinched by the edge with two fingers. I had not managed to hide the stains, nor the smell.

I ran. Nearly tripping as I jumped down the stairs three at a time, I headed for Parvaneh Street, but only made it to the end of the Jahanis' yard.

Hours later, carrying my red doll suitcase, I was climbing the steps of yet another family friend's home. At least in that house, I had my own bedroom and I could hide my urine-stained clothes under the bed, in my suitcase.

When the mother of my new temporary family, Mrs. Omadi, sniffed out the problem, she washed my clothes. I found them clean and folded on my bed when I returned from school. Even my suitcase had been washed. Every morning from that day on, we had a routine, just as I had with Maman: I removed the sheets and when I returned, they would be clean on my bed.

At school every morning at 7:30 a.m., when the principal asked me to stick out my hands to check that my nails were freshly cut without polish, she had to repeat herself twice. My body was in line with the other girls, but my mind was elsewhere.

I envision Maman clearly. *It is a bright day and the blossoms are out, just like she loves. Hidden behind my back, I carry a bouquet of parrot tulips and forsythia picked fresh from our yard. The normally busy airport is clear. There's no noise, no pollution, no stench of body odor and sweat. The only sound is the wind cooling my face while I watch the disembarking passengers, looking for a black chador and the round shape of Maman's head under it. I could tell her apart from 50 other women in a chador even if I couldn't see their faces. I could tell if she had gained or lost a kilo; sometimes I could even guess which jacket she was wearing, just by the way it shaped the chador draping over it. I run toward her, and she wraps me in her arms and showers me with kisses. We stay that way forever.*

"For the third time, stick out your hands and show me your nails, Rahimeh." The principal's voice startled me. I stuck out a hand. "The other one too," she repeated, raising her eyebrows. "We'll have to talk to your father about your lack of attention when he comes back next week," she snapped as she walked away.

I showed her my other hand and then continued greeting Maman at the airport until school was over and it was time to go home. I was missing Hadi and Zain. But I missed Iman terribly. I was beginning to forget his face.

REFUGE IN LONDON

~❧~

MAMAN AND BABA

Thousands of miles away in London, Iman was pulling at Maman's chador as she wailed and clawed at the oversized wall-to-wall posters of Khomeini and Khamenei that covered the walls of the Iranian religious center where my parents and Iman had been sharing a single room. Baba had found himself in London with no language, no status—and because Khomeini was preventing the removal of assets from Iran—no money. The doctors had advised against Maman going back to a war-stricken country, and Baba couldn't get our money out of Iran. So this center was their best option.

Originally, Baba had rushed Maman to London for a second opinion after she had been diagnosed with breast cancer. Even though the London doctors had declared Maman cancer-free, a host of other physical conditions, including a heart murmur, numbness in her hands, a sleeping disorder, fatigue, extreme panic attacks, and gastrointestinal problems led her from one doctor to another. Their trip was extended, week after week, month after month. The psychological symptoms she was suffering worried the British doctors enough to insist that she not return home, where any symbol of the new government could trigger another breakdown. They also told my father that further separation from her other children could cause more problems. She also was going to need surgery for an ovarian cyst, later found to be benign.

Living in an Iranian center supported by the same government that had caused her so much torment while being separated from her other children, Maman snapped.

With Iman pleading, "No, Maman," she shredded the clerics' posters, her fingernails scratching through to the concrete.

In London, the 10-by-11 room that Maman, Baba, and Iman had called home for the past nine months was bitter cold. The frost blocked a view from the small, oddly positioned window, and the London draft penetrated the cracks in the cement walls, creeping into Maman's bones. Curled up in pain from surgery, she turned and twisted on a blanket on the floor that served as their mattress every night.

Baba pulled the top blanket over her, tucking it under her cheek. But the moment he turned away, tears rolled down the side of her face and trailed into her ear. *When would the tightness in her chest lift and the pain in her throat loosen?* Maman peeked at Iman to her right, and reached over to protect his curled-up body from the sharp cold. The small radiator provided inadequate heat for the London winter.

Maman looked at the door; the bathroom was down the hallway. She pulled the blanket off her chest and slowly tried to push off the floor with one hand when pain shook her back onto the makeshift bed.

She looked at Baba and listened to his even breathing. He had been to every doctor's appointment with her since they arrived in London. Between money transfers, converting tomans to British pounds, taking care of Iman, and nursing Maman, Baba had been existing on three hours of sleep a night. Tonight, when his heavy eyes closed, he had fallen asleep instantly.

He didn't wake when Maman dragged herself off the blankets and pulled herself to the door. But when she tried to reach the handle, a stab of pain ripped into her lower belly and she cried out. Baba raised his head immediately and sat up. "What is it?" he asked. "Another nightmare?"

Every night, Baba had been awakened by the same dream Maman had suffered since Abdollah's disappearance. He opened his eyes and searched for his wife in the darkness. "What are you doing? You have to call me when you get up." Throwing the blanket to the side, he crawled his way to Maman, who was now curled up on the floor. "What do you need? Your pills? Water?" Slowly, he stood, lifting her in his arms.

At his touch on her neck, she began to weep. And for the first time in four years, she laid her head on his shoulder.

"What can I do for you?" He squinted in the dark, noticing she was wearing her scarf. "The bathroom?" Maman nodded.

In the bathroom, Baba took off her scarf, pulled her hair back from her face and wiped the sweat from her forehead as she struggled to relieve herself. He breathed onto her neck. Her body was hot and shivering.

"*Boro* Baba, go." Maman kept begging Baba. "Go check on Iman."

Instead, Baba placed a warm hand on her shoulder as he blew more air onto her hot neck. He used her scarf to fan her and rubbed her back. After an hour, when she was ready to go back to bed, he tenderly helped her clean up. Her eyes welled up.

"I'm sorry, Haji. I'm sorry you had to do that for me," Maman whispered into Baba's ear.

"You're my angel. You're my life. I would do it for you every day, forever."

When she saw the longing and sorrow in his eyes, the lines that had doubled around his forehead, and the guilt that threatened his spirit, she took a deep breath. A tear slid down the side of her face.

Maman knew her grief had nearly ruined her, and them. She softened as she remembered how much she loved Baba. And now, she missed his kiss.

LEGAL ALIENS

1985
Tehran and London

HADI WAS TRYING TO BALANCE HIS FEET on the ground to stabilize the motorcycle as he waited for me to climb on. Pulling my chador over my face, I squeezed my eyes shut during the ride to Parvaneh Street. My little red suitcase was between us, and I didn't let go of his waist. My fingernails dug deep into his flesh as cars honked and bikes swerved by. Hadi ran red lights and scooted around traffic as if we were invincible. I feared I was going to die.

Dying might have been better than going back to school on Saturday after our Fridays off. We were all in trouble. The morning before the school's five-day camping trip, Hadi had been expelled for sneaking onto a bus and removing all the bolts in the last eight rows of seats. Even so, he continued to attend every day instead of telling Baba what happened. After getting dropped off, he watched the other kids go in, and then sat on the sidewalk talking to the street vender who sold corn on the cob behind the school. Meanwhile, Zain had been told he would have to repeat two of his classes, even after Baba had hired a tutor for him.

I normally sat alone in the lunchroom. I had stopped participating in theater and drama groups, my favorite after-school activity. Sleepless nights became a given, and my straight A's had become C's. When I did make it outside after lunch, before the bell rang for class, I would sit in the corner of the yard and daydream about Mashhad while my classmates played hide-and-seek.

Hadi's motorbike backfired as we churned around the last corner onto Parvaneh Street. My teeth suddenly felt sore from biting into my chador. Without thinking, I let it fall to my shoulders. While Hadi parked the bike and lifted me off, I paused and closed my eyes—fantasizing, as I always did, that maybe this time Maman and Iman would materialize on the other side of the front door when I walked through it.

The chicks were peeping and flapping yellow feathers about the yard. But Khaleh's car wasn't there. Someone else had opened the pen. I started to run.

Inside, the house was quiet, and the curtains, which had blown around when I opened the door, settled. Suitcases had been tossed into a pile in the foyer. Hadi and I looked at each other. *What was going on?*

When we heard Zain's laughter coming down the hall, I caught my breath. He couldn't be here by himself. Then we recognized the heavy thump of Baba's footsteps trailing him down the hall. When Zain burst into the foyer with Baba behind him, we ran and threw our arms around our father. It had been over a month since his last visit, and we weren't expecting him for another week.

A day later, we were on our way to the airport, Hadi's motorbike still leaning against a tree in the front yard. As we drew closer, we saw people yelling and screaming and running in the streets. A bomb had hit Tehran and planes were grounded, but Baba made sure we were on the next available flight out. I had my little red suitcase, a few clothes, and none of my toys. We said no goodbyes. We didn't know why we were going to Maman instead of her coming to us. We didn't care; it had been more than a year since we had seen her.

Baba couldn't take all of us with him. Not right away. Britain was becoming inundated with immigrants fleeing the growing dangers in Iran. They were not issuing visas to whole families, or to remaining family members for fear they would settle in the U.K. once reunited. After overcoming tremendous challenges to get Hadi and Zain out of Iran, Baba was forced to drop my brothers at a friend's home in Germany until he could secure British visas for his sons.

In the airport in Germany, Zain—now almost 11 years old—had both palms against the glass of the observation window as Hadi tugged on his arm. Zain wiped his nose with his hand. He was crying.

I started back down the steps of the plane. "It's not fair to leave them," I said to Baba, digging my hand into his.

Baba grabbed my other hand. "Come on, *azizam*. They're with close friends. It's only for a short time. I promise."

"Can't I stay here and come to London with them?" I begged. "I don't want to leave them here alone."

The air from the engines was lifting the hem of my short chador in the air.

"They'll be with us soon. We can't miss the plane. Come on, *azizam*. Iman's waiting for you."

I took a deep breath and followed Baba. When I turned for a last look, I saw only Zain's handprint. My brothers were gone. *What if*

they didn't get visas? Would they have to go back to Iran and fight in the
war? Would I ever see them again? And how would Maman react when
she saw it was only me getting off the plane?

⊰⊱

An Afghan woman who had offered me walnuts on the plane smiled.
"This is London." Her accent was Dari. "Good luck, little one." I
tightened the grip on my little red suitcase.

The lights were blinding, and the crackling from the overhead
speakers sounded like hot oil spitting in a pan.

"*Dokhtaram,*" Baba called every few minutes to make sure I was
still behind him as he struggled to push the cart of luggage that
weaved side to side. It was the first time I remember Baba calling me
"my daughter."

I had never in my life imagined there were so many people with
blonde hair. As I squeezed past them, I was fixated on the blue and
green eyes that stared at me: a nine-year-old girl dressed in a minia-
ture black chador.

Only one other person in the airport wore one.

"*Dokhtaram,*" Baba said as he pushed me forward.

I stared into Maman's welcoming, beautiful brown eyes. Weeping,
she sank to her knees, opened her chador, and pulled me inside her
robe, pressing her forehead against mine, showering me with kisses,
whispering sweet things in my ear.

I held my breath and waited, but all I felt was cold and distant as
if a stranger were holding me. This felt nothing like the hugging and

kissing in my daydream. I felt Maman's wet face against mine, and I stared at the bright lights around us. No words.

When Iman stepped forward, his eyes told me a story. "I've missed you. Where were you, little mommy?" Taller, with short hair, he was older, changed. He wore a gray V-neck sweater tucked into black pants, and a white shirt buttoned up all the way. But his chubby cheeks hadn't changed at all. Holding my hand, Maman walked me in Iman's direction. I wanted to pick him up and kiss his cheeks. But I did nothing.

When Maman released my hand and grabbed my red suitcase, I hesitated. I was floating away. Everything seemed gigantic. Strange sounds were ringing in my ears, and there were signs everywhere with lettering I didn't understand.

Chador to chador, Maman and I followed Iman out of the bright, loud terminal into the darkness of the night.

On the ride in the huge, black taxicab to my parents' new apartment, Maman smoothed my hair. "This is London, *azizam*. It's different here. The lights are brighter, the cars move faster, and there are signs everywhere."

The chill London wind blew in the open window. I gripped my chador more tightly under my chin and leaned my head out to smell the air. The sea of lights made me dizzy. I thought about my brothers. I wondered if they felt as lost as I did.

When the taxi finally came to a stop, my heart began to pound. I followed Iman and Maman across patches of grass that appeared yellow in the faint porch light. The wind was cold and shook the row of bluebell flowers along the walk.

When I first saw the apartment, I thought it must be a small living room, part of larger quarters. I was wrong. This single room was to be our home. The bathroom frightened me. In the dark earth underneath the loose toilet pedestal, slugs and worms weaved among mushroom caps. I didn't say anything as Maman opened a small cabinet refrigerator and pulled out a bowl of *shirazi* salad covered with plastic wrap. The refrigerator was shorter than Iman.

That night, Maman was making celery lamb stew especially for me. The small two-burner stove reminded me of the one in the RV parked in our backyard in Mashhad. How would she make a lavish dinner on a stove the size of one pot?

"You want something to drink, *azizam*?" Maman walked toward me with a glass of freshly squeezed orange juice. "We moved here as soon as we knew you had a visa; we wanted to get a larger place so you and Iman would have some room to play." As Maman handed me the glass, her smile faded. She sat beside me and pressed my hair to her cheek. "We'll need more space when your brothers get their visas. I hope it's soon. I can't be without them much longer."

I stared at the orange juice. One child was a poor substitute for three.

Baba stared at the floor. "I'm going to try the embassy again in three weeks."

As Maman rattled the pots and began heating the celery stew, Iman's eyes followed me everywhere. Finally, with Maman gently pushing him, he sat near me, a foot away, and placed a wrapped gift in my lap.

Maman smiled. "Iman has one, and he wanted you to have one just like it."

We helped each other unfold the duvet cover he had so neatly wrapped. We carefully laid it out like a sofreh, and then sat on it, shoulder to shoulder, looking out the window. On the duvet was a picture of a little boy, his head resting on a little girl's shoulder.

The wind blew open her chador, so Maman let the air inside to cool her chest. It was a warm day in London as my parents waited on the street for Baba's cab to the airport.

"Here's 50 pounds." Maman handed Baba the notes.

"But that's all you have for ten days."

"You take it. We have enough groceries for now." The week before, she had shown Baba how to separate the toilet paper. If we were careful, we could get two whole rolls out of one, without even a tear in one square.

Maman fanned herself with the chador. "Your sister called this morning and said she would give you a return ticket from Tehran. She must have known that we can't ask any of our friends for more money."

Baba kissed her cheek. "You keep the money. Soon I'll have all we need. Start looking for a bigger apartment, one with room enough for Hadi and Zain."

Maman squeezed his hand and kissed Baba. "Until we can go home to Iran, of course," She said. Her voice had the strained sound it did whenever she mentioned the future.

A few days after Baba returned from Tehran, Maman sent Iman and me to play outside in the small, dusty rectangle with balding patches of dead grass. When we looked up, we could see our parents through the window, and we could hear them as their voices rose.

"You sold our house without talking to me! And I had to hear this from my brother-in-law? You knew I would stop you. You got rid of it all, just like you did the hotel? Not even a call to my sisters? To have them come get my things, pack my jewelry, take a few of the antiques, nothing? Our kids' toys? My God, the chickens! The house was to be the kids' inheritance. They could have built on the land and raised their children there. How could you do this?" Maman was furious at Baba again.

"You don't understand these things. We have no money. I can't work in Britain on a medical visa. You see where we live, right? To move to a bigger, nicer apartment, we need money, *zan*, money. Our money is not worth the same here, it's toman to pound, you understand? We need to live, and now we have the money to do it." Baba turned off the gas burner.

Maman ran to the stove. "How many times have I told you not to touch the heat!" She turned the fire back on high and stared at Baba, "Don't touch my stove." She picked up the pot cover and slammed it on the pot twice.

She closed her eyes for a moment. "You can't keep doing this, Haji. You can't keep making decisions without asking me. You can't protect me this way." She took another breath. "You're robbing me of the chance to do it my way, or for us to do it together." Maman placed the lid on the pot and turned down the burner. With softer eyes, she looked at Baba again. "I want go back someday, Haji. I want a home to go back to."

"Mashhad is not home anymore, *azizam*. Iran is not our home either. I don't know where home will be—maybe somewhere in between these two worlds. But Iran is not an option." Baba's voice softened as he walked a step closer to Maman. "The government is still terrorizing people. Any good ayatollah, professor, or filmmaker is either dead, in prison, or under house arrest. Look what they did to Ayatollah Shariatmadari. He stopped the shah from killing Khomeini in 1963; a man of peace, a visionary who believed in keeping clerics away from government positions, is under house arrest until he dies. There's no way to tell a good ayatollah from an evil one anymore. All the women wear chadors so you can't tell a call girl from a good woman. The pretense, the backstabbing. People there have changed. Everything is different, *zan*." Baba's face was near Maman's now. "I'll never go back to live there. I'm sorry to tell you that, but we simply can't."

Maman held her chest and leaned against the wall. Her breathing was labored. "But this is not my country. You could have bought a small apartment for us so we had something left there, anything." She was still angry but now her voice gave way to an old sadness. "You shouldn't have done this without me."

"Our sons would be drafted to be killed in a senseless war." Baba took a breath. "Over a million men—boys—Shi'a and Sunni—have been killed so far. For what? And you're upset about the house?"

Baba always emphasized the difference between the two subgroups of Muslims, explaining that the Sunni and Shi'a initially split not because of spiritual differences but political ones. The Sunni believed that after the death of Prophet Muhammad, the Muslim leadership should be in the hands of his companions; the Shi'a believed the leadership of the faith should stay within the Prophet's family, starting with his son-in-law, Imam Ali. Baba felt that the two groups killing one another was irrational.

Baba rubbed his forehead. "We can't go back, *zan*." Calling her "woman" signaled he was finished talking. "You know how many people are dead. You're sick, *zan*. You're getting the best medical care here. Do you know how many people are being denied medical treatment because of their faith? Anyone who opposes the regime or speaks out is arrested, beaten, or executed." Baba closed his eyes. "I did what I had to do, and I did it for all of us. I had no choice, and I will not apologize for protecting my family."

Maman wielded a pot lid in one hand, closing the gap between her and Baba. "The war will be over someday. This isn't just about money or the war. You hate what people said about you and about him." Maman rarely mentioned Abdollah's name aloud anymore. "You don't want to go back and have to face that. You would rather hide from our past."

The next morning I stared into my bowl, chewing my cereal slowly as Maman did her best to smile.

I'd been enrolled in a new British school for over a month. Each time Maman asked me about my day, I couldn't bear to tell her the truth. Seeing her face after she talked with Zain and Hadi on the hallway pay phone was painful enough. We were still digesting the news that our house had been sold and that we might never see it again, and I couldn't add to her worries. I had to handle my problems myself.

It was the tall girl at school who made me snap. She was always cursing me in English. It was different than calling me "Gandhi" and "towel head" and saying I was bald, as everyone else did when they mocked me for wearing a chador. Even though I couldn't understand her words, I felt their venom. Since the day I walked into the school compound, I felt hundreds of eyes on me. Two other Iranian girls wore head scarves, but I was the only one of thousands of students who wore a chador.

Eventually, I built up enough courage to take off my chador before class, hanging the black robe on a hook next to the jackets on the wall to wear only a head scarf like the other two Iranian girls. I struck a bargain with these two girls, my new friends: I would do their artwork, and in exchange, they would do my English homework. I refused to learn English: writing, reading, or speaking. It was my way of saying, "I don't actually live here. I'm just occupying space in the back row until I can go home."

At the end of the day, when I went to take my chador off the hook, the tall girl was there with a wicked smile, putting something in her pocket as she left. My black chador, which had been the object of envy and praise in Tehran, now had three holes in it—the result of a burning cigarette.

After that, I kept my chador on at school, hiding the holes in the folds of the fabric. I hid myself in it, too. I closed my eyes and went back to our home in Iran.

We are standing under the tall willow tree, its branches protecting us from the summer sun. The sofreh lies on a blanket in the shade, and we breathe in the scent of blossoming lemon, plum, and sour cherry trees. Baba is feeding Maman a bite of sangak bread dipped in yogurt while Hadi and Zain chase Iman and me around the tree trunks, pretending they can't find us during hide-and-seek. Then, Baba calls us around the sofreh, where he cracks open a pomegranate. Abdollah is there, visiting from America.

This was how I would handle the tall girl. I would remain an outsider, biding my time in dreams until Maman and I could kneel again at the window and watch the shining cherries bob in the sunlight.

But first, we had to get Hadi and Zain out of Germany.

⚛

"I had a nightmare last night." Maman moved the tissues closer to where she sat cross-legged on the floor. "The boys were hungry and Zain kept begging me for rice and *kebab*." She looked up at Baba, who was standing above her, staring at the numerous pots of hot meals on the sofreh.

"It's been months, Haji." Maman held the heavy pot handle up with both hands. "When will we be together again? I'm running out of prayers."

"How can I take all this to Germany?" Baba's voice was gentle. "You've made entirely too much food this time." He put his hand on her shoulder. "Freeze some of it. I promise they'll be here soon. We can eat it together then."

"I didn't make Abdollah's favorite dish. We'll have that together." Maman filled another plastic bowl. "Zain loves *lubia polo*, Haji," Maman looked up at Baba with sad eyes.

"I promise you. Next time, I'm bringing our sons back, no matter what."

A half smile played around Maman's mouth as she placed the pot next to the other four large ones already cooling. The smells of parsley, sautéed green onions, and spinach filled the room. "I can freeze some soup, but you have to take all the rest. I'm telling you, I can feel it. Every cell of my body tells me that my boys are hungry."

⊰⊱

Hundreds of miles away in Germany, in their shared room in the home of family friends, Zain pushed away his meal, spilling the cold, sticky beans from the corner of his plate. "This is no *lubia polo*. It's stupid canned beans and rice."

Hadi pointed his fork at Zain. "I told you, this is all we have. You eat it or you'll be hungry again. These beans cost us money we don't have. I'll warm up a slice of bread for you. OK?"

Looking at him with sullen eyes, Zain propped his chin up with one hand. "I'm sick of this. Nothing tastes right anymore. And my stomach hurts. Who makes green beans and rice from cans? I'd rather starve."

Hadi had been holding on to their money after they had spent too much on ice cream the week before. They weren't sure when Baba was coming again, and Hadi was not going to ask him to send anything more—certainly not now, when our family's entire savings were tied up in Iran.

Zain's belly rumbled. Playing with the sticky rice grains, he finally took a bite of beans. He ate all the rice and poured the beans back in the can. "*Merci,* brother." He put his slice of bread on Hadi's plate. "You can eat the beans if you want."

"Maman told me on the phone this morning that Baba's bringing *lubia polo* and *ash* with caramelized onion, garlic, and mint—your favorite soup. OK?" Hadi forced himself to smile.

Zain nodded and lay on his folded blanket on the floor. He had spoken to Maman on the phone that morning too—but, as usual, he had hurried to get off. The sound of her voice made him curl into a ball. It was best not to have any reminders. He hugged his legs to his chest and forced his eyes shut.

At our two-burner stove, Maman's humming made me smile. And it was then that I noticed her lipstick. It wasn't the passionate red she used to wear, but there was pink on her lips for the first time since we had left Mashhad.

Maman spent three days preparing a lavish meal, busily switching pots on the tiny stove. She was making four dishes: eggplant, lamb, and rice *tahchin,* Hadi's favorite; *kebab* for Zain; spaghetti with ground beef and mushrooms for Iman; and tomato paste celery lamb stew, Abdollah's—and now my—favorite. Making one elaborate Persian stew on this stove was a task; making four was monumental. "We'll have to warm up one dish at a time," she explained.

After the last four trips to Germany that year, Baba had returned alone. But this time, we hoped, it would be different.

When the doorbell rang, I jumped. *Who would ring the bell?* Unlike in Iran, where people visited us daily with food and sweets, no one here ever called on us—not once in the last 12 months. Maman rushed to the closet, took out her colorful chador, and pressed one hand to the door, "*Kieh?*"

There was no answer.

Fear took over Maman's face. "*Kieh?*" she called out louder this time.

"Stand next to Iman, honey." Maman held her hand in the air, gesturing us to stay back as she flipped the chain and slowly slid the door open, peeking around it. With a sigh, she swung it wider and let her chador fall to her shoulders. "Haji?" Maman said with shock. "What are you doing here? I almost had a stroke."

"Baba jaan," Iman cried out and ran to be lifted into the air as Baba kissed his head.

Maman and I exchanged looks. No boys? Again?

Baba was silent.

Then I saw it. Abdollah's navy blue jacket that Hadi had taken with him when we left Tehran was folded over Baba's arm. I jumped up and down and pounded my fist on the suit. "They're here Mamani, they're here!"

Maman flung open the door. "Where, Haji?" She stumbled into the street with her chador only covering half her head.

I looked at Baba, who waited at the door, now smiling.

"Hadi! Zain!" I screamed as I grabbed Iman's hand and ran outside without bothering to put on my scarf.

Maman's hair came loose in the breeze as she tugged at her chador. She sprinted to the middle of the street. When Hadi and Zain stepped out from behind a red car where they had been hiding, Maman fell to her knees. They ran toward her screaming, "Mamani!" and dropped to the ground in front of her.

As she cried and smiled, kissing their foreheads and cheeks, Maman's chador slid down to her shoulders and finally floated to the ground. While Zain pressed his head against her chest and put his arms around her, Hadi held them both in his.

"*Dadashis!*" I screamed and pulled Iman with me. We piled on top of them, hugging in the street.

When I looked back at Baba, he was standing in front of our apartment, his right hand over the jacket on his arm, watching Maman. Tears rolled down the dark circles around his exhausted eyes. I had never seen my father cry before.

Crowded into our single-room home with our feet and elbows bumping against each other as we sat around the sofreh eating Maman's feast, we were oblivious to everything that was still difficult. It didn't matter that the money from the house sale hadn't arrived, or that we had a bathroom with slugs under the toilet. Crammed together, we laughed and shared stories. After nearly two years, scattered in different homes, we were almost whole again.

Only Abdollah was still missing.

❊

In the weeks after he arrived from Germany, Zain, now 12, did not leave Maman's side. And he didn't stop eating. All day, he sat at the small sofreh and asked for more food. Maman catered to him, taking care of her son, trying to make up for all the lost time. Each day, she cooked three of his favorite dishes, and then he asked for more.

It was Zain who always heard the music of the ice cream truck before the rest of us. One day he left the sofreh so fast he spilled his hot tea. The sounds of a screeching car immediately followed; when we ran downstairs, I was afraid to look. Zain's crooked body was lying on the ground, his forehead bleeding where the headlight of an old car had grazed him. His eyes were open, though there was blood all over his face. Around him, the driver and the neighbors were speaking in English, but we could only understand Zain who kept saying in Persian, "I don't need a doctor. I want my ice cream."

He was not seriously injured—all head lacerations tend to bleed profusely. After he was cleaned up and deemed well, we began to worry: He had almost killed himself to get to more food. His appetite, at first understandable, then laughable, was now a reason for concern.

While Zain was busy smothering his feelings with food, Hadi was playing daredevil on the streets of London. He demolished the Audi a family friend loaned to us. Zain and Iman, who were in the car, were OK; Hadi had been lucky not to be arrested for driving three years under age and without a license. However, he suffered serious injuries. In the hospital, I visited and found him with a bandaged head, still wearing a ripped and bloodied white shirt. The bandage looked like an ayatollah's turban, but this one was streaked with blood.

Baba tried to quiet Hadi. "She's a woman, yes, but she's your nurse. You're rewriting Islam if you prevent her from helping you because she's a woman. Doctors are *halal;* it's permitted. Now let's get this done."

"She's a woman. She won't touch my head, and I'm going home. I'm not committing a sin." In a strange twist, Hadi was now more Muslim outside Iran than he ever was when we were living there.

Baba didn't know how to argue with that, especially as Hadi was becoming more devout. In fact, Hadi had transformed into an old man—no longer one of us children. He grew a beard, prayed for hours with his *tabeeh,* and never opened the top button of his shirt. He may have acted devilish as a boy, but now, at 15, he was a "man of God." And his rules were our rules. Hadi forbade music in the house, and during commercials, he would change the channel on the radio in case there was a jingle. In London, he didn't go out on hot summer days so he wouldn't be exposed to women wearing miniskirts and halter tops.

Hadi was late to his prayers the day we came home from school and found Baba pounding on the table. "I'm going to kill that bastard for what he's done to my family. He calls himself a man of God. I trusted him. Now no one knows where he is. Or our money." Baba stood up from the table. "I swear, I will find him."

Baba had sold the estate in Tehran about a year after our move. He entrusted the proceeds to Mr. Madressi, a contact he made through a trusted ayatollah. When Madressi excused himself to pray during their meeting, Baba had believed that he could trust him.

When Maman learned we had lost the money from selling the house she didn't want to sell, she said nothing. She just turned off the stove and went to lie on the bed in the corner. She closed her eyes and dreamed of her mother and sisters in Iran, whom she might never see again.

While Baba spent months tracking down the swindler, he discovered that Mr. Madressi had conned dozens of other unsuspecting

Iranians. "That bastard won't get away with this. I'm going to get it back, *zan*."

A few weeks later, Baba's eyes were wild as he came dashing into the house. He grabbed for his suitcase. "I just talked to her, his wife in America. He has a son with her. When she found out that he has a whole other life in Iran, with another woman—and that he's a thief—she was on board."

Maman looked at Baba and forced herself to stay quiet.

Baba started to pack. "I'm going to get our money back. No matter what. I have his address. He will pay for what he's done to us. He will know what it's been like living hand to mouth for over a year, not a penny to our name, borrowing money from friends and begging from strangers. He *will* pay me our money."

Maman looked down at the dirty brown carpet of our studio apartment. Her eyes went with her to the place deep in her memory.

Iranians." That bastard won't get away with this. I'm going to get it back, zan."

A few weeks later, Baba's eyes were wild as he came dashing into the house. He grabbed for his suitcase. "I just talked to her, his wife in America. He has a son with her. What she found out that he has a whole other life in Iran, with another woman—and that he's a thief—she was on board."

Maman looked at Baba and forced herself to stay quiet.

Baba started to pack. "I'm going to get our money back. No matter what I have his address. He will pay for what he's done to us. He will know what it's been like living hand to mouth for over a year, not a penny to our name, borrowing money from friends and begging from strangers. He will pay me our money."

Maman looked down at the dirty brown carpet of our studio apartment. Her eyes went with her to the place deep in her memory.

JUSTICE

BABA

Baba arrived in Tehran in the dead of night. The sweet call to prayer, the sound of the *azan* from the speakers of the nearby mosque scared the crows off the roof. With money borrowed from his sister, Baba paid 15 rogue officers to be his private interrogators. This time, they weren't working for the regime. They were working for him.

"Haji, you stay in the car," said Commander Hosseini. "I want to catch Madressi by surprise. I don't want him to have a minute to think."

Baba clenched his fists. "I want to look into his eyes. Understand?"

Pressing his palm on the roof of the car, Hosseini leaned in to face Baba. "Don't you worry, Haji, you'll get every penny of your money back. You'll see the surprise in his eyes before I bag his head and fear overtakes him."

After he sent guards dressed in camouflage around the back of the house, Hosseini rang the doorbell.

"Mr. Madressi's house? Open up! Police."

The man who opened the door was wearing a white pajama shirt. He quickly walked outside. "What can I do for you, officer?" He met the commander's gaze unfazed.

"Are you Madressi?" Hosseini asked, putting a hand on his side pistol.

"No. My name's Aslani, sir," he said, bluffing. "Why are you looking for Madressi?"

"Does your wife know that you have another family and two kids in America? Or that you are a swindler, a thief?" Hosseini yelled. "Do you want me to call your wife out here and break the news to her, or do you want to go with me quietly? Yes or no? You have one second to decide." He made a hand motion and six soldiers jumped from the corner and pointed their rifles at the man in pajamas.

"My personal life is not any of your business. In fact, unless you have a warrant for my arrest, you can show yourselves the way out." Madressi began to turn when Hosseini pulled out his gun.

"Do you remember the owner of the Rose Hotel?"

Madressi's head jerked up, his hand on the door handle. He slowly turned around to face the guards. "Who?" he asked, his voice cracking a bit.

"Me, you son of a bitch." Baba emerged from the darkness without waiting for the flashlight signal from the commander. "Do you remember the day you put your hand on the Qur'an and swore you were a man I could trust? You remember when you took my family's life in your hands and then disappeared? You remember me now, you ruthless bastard?" Baba sprang to the door, his raised hand about to land on Madressi's throat.

"I have no idea who you are. But clearly you're a crazy man . . ." Before he finished the sentence, duct tape was on his mouth, and one of the policemen threw a brown burlap rice sack over his head.

At the police station, Baba's stomach was grinding with pain. He hadn't slept in more than 35 hours since his departure from

London, and he hadn't eaten for over 11 hours. While Madressi was screaming his denials, brutality begot more brutality. Baba was sickened. The cries from the other room seemed to shake the dark gray walls of the cell where he waited. Delirious with exhaustion, he noticed that the bars of this cell were cleaner than the ones in the Mashhad prison where Abdollah had been held. For hours, Baba listened in until Madressi finally acknowledged his name and identity, admitted knowing Baba—even acknowledged he had taken Baba's money. But even at hour 11, his screams filling the air, the man who stole from us kept repeating that the money was spent and that he didn't have any way to pay Baba back. He insisted that he had no assets and no foreign accounts.

"How much longer? What else can we do?" Baba asked Hosseini.

The commander shrugged. "You paid us for a job, Haji, and we won't let you down. There are a million of these ruthless thieves running around. There are hundreds of families like yours who left Iran and relied on these criminals to help them get their money out. You're not alone. We already have three other families in line after you. Trust me, more will come out. This guy's a professional. He knew what he was doing. And he knows how this game is played. Don't pity him, this is a part of his business." The commander glanced at the room where Madressi hung. "I'm pleased to help you gain some justice for your family."

Another scream came from the interrogation room. Baba dropped his head. "God help me."

With every scream, Baba thought of what it must have been like in that cold, dirty jail in Mashhad. He felt an ache in his chest when he imagined how the guards had flung open the bars, dragged his son from his cell, and separated him from his *tasbeeh* and his Qur'an.

But this was nothing. Madressi was enduring this pain to protect stolen money. The real torture would be for Madressi to find his own son, cold and lifeless, with bullet holes in his head and chest.

Baba thought back to the time when Abdollah was a baby. He remembered his big brown eyes as he had stared up at Baba in wonder on their first picnic as a family. Watching Maman feed him, Baba knew he would always come second after this child. And for that he was grateful. He remembered how quickly Abdollah became a boy, twirling his *tasbeeh,* combing his hair, and grabbing a briefcase to make believe he was going to work with Baba years before he was ready. At 15, it had been Abdollah who insisted on going with Baba to feed the earthquake victims in Tabas.

If Abdollah were alive, Baba wouldn't be in this cell, paying policemen to force a man to return his family's money. If Abdollah were alive, his family would still be living in Iran, together. His mind raced from the distant past of his son's childhood to the night he had held his cold, dead hands. Tears dropped down his cheeks. When another scream filled the air, Baba began to whisper a curse as he paced the dark room.

"Haji, there's no room for guilt here. Think of your family. We go all the way or you don't get a penny. He's going to outpace, outsmart, and outrun your patience. If you can't tolerate this, step outside."

Baba was playing with the two bills left in his pocket. He had two thousand borrowed tomans, and a wife and four children to support in a foreign land. He took a deep breath and nodded. Being involved with torture felt corrupt; there was no way not to be tainted by it. But he had to take care of what was left of his family.

"Do what you have to," Baba finally said. Sitting back on the flimsy cot where he had been waiting, Baba stared at the ceiling. "*Khodaya komak kon.* This is for my family. God help me."

Twenty-eight hours later, the interrogators got the bank account information they needed to pull out the two-thirds of Baba's money that was still unspent. For more than ten years, Baba never spoke of this to anyone.

with torture felt corrupt there was no way not to be claimed by it.

But he had to take care of what was left of his family.

"Do what you have to," Baba finally said. Sitting back on the flimsy cot where he had been waiting, Baba stared at the ceiling. "Khodaya towná kon. This is for my family. God help me."

Twenty-eight hours later, the interrogators got the bank account information they needed to pull out the two-thirds of Baba's money that was still unspent. For more than ten years, Baba never spoke of this to anyone.

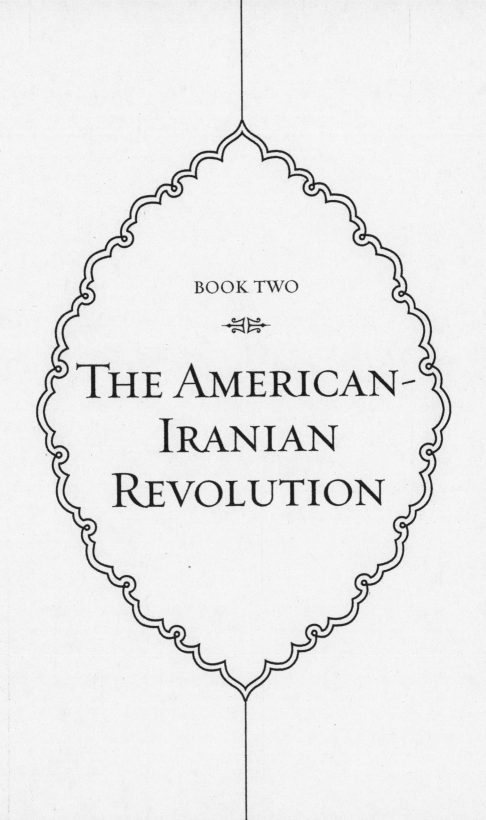

BOOK TWO

⁂

THE AMERICAN-
IRANIAN
REVOLUTION

THE KING'S ENGLISH

❧

1986

OUR AMERICAN-IRANIAN REVOLUTION started in England with a protest against the King: not the King of England, but the King of Rock-and-Roll. Although at the age of 11, I still refused to learn English at my British school, I was all ears whenever I heard Elvis Presley sing. He was simply too handsome to be ignored. Our new apartment had upstairs bedrooms, a full-size stove, a toilet without slimy bugs—and, most significantly, a television station that played Presley movies. I clicked it on, and the first shot of the revolution was fired: "Jailhouse Rock"!

> *"The band was jumping and the joint began to swing.*
> *You should've heard those knocked out jailbirds sing.*
> *Let's rock, everybody, let's rock.*
> *Everybody in the whole cell block*
> *Was dancing to the jailhouse rock."*

At that moment, two victories occurred on the rebel side. First, I gave my heart to an infidel, Elvis Presley. And second, I accepted the fact that I had to learn English.

Though we knew nothing of Baba's nightmares, of the price he was paying as he lie in bed at night reliving Madressi's wails of agony, we had come to understand that we were exiled from Iran: England was home now. Home would have to be where we were, not where we had been.

I realized that I was also making a break with the traditions my father had upheld. And it turned out he was not the only enforcer of strict rules at home. One afternoon, as I was watching my fourth consecutive Elvis movie, Hadi entered the living room and slammed the door closed. "This is not approved!"

"Maman said it was OK." I jumped up and stood in front of the television set, hoping to obscure Elvis's swiveling hips and sensuous bedroom gaze. "I've been watching TV for weeks, Hadi. Leave me alone." I clutched the fancy new remote control like a weapon.

Hadi stomped into the kitchen. I could hear him upstairs as his voice overpowered the Elvis's. "Maman, these shows have inappropriate content. They're all about rock-and-roll, drugs, and sex. She's eleven. She should be reading instead. No movies like this, Maman. These are rated for adults."

As always, Maman was conciliatory: "I'm sure Rahimeh will change the channel at any bad scenes. You know she's a good girl."

"She will not watch television in this house, unless it is cartoons or videos we approve of. It's for her own good." Hadi was now the enforcer of Islamic ideals in our house, and acted as my second father—and an even stricter one than Baba.

It was Elvis marathon week on TV, and I was not about to miss any of it. "Do you want to watch the next movie with me? It's not bad, I promise. This one has a Cadillac Fleetwood in it. And besides, I need to learn English if we're going to Disneyland," I said, feigning innocence.

Baba had just announced that he was taking us on vacation to the United States. But, unbeknownst to us, he was also searching for economic opportunity. Unable to work in England with a medical visa extension for the family, he had been sustaining the family on the proceeds from the hotel sale, now quickly dwindling.

I didn't really care about Mickey Mouse. All I cared about was that now, I would finally get to visit Abdollah at his college. Although Khaleh had tried to tell me that my brother was dead, I denied it. The hope of seeing him again was thin, but I clung to it.

Hadi said nothing, but hours later, as I sat curled up and watched Elvis rev up the engine of the Fleetwood Cadillac, I felt the couch shift with new weight. Hadi had sat down to join me.

The flickering from the screen reflected on our faces; we didn't speak, but stared straight ahead as Elvis continued to talk to me in my new language, the language of Abdollah. *"Love me tender, love me true . . . all my dreams fulfilled . . ."*

California, 1986–1995

Dear Abdollah,
The mind is a pretty powerful thing. I had long dreamed that I was wrong somehow about you. But when we arrived in America and you weren't here and no one said your

name, I finally understood the truth. You're not coming back, are you?

I always wonder what our life would be like if you weren't gone. Maybe we would be home in Iran. Our family would be normal again.

If only you were here to help me. I'm trying to keep our family happy, but I'm not sure what to do. And no one takes me that seriously.

We are staying at the top floor of the Hilton near the airport in Los Angeles. I've been staring down at hundreds of speeding cars across this huge road they call the "freeway." A trip to Disneyland tomorrow isn't going to fix us. We haven't been here for more than four hours and already I hate it. We all do, especially Maman. It's good we'll only be here for two weeks.

Your face is starting to fade in my memory. I'm worried I'll forget you.

I love you.

Your little sister,
Rahimeh

As he had done with the move to London, Baba usurped any decision making from his children when he took the dramatic step of moving his family to a new country. After exploratory meetings, he had managed to obtain a work sponsorship from a clergy in California, enabling him to legally start a business. He had decided to make our "vacation" permanent. For the second time in our lives, what was supposed to be a two-week trip stretched to two years, catching Maman and the rest of us off guard. We landed in America with just four small suitcases and again, no goodbyes.

With characteristic determination, Baba established himself as a leader in the local Iranian community within a few months of our arrival. He opened a carpet store that carried rugs made in Iran, and he worked hard—very hard. Sometimes, I thought I could feel the exhaustion in his eyes when he came home late at night—the weight noticeable from carrying his entire family on his shoulders while starting, once more, from scratch.

Baba would not be defeated. Within two years, my parents bought a three-story home in Irvine, and tried their best to re-create an Iranian household uncorrupted by the influence of American culture. On the outside, palms and flowering fruit trees bloomed. Inside, deep plush rugs and the sacred Qur'an gave our new household the feel of a traditional Persian home. It even smelled the same: the whiffs of cardamom and jasmine, the aromas of Maman's cooking—caramelized onions with turmeric, saffron, garlic, and mint. The new house held the same profound encapsulated silence, as if the decor had also imported an atmosphere from the Old World. I could inhale the scented peace and quiet—until it shattered.

Baba's success in creating a business and purchasing a home was not matched by his ability to police his household. It was the eighties, and things were changing for all American teenagers. For young Iranian immigrants, it was a cataclysm—one that my two older brothers could not wait to enjoy.

Zain was the first to test our father's limits.

One evening, I walked into the living room to see Baba knocking a set of keys to the floor as he tried to snatch them from Zain's hand. "And you better take off that shirt or I'll rip it off you!" he added.

Zain pulled the orange tank top over his head and threw it on the floor. "It's summer and 90 degrees outside. I'm no ayatollah, Dad." This was the first time I had ever heard Zain refer to our father as "Dad" instead of the usual "Baba."

"You brought me here. I'm going to make it worth it and do what other kids my age do. Everybody wears T-shirts and tanks, Dad."

Maman placed a hand on Baba's shoulder to calm him.

"He's going through a phase. He needs time," she said. "Please, Haji."

Circling Zain as he slouched on the sofa, Baba began yelling, his hands stabbing the air. The scene had a cinematic intensity: Zain was naked from the waist up, face full of defiance, with a tiny diamond stud sparkling in his left earlobe. He leaned over and picked up the keys, jiggling them as he sat back down, legs sprawled open—a pose I knew my father would regard as disrespectful and vulgar. His hair was cut into a Mohawk ending in a two-inch ponytail.

"Zain, you're 15. It's time to be a man, to take responsibility."

To Baba, wearing an earring and going to a dance made his older son Hadi's recent behavior—getting expelled from school, collecting speeding tickets, and rejecting authority—seem like child's play.

"You don't understand how serious this is. A diamond earring! A dance! You need to get your hair cut to a respectable length, put on a shirt, get rid of that earring, and go to school and work. Then maybe you'll have permission to drive the car. Otherwise, it's over."

Baba's voice was shaking as he pointed his index finger at Maman. "This is your fault!"

"I'm going to the dance, Baba," Zain looked straight into his eyes. "That's what all the kids here do."

Baba pounded his fist on the coffee table. "Give me your car keys. Now!"

"Sure. Take them. But I'm going to the dance even if I have to walk there." Zain tossed his keys on the table. Then he turned, stomped up the stairs, and slammed his bedroom door.

The house seemed to take a deep breath. This was a new development. Even at his most reckless, Hadi didn't dress like an infidel or swear at Baba.

"You see what's happening here?" Baba said, pointing a finger at Maman. "You told me to let the long hair go, then you told me to get the car repaired after he crashed it, and I listened. Now what? Now this?" He was turning red. "You see how you've raised your son? You see how he has turned out?"

From the doorway, I felt my entire body flush hot with anger. In my mind, I couldn't help hearing the sound of Baba's hand smack Abdollah's face when Abdollah refused to button his shirt collar. *How could Baba blame Maman for this? Had he learned nothing?*

Maman remained calm. "You can't yell him into submission, Haji. He's a teenager. We've lived in America for two years. What do you expect, *azizam?*"

He had not expected this: a son who now wanted to be called by an American name—Mike—and who had adopted all these "American" ways.

Maman tried to help Baba understand that he wasn't going to win the battle to save our souls even with stricter rules.

"Haji, he just wants to fit in. That's natural. We have to accept some changes." Maman's voice was soft.

"I can't have a son who defies God!" He raised his voice and gave her a disapproving look.

I couldn't help wondering how Baba knew that God disapproved of diamond studs, tank tops, and dances, but he seemed sure.

"We have to talk him through it," Maman said. "We have to help him." She placed her hand on Baba's arm and guided him into a chair.

"You're not a raging teenager, woman. You don't understand what goes on in that boy's mind. You think he innocently wants to go to a dance? Do you know where that dance leads next?" He took in a deep breath. "If I don't stop him now, it'll be too late." Baba's body appeared to deflate. "He's the same age as . . ." Baba turned his eyes to the ceiling. "God help me. This will not happen again." His shoulders sagged and he looked at Maman. "I will not let this happen again."

We all turned as Zain pounded down the steps, clothes folded over one arm. "Maman, *khodafez*. Bye, don't wait up for me tonight." He slammed out the front door, shaking the mirrors hanging in the foyer. I imagined that the Qur'an caught a splinter of glass, and shivered in its case.

Tears trailed down Maman's face. "Don't you see? You're just pushing him farther away from us."

"Don't cry, woman," Baba snapped.

I trailed behind as Hadi caught up with Zain on the front steps.

"You can't go, Zain. There'll be girls and alcohol." Hadi yelled.

"Exactly."

"Zain, you can't do these things. It has to stop."

Zain shrugged. "I'm leaving. I don't need another father, Hadi."

In America, Hadi had gone from brother to parent. He had also become even more religious than he was in England. *Where was the prank-playing brother who swung upside down from tree branches?* I missed him. Of course we didn't want to lose Hadi, our brother. But didn't Zain see? Beyond the walls of our home where English was spoken, Hadi was our protector. Because Baba didn't speak English that well, the school relied on Hadi for communication. One school even thought Baba was living abroad. On the streets, Zain and I needed Hadi to be a father.

"Let me see it." I pointed to Zain's ear.

Zain smiled for the first time as he moved his hair out of the way, "It's got a diamond in it." The little diamond stub was so small, it was hardly noticeable. *This is what the fuss was about?*

Zain kissed my cheek. "Well, got to go, Sis, I'm late."

Hadi pulled his car keys from his pocket. "I'll drive you."

"No thanks." Zain—now Mike—flung his jacket over his shoulder and headed down the street.

I didn't blame Zain for refusing a ride. For all his strictness over dress and religious codes, Hadi was still wild in other ways. The little boy who raced and crashed cars was more dangerous as a young adult at the wheel. A typical drive with Hadi meant weaving between cars and 18-wheelers at 100 miles an hour. The last time we had let Hadi drive, we had to grit our teeth when he almost sideswiped a semi. Even after two dozen traffic tickets, Hadi kept a heavy foot on the accelerator.

Hadi gave me rides to many schools. Anytime there was trouble with me refusing to wear shorts for gym class because of my dress code, or I was harassed for being the only girl wearing a scarf, or a teacher demanded to meet my parents because I refused to speak English, Hadi would step in and help me transfer to another school.

Some incidents were so bad, I did not even tell Hadi. One hot day, as I was walking home from school, my scarf felt extra-tight around my neck, sweat gluing the knot of the fabric under my chin to my throat. It was a 20-minute trek uphill to our house in Turtle Rock, in Irvine. This was the part of the day I dreaded most.

Keep going with your head down . . . don't look up . . . you're almost there, I told myself. *Today he won't see you walking home. Today you're safe.* I was hopeful, but I knew it was wishful thinking. For the last two weeks, the insolent teenager had been there, hiding in his house or the trees, ready to let me have it. But I could never see where he was. I never looked.

On this hot day, my back was wet, and I could feel the drops of sweat roll down my chest to my belly. Home was only 20 feet away. It was then that I felt the heavy slap of a water balloon against the back of my neck, jolting me forward. Ice-cold water spread down my spine. My heart stopped. My head dropped and my hands covered my face; I froze for the now familiar assault. I heard the screams—"Towel head!"—as the second, third, and fourth water balloon soaked my cloak. Finally, with my eyes glued to our house in the distance, I walked the rest of the way home, drenched. If Hadi had been with me, this wouldn't have happened.

Hadi was my hero. He was the first in our family to learn English and master the system. We all counted on him. Hadi did everything for us, and often. As he darted through traffic to get us from one place to another, I would catch his eyes in the rearview mirror. He was running from something; I understood that.

Now, Hadi headed down the road after Zain.

Standing in the door, my little brother Iman was silent. He had only one father—Baba, the man he loved and admired—and even at the age of ten, Iman was calmer, an old soul respectful of his father's faith and tradition. Iman would never want to cause Baba the kind of pain his older brothers did. He loved Hadi and Zain, but didn't want to act like them.

Without realizing it, Iman was living the life Abdollah might have lived. Abdollah himself inhabited our home as a shadow presence; though we seldom referred to him, he was not forgotten. The evasion of truth about his fate had become a toxic cloud.

Back in the house, Baba stormed out of Zain's bedroom with three muscle T-shirts ripped into shreds. He headed for the kitchen, threw the shirts in the garbage can, and slammed down the lid.

Swallowing my fear, I followed him and fixed a cup of water packed with ice. "Here, Baba, drink this," I said.

Dropping into a chair at the table, Baba rested his forehead on his fists and closed his eyelids.

"It's filled with ice. Just the way you like it," I said as I placed the cup close to his hand. "Zain loves you, Baba, but he wants to be like the other kids here. We're in a different country. It's like a completely different world here, Baba."

Baba began chewing on the ice. "He's so obstinate," he said, defeated.

"He's no different than he ever was. Strong willed, the way you raised all of us to be."

I didn't tell Baba that Zain was sneaking home in the early morning, just in time for prayers, and then sleeping all day.

"Yelling at him won't make him do what you want. And blaming Maman isn't right. You have to listen to Zain and help him be a man in this place. Otherwise, he'll push you away and not tell you anything." I put a slice of cold red watermelon on his plate.

Baba's face was no longer flushed. He was thinking and I could see that he was listening.

"Your mother always did say you were a wise young girl," he said finally.

"Talk to him, Baba jaan. It's not easy for us here, Baba."

I didn't tell him about the "towel head," or the water balloons, or that my classmates in America called me "camel jockey." I didn't tell him that every time I put on my head scarf, it was a reminder that I would never be at home in California. I had been through middle school and was now in high school, but felt even more like an outsider. I felt utterly alone, desperate to hear Persian spoken, to smell hyacinth blossoms at the nearby florist, and buy *roulette* and *zaban* sweets at the bakery on my way home from school. I ached for all of us, and, most of all, ached for my father.

Baba stared at me, lost.

"I'm sorry, Baba jaan. I know this must be rough for you. I hope that you and Zain can find a way to get along better."

Baba cut a watermelon slice, stabbed a small piece with a fork and offered it to me.

Now I needed to take care of Maman.

Maman was in her bedroom; she was breathing hard, her face flushed, her eyes closed, her head shaking as she talked into space. "*Khoda,* please. Help me God! Tell me this isn't happening again." Tears rolled down her face; she began to pull at the buttons of her shirt and slap at her chest, turning her pink skin a darker, almost scarlet shade. "I don't know what to do. God, I don't know what to do!" In the two years we had been in America, this wasn't the first time Maman had experienced an episode like this. But this was the most severe.

I ran a cool cloth over Maman's forehead and watched her face for signs of calm. I hoped that the glass of hot water with melting sugar crystals and rose water would help settle the flashbacks of Baba fighting with Abdollah. But her uncontrollable sobbing and labored breathing continued for another 25 minutes until she finally slumped onto the bed, exhausted.

As I put the bottle of Valium she had refused back in the medicine cabinet, I noticed a round, metal cookie tin up on the top shelf of her closet. In Iran, Baba brought these pretty boxes back from every Kuwait trip, and family members would line up at our house in Tehran to take one or two home for their kids. I knew these cookies well; they were as delicious—deep, chewy, sweet—as the boxes were decorative, an intimate memory from our past.

When I looked and saw Maman deeply asleep, I reached toward the tin. A flash of guilt came over me. It was Maman's closet, I told myself, and I was just straightening her things. As I took down the box and popped open the lid, I knew why I'd felt like a thief. Instead of cookies, the box contained a four-by-seven-inch plastic-covered photo album on top of a stack of letters written in red ink. My hands began to shake.

I flipped the album cover open and my lost brother, Abdollah, stared back at me from a photo I had never seen before this moment. I flipped through the pages. Some of the pictures had ripped and were repaired with curling yellowed tape. In one he posed confidently, sitting in the sand with two other cousins; in another, he is a little boy, Maman holding him to her side. Then, there it was: a wallet-size photo exactly as I saw him last. Abdollah, with his big brown eyes, stares right at me. He is wearing his navy blue suit, the one that now hangs in Hadi's closet. I shut the album, put the lid back on the container, closed the closet, and took several deep breaths before going back to pull a sheet over my sleeping mother.

In my room, I stared out the window.

Dear Abdollah,

All this is tricky. I wish I were older than 13. Maybe you would know what to do. Brother, I've missed saying your name. I had secretly hoped that Hadi and Zain would find their own way, but now I'm worried that Zain has gone too far. I know he's just trying to become his own man, but I'm afraid for him. I'm afraid he'll be lost to us soon.

I wish you were here to help.

Love,

Rahimeh

Could Abdollah help? In America, they say "The truth will set you free." Now that I had seen his picture in Maman's secret album, I decided that no matter how scary it was, I would ask what really happened to him.

The next day, I gave Maman a cup of tea and spoke Abdollah's name aloud for the first time since he had disappeared. "I miss Abdollah." I said his name so low, so hesitant, I wasn't sure she'd heard me. Sweat started to roll down my lower back. I watched closely and held my breath.

Maman's face and body shifted. A decade of being silenced—first by Khomeini's secret police and then by my parents' decision to hide the truth from us—had passed. Maman locked eyes with me. "I miss him, too, *azizam.*"

I felt as if I were waking from a long sleep. "I didn't want to upset you by asking, Maman jaan. But I think of him often."

"I was waiting for you to be ready, darling."

I kissed her cheek. "I would like to make a copy of that wallet-size photo of Abdollah. I can enlarge a copy in my photography class and we can frame it."

Without asking how I knew about the picture, Maman ran to get the metal cookie box and pulled out the little album. Suddenly animated, she lifted out each picture and explained where each was taken and when. "That one is at the beach near the pomegranate farm," she said, pointing to the one with Abdollah posing on the sand. She carefully laid out the ripped photos, repaired with yellowing tape, on the bed. Baba and a relative, she explained, had cut Abdollah out of those photos so Maman wouldn't be triggered into a crying spell. She turned to the last page. There it was, Abdollah's last picture: the black-and-white photo in his navy blue suit, taken just before his arrest.

"Take this one. It's yours," she said, handing it to me gently.

I cupped the picture in my hand and kissed it. That night, when I talked to Abdollah, I was able to look into his eyes, grateful that the faded picture in my memory was coming back into focus.

Although I didn't have the words to explain the change I sensed in my heart, I felt that Maman and I had just stepped together onto a path covered in sunlight. I wondered when my brothers would fall in place beside us.

As it turned out, I wasn't the only one who was ready to talk about Abdollah. Two days later, Zain found Maman fanning herself with a laminated Hafez poem sheet, sitting cross-legged on her prayer rug in the afternoon.

"You came back from school early? What's going on, Zain? Is something wrong?" Maman took off her white scarf and folded it.

Placing a bowl of fruit near her prayer rug, Zain sat facing her. "I think I might upset you by what I have to ask."

"What's wrong, *azizam?*"

Zain lowered his head and began to speak.

"Everybody told me a different story, Maman. Back then, when I was a kid, Hadi said Abdollah was in America. Then we came to America and he wasn't here. I want to know the truth." He lowered his gaze. "What happened to my brother, Maman? What really happened to Abdollah?"

When, at the same age, Hadi had asked the same question of Mr. Gaffari and Baba back in Iran, he had never gotten a real answer. But Zain had better luck. He asked the parent who never liked secrets.

Maman took Zain's hands in hers. She didn't tell him everything, but for an hour as they talked, she told him in parts about the terrible events that led to Abdollah's arrest. She told him about the aftermath that we lived through, but were too young and confused to understand.

"Why didn't you tell me all this sooner?

"At first, we were in disbelief, shocked. I don't even know who told you he was studying in America. He loved you children so much. We even thought if you knew the truth, we would lose one of you to grief. Back then in Iran, you hid painful things from your kids."

Baba had a younger sister who died at 17, just a year older than Abdollah. Abused by her husband, she was beaten badly and her death devastated the family. Even though Baba was just a child, he carried tremendous guilt.

Baba's brother also had a daughter, who was married at 17 to a clergyman with substance abuse problems. Their marriage produced three children and withstood hundreds of fights. During a road trip, when he had promised sobriety, their car crashed. The couple and the baby died instantly, leaving two children behind. Baba's brother and his wife never recovered from the loss. After raising their surviving grandchildren to adulthood, they divorced.

Maman, too, had lost a sibling—a younger brother at the age of two to a fever. But unlike Baba, she openly talked about him.

When Zain confronted Maman, she spoke candidly for the first time. Patterns emerged. One was marrying off teenagers perceived as "going down the wrong path." Another was mourning loss in secret to "protect" others.

"Everyone told us to handle it with secrecy," Maman told Zain. "I was in my early 30s then, and I started to think maybe it was better for you not to know what happened until you were older. I told myself that you would come to me when you were ready." She squeezed Zain's hand, and he rested his head on her folded leg.

"But to let us think he was alive? Maman, that was much worse."

Maman stroked his hair. "It was probably the wrong thing to do. I'm sorry, *azizam*. I'm so sorry." She kissed his cheek. "We didn't know any better. Your father and I spent so many years trying to accept that your brother was gone, and we could only manage to tell you what we wished could be true."

REVOLUTION AT HOME

❧

ALTHOUGH I STILL WAITED to hear the word "dead" spoken aloud, I had begun to repair the path with my mother. Zain, too, wouldn't hear more details of the story for many years—but what he had been told was enough for him to forgive Maman. Still, he didn't forgive everyone. Now that he knew the Iranian government had killed his brother, he had one thing on his mind: revenge. After he heard Maman's story, he vowed to study law and sue Iran in the World Court. Someone needed to pay for killing our brother and destroying our family.

And destroyed we were. Because we did not mourn our losses or talk openly about what had happened, the festering wound—the secret—got buried deep within our family, like a land mine. It was only a matter of time before it would explode. We had escaped war-stricken, postrevolutionary Iran, but we faced a different kind of revolution in America: a revolution from within.

Our family was blown apart as one child after another vented their long unspent feelings. We each faced inner turmoil and outer conflict with our new culture, opposition from our old-world father, and struggles within ourselves. During the next few years, waves of anger reverberated through our home. Wild behavior and attempts to control the destruction were the new normal.

Our father also battled inner rage and guilt that he could not share. His life's mission was now to save us—and he would do anything, absolutely anything, to achieve that. But his culture and code of behavior struck us as dictatorial, and we all fought back in our own way. Everyone appeared to be in rebellion, especially Zain and Hadi. We all needed to reenact Abdollah's battle with Baba and with the old codes of behavior; our lives revolved around the gaping crater in the heart of our family.

We would soon break ranks.

THE SECOND
IN COMMAND

⊰❦⊱

HADI POUNDED ON THE HOOD of the car and faced Zain through the windshield. "Get out, now!"

The blonde girl sitting next to Zain in the front seat stared at Hadi, shock in her blue-green eyes. She and Zain were parked on a street around the corner from our house.

"I said, get out!" Hadi slammed both fists on the hood and moved to the driver's side. He was remembering another brother alone in a car with a girl, without a head scarf or obvious morals. Hadi acted as if he were interrupting a crime, or adultery.

"Hold on. Why are you making a scene, Hadi?" Zain took his time stepping out of the car. He had learned something important from his talk with Maman: that Abdollah was a victim, a martyr. Therefore, in his death, Abdollah had become a saint. Now, Zain understood he would always be living in that shadow. There would be no way to measure up, certainly not with Baba. So why try? And no one could stop him. Especially not his *other* father, Hadi.

"Who is she? What the hell are you doing in a car with her? This is not why I work with Baba to pay for your car, your insurance, and your gas. We don't work so you can run around town with girls," His eyes traveled back and forth between the two of them.

The girl, pretty and pale, looked terrified.

"Her name is Shanna. And by the way, I work too, at the same place you do. Why are you yelling? I'm not doing anything wrong." Zain had a slight grin on his face. "Come on, Bro, come with us for a ride." Zain had his fists out jabbing the air, pretending to box. His smile stretched across his face.

"What's your problem, Zain?"

"What's yours? You're acting like an old man."

"Give me your keys and get in the house. I'll take her home."

"No way." Zain jabbed the air at Hadi's head again.

"Give them to me before I . . ." A vein in Hadi's neck throbbed.

Zain didn't move. He didn't know what Abdollah had whispered to Hadi—or how Hadi was bending under the weight of that promise. He only saw the anger in Hadi's eyes. Now, he looked like Baba.

"Just because you wear a beard now, eat only *halal* meat, pray all the time, and forbid us to listen to music doesn't mean I have to do the same. In fact, I want to be nothing like you!" Zain shouted.

Shanna squeezed her eyes shut as the slap landed on Zain's face. When she opened them, she saw Hadi's back as he walked away from the car.

After that day, the only time we saw Zain was when he was out cold on the couch during the daylight hours, sleeping off the previous night's action. Baba left threatening messages on Shanna's answering machine, frightening her more than her own abusive father. Zain disappeared to live a life we knew nothing about, leaving Maman praying and fighting off more frightening episodes of emotional turmoil.

This left me, as I approached 15, to be the next child who would need protection and insulation from these two fathers who carried the burden of Abdollah's death.

THE TWO
IRAN-IRAQ WARS

❧

THERE WERE TWO PERSIAN GULF WARS FOR ME: the public one, which transpired after Iraq invaded Iran, and the private war, in which I felt personally under attack in high school.

One day in the thick heat of summer, as I walked home in my scarf and oversized clothes, I was approached by a man in his late 20s with a microphone and a recorder. He was a journalist for the local newspaper and was interviewing high schoolers about their views on the war. With my big Persian nose and braces, I felt awkward but determined to be who I was without apology. Though I told him I was from Iran, he kept referring to me as Iraqi. Finally, I asked him if he knew that Iran and Iraq were two very different countries. He had no idea. He had not even heard of the Iran-Iraq war.

This was a common experience. I was always forced to educate the people around me about the "other" part of the world: that Iran and Iraq are separate countries, and that the Iranian language is Persian (or Farsi), not Arabic. It wasn't until 9/11 that maps appeared on CNN and the masses became more familiar with the greater Middle East. But during the early 1990s, when I was still in high school, I constantly worried about when the next water balloon or next insult would be hurled.

One banner day, after secretly spending weeks worrying that no one would hire the girl with a "towel" wrapped around her head, I had found a job—and to my surprise, pretty easily—at a telemarketing company. After all, no customers would see me; they would only hear my voice on the phone. The company hired me three days a week, after school and on weekends. Although I wasn't sure what time-shares were, I was certain I could sell them. There was only one hitch: I needed a ride. Because Maman didn't drive, that meant crossing the Rubicon: asking Baba.

"Time-share?" Baba hadn't heard the word before either. "It's not going to happen. I'm not taking you. My daughter is not going to work. If you need money, I'll give you money." He started to walk away toward the kitchen.

I took a breath. "It's not for the money at all," I lied. Baba had been struggling since the Gulf War hurt his carpet business, and I hadn't asked him for lunch money for over six weeks. I didn't want to embarrass him. So I exaggerated the truth. "I need to learn how to work, Baba. I need the work credits to graduate from high school early."

"*Dokhtaram*," he said with his eyes softening. I knew when he called me "my daughter," he was going to gently say no. "I'm your provider. It's my job to take care of you. You understand? It's my job to make sure you have enough money, and food, and that you are safe. It's my job to protect you."

"But Baba, I need the credits. They say it's a good preparation for college, too."

Baba put his hands on the counter. "You will not be going to work for God-knows-who in God-knows-where for God-knows-why." He hadn't heard a word I'd said. "You understand?" His voice burned my ears, threatening my eardrums.

My mind began to spin. I had to figure out how to win over Baba *and* God.

"Anything can happen to you. Someone can pick you up and kidnap you. This is America. Do you know how many children go missing here? It's unsafe. And I won't have it." Baba was calm. He expected no argument from his only daughter.

I loosened my scarf, which suddenly felt tight around my throat. Hadi and Zain had cars, and came and went as they wished.

"It's not fair, Baba. Hadi and Zain work! I want to work, too. I'm the one in school, getting good grades and helping the family with religious ceremonies, wearing a *hejab*, praying three times a day. I do everything you ask of me." My voice began to crack. "I hate high school, Baba, I really hate it. I can't stand to be there another day. I need to work."

Baba set the cup he had been holding in the sink and turned his back to me.

"I just want this one thing. Baba, please." My throat closed up as I tried to swallow my tears. "I can't stay home forever, Baba. It's not like Iran here. I want to be somebody. Maybe one day I can even help you with your business." I wasn't sure what I was saying anymore. I had lost control when I had loosened my scarf. But I knew I never wanted to ask Baba or anybody for money again. Ever.

When he didn't respond, I fled upstairs to the room I shared with Hadi. In Iranian families, the eldest child would generally have his own room, as would the only girl. But for the past few months, I'd been staying with Hadi, so Iman and Zain could have a chance to have their own rooms.

As I heard Hadi coming up the stairs, I was relieved. He knew how trustworthy I was. He would help me convince Baba. But Hadi didn't think of himself as a brother anymore. Not looking at me, he walked into the room. "I overheard. So you want to work?" He crossed his arms. "Well, forget it. You're 15. We'll take care of you. You'll have everything you need." And with that, he walked out.

I chewed on my lower lip and turned toward the wall. I had cousins in Iran who had been married at 15. I pictured the sadness in Abdollah's eyes on the day of his wedding. Right there, I made up my mind. I wouldn't stay here forever, a child in my parents' home. I would go to college. I would travel to all the places Abdollah never got to go. Nothing was going to stop me. Not two fathers, not the way people looked at my scarf—not even my loyalty to my family's values. I would make my own way. And that meant working, even if it meant lying to Baba. Maman, who wanted a life of financial independence for her only daughter, now had enough ammunition to soften up Baba. This victory would be the beginning of a new destiny for us both.

Every afternoon for four months, on the hour-drive back and forth to my first job, Baba needed to know who my supervisor was, how much they would pay me, where I would sit, what color the walls were, did they have wastebaskets near my desk so I wouldn't be inconvenienced or ogled as I crossed the room of mostly men, and how the other women dressed who worked there. Although he had endless questions, every day he took me to work.

Hadi, however, never relented. I had gone against his orders and his increasingly rigid values. My real conflict was not with Baba, who was becoming more flexible, but with my second father.

ANOTHER BATTLE AT HOME

❧❧

1990

THE WIND SHOOK THE LEAVES of the eucalyptus tree, and as I walked up three steps to our front door, I could see my bedroom light was on. The moon's grayish light wasn't helping me to get my key into the front door lock. A cold wind kept blowing my scarf out of place, and my spine quivered.

The brother of an Iranian friend had given me a ride home after my girlfriend and I had spent the evening studying together. Because Hadi had been monitoring my behavior closely, I had asked my friend to drop me off a few houses down from ours, just in case he was home and looking out the window.

When I entered the room, I found Hadi lying on top of his bed covers, watching our favorite show, "Cheers." He sat up and turned off the TV. "You're 15 and you were in a car with a guy? Alone? I give you rides everywhere. Why didn't you give me a call to pick you up?"

"I didn't want to bother you, and besides my friend's brother offered." I took off my scarf. My knees would buckle around Baba when he was this angry, but I wasn't going to take it from Hadi. "He's my good friend's brother. We're just friends, and he lives up the street. What's the problem?" I knew he was thinking about Zain and the blonde. "It was just a ride."

"I'm older than you. I drive you to school. I talk to you about your schoolwork. I tell you what to do. I do this for your own good. Going to work was bad enough, but what you just did is totally out of line."

I couldn't contain myself. "I did nothing wrong. Even Baba doesn't act like this. You're not my father, Hadi. Even Baba trusts me. Why are you questioning me?"

My ears rang, and I saw a blast of white light. As the sharp pain and the high-pitched ringing in my ear began to clear, I realized that I had just been hit. I had never been struck by anyone before. Baba had never hit any of us since the day he slapped Abdollah.

My vision came back slowly and I was holding my cheek when the rage left Hadi's eyes. I ran out of the house and refused to come back inside.

At 9:00 p.m., when I was still sitting in the family car, Baba knocked on the window. "I'll talk to him. He'll apologize. I'm not leaving until you come inside."

"He won't apologize, and I'm not coming in while Hadi's there. He's out of control."

Maman's voice was soft. "You can't sleep in the car, *azizam*. Hadi only wants the best for you, and he must have been scared to see you with a guy. He must have been worried about your safety."

When I began shouting and sobbing that I hadn't done anything wrong and that I would never talk to Hadi again, Maman admitted it was wrong of him to hit me. But she asked me to forgive him and allow him to explain.

I spent the night in the car. With Baba.

What Maman and Baba didn't realize was that Hadi had no intention of explaining or apologizing. After school the next day, I arrived home to the sound of the vacuum. Baba, a man I had never seen hold a cleaning appliance, kept pushing the vacuum over the same spot.

"Baba *Chie?* What's wrong? He turned his face away and moved the vacuum to the other room. He was crying.

In the kitchen, Maman was crying too. "Hadi moved out today." She hugged me. "He said he doesn't know when he'll come back."

Even though Hadi and Baba argued constantly about business, Baba cried for three days after Hadi left. That night, I heard him on the phone: "When are you coming home? Who are these people you're with? What's your plan for work, for a living situation, for marriage? Come back and let's work together again. The market is better now. Come back and do whatever you want. Just be under this roof with us . . . Please."

Maman's questions were different: "What are you eating? Do you need fried onions or dried fruits or homemade jam?" She had already prepared frozen bags of food to give him when he visited.

As angry as I was, I still found myself in the role of peacemaker, reassuring my parents that Hadi needed to have his own place. He was 21, past the launching age in America, and it was 1990. If he was going to become someone other than another version of Baba, he had to do it outside the house. Meanwhile, when Hadi came by, I went into another room; if he called, I refused to talk to him. I missed him terribly, but I was determined to wait him out for an apology.

❧

Eight months later, I had my best day yet in high school. First, a rose, then, a balloon and a note arrived in my classroom. In the note, Hadi had reconstructed his last eight months out of the house: how he had taken my hairbrush with him so he would be reminded of what he had done, how he had thought of me every day. He wondered if I could ever forgive him.

After I finished reading the letter, I ran out of class, unable to control my tears. I left school early, and walked home, hoping to find Hadi waiting for me.

In front of our house, I stopped in my tracks. A shiny black VW Corrado was parked near our driveway. It had a big red ribbon on the hood, and the driver's door was open. If I dreamed of cars, the Corrado was my dream. As I walked past it, my eyes glued to the shiny hood reflecting the bright sunlight, I wondered which neighbor had made the purchase.

"What do you think?" Suddenly, Hadi stepped out from beside the car. I jumped in shock, my mouth open, and then I ran into his arms and he lifted me up in a hug.

"Thank you for my rose. It's beautiful."

Hadi kissed my cheek and guided me toward the Corrado. "Take a seat," He said, closing the door with a gentle click.

I inhaled the fresh car smell. The dashboard was beautiful, the leather steering wheel shiny, and the black striped fabric of the seat like velvet on my back. "Take it for a ride." Hadi said.

"What?"

"It's yours, baby sister!"

"No, no, I can't take it. This is too much," I said. "I don't even know how to drive a stick shift."

"I'm going to teach you," Hadi's smile widened as he sat in the passenger seat.

The car was great. But the best news was that Hadi, who had now officially moved out and changed his name to Todd—a change I could not quite accept—had made some other changes, too. In the eight months that he had been gone, he had lived with a few different friends, started to date, started working for a Persian rug store, and shaved off the black beard. When he visited on the weekends now, Zain and Iman and I were hopeful our real brother, and not the dictatorial bully, was returning to us.

Now, thanks to Hadi's generous gift, I had wheels, I was making money, and I was on track to graduate from high school at 16— finally free from the torment of other teenagers and the gloom that followed me everywhere. I was going to college at Cal State Fullerton in the fall. Things were looking up.

With Hadi now out of the house, Baba turned his attention to Zain, who was assimilating deeper into the Western culture. But, instead of leaving home, as Hadi had done, Zain brought the West home to us.

The next crisis took an unexpected form, shapely and blonde.

When Maman and I sneaked Shanna, Zain's 17-year-old, American girlfriend into his room, we hid her from Baba as long as we could. Each day, Maman knocked softly and entered carrying a serving tray with *sabzi,* Persian hot tea, and turmeric chicken sprinkled with barberry rice, Shanna's favorite. Maman had defended Zain's mullet haircut, but defending this new secret was entirely different. Before I entered the kitchen, where the yelling shook the walls and rattled the cups in their saucers, I paused for a deep breath.

"We have no choice. They want to be together." Maman placed a cup of tea in front of Baba.

The chair screeched as Baba ignored the tea, pushed away from the table, and stood, staring into the yard. "This is a mistake. He's 18. He doesn't know anything. Today, it's a blonde girl named Shanna, tomorrow it will be another. If he is not married to the right woman, his life will be ruined."

"They love each other. We need to accept it."

Baba slammed his fist on the table. "I will not. I cannot. I will not sell my son out to his hormones . . . It's my own fault for bringing them here." I could hear the pain in his voice. Not only did he carry the guilt for Abdollah's death—but had that trauma not caused our exile to America, my brothers would never have been exposed to dancing, non-Muslim women, and a host of other forbidden things. They would be good Muslim businessmen in Mashhad, married to women approved by the family.

"I am responsible for this." Baba started pacing. "I have to put a stop to it."

"It's too late, Haji. They're married."

Baba stopped moving, and then he slammed his fist against the wall, causing a picture to crash and break.

After a long silence, Maman took a deep breath. "And they're going to have a baby."

The door to the kitchen shook as Baba slammed it on his way out. Maman put her hand on the shaking panel to settle it.

We both knew Baba was right. Zain wasn't ready. Zain's face betrayed the same expression I had seen in the mirror at Abdollah's wedding: that of an unsure, unhappy adolescent. During Shanna's pregnancy, Zain had denied the baby was his, fell in love with Shanna again for a few days, and then rejected her, claiming she was trying to trap him.

Later that afternoon, I heard a strange sound emanating from behind my parents' closed bedroom door. I froze. Baba was wailing and slapping himself so hard that the door vibrated. But his anger and pain didn't last long.

⊰⊱

With the birth of Baba's first grandchild, our family had captured a bit of the American dream for a brief moment. Maybe Zain wasn't ready for parenthood, but Baba found himself ready for grandparenthood. When baby Zahra's tiny fist gripped Baba's index finger, he whispered a prayer of safety—first in her right ear and then her left—and kissed her forehead. Our once totally sealed Iranian family was officially integrated. Zain resembled an American television version of a dad, smitten with Zahra and back in love with his young wife. Briefly.

Meanwhile, instead of being married as many of my Iranian cousins had been at 16, I was living at home and attending college at nearby Cal State—the first in my family to attend university. Hadi was in his own apartment, establishing himself independently of our family, and, unbeknownst to any of us, scheming to restore the family fortune in this land of opportunity. We weren't completely assimilated into the host culture. Maman only spoke 15 words of English: "I do not speak English well," "Please," "Would you like food?" "Thank you," and "Excuse me." But there was progress.

THE AMERICAN NIGHTMARE

⚜

1991

OUR AMERICAN DREAM WAS SHORT-LIVED. One fall night, there was a great commotion outside the house. I looked out the window and saw a man towing away my new Corrado.

Baba, with Hadi working alongside him, had initially been successful in his new business selling carpets and Persian rugs. But some years were leaner than others, and Hadi had overreached: He had no real money for ongoing payments. This was the beginning of a pattern for Hadi, who often hung by his fingernails at the edge of a financial cliff. He mimicked Baba by asserting his power and strictness, as well as his grandiose dreams that would rise and then fall.

By the end of 1992, just before Zahra's first birthday, my proud father—who from his start as a street vendor had built an impressive financial base in Iran and a profitable carpet business in his new country—went bankrupt. All the fruits of his hard labor disappeared as his business failed and we lost our home to the bank. Frustrated and ashamed at having to accept help from the community, Baba began living paycheck to paycheck as an employee of the new owner of his former store, and we moved to the first of a series of rental properties.

When Maman wasn't in despair over the loss of yet another home, my parents argued bitterly over Zain's failure to take responsibility for his new family. After the initial bliss of fatherhood, Zain felt that he was imprisoned forever. Worse, however, was a roller-coaster ride of violent mood swings that featured partying and prolonged disappearances.

Zain left the care of his wife and daughter to us. With a son who was shirking his responsibility, Baba felt disgraced in the community where he had preached the value of marriage and family.

And, although we were legal in the United States, our green card application had been delayed for the sixth consecutive year. Maman was deeply depressed, homesick for her mother and sisters in Iran. Unable to mourn for Abdollah at home with her family, or to realize her dream of placing her palm on his tombstone in Mashhad, she suffered renewed crying spells that threatened her health and frightened us all.

Just when we believed life could not get any worse, it did.

History was about to repeat itself.

Now—
In the Past

⟡⟐⟡

ONE SATURDAY MORNING, deep asleep after a hard week of college classes, I awoke to a loud car screech. Sirens blared while red and blue lights flashed in front of our house. From my second floor window, I could see a squad car—"Irvine Police Department" was written on the side—and two uniformed police officers. One had his hand on his gun, his posture rigid. "Open the door!" he called out.

I ran downstairs without my scarf.

"Who is it?" Baba yelled with his thick accent, alarmed as he squinted through the peephole of our front door. "Rahimeh, come translate."

The heavy knock was now shaking our heavy, wooden door. I wanted to yell for Hadi, who had spent the night, and Zain and Iman. But a weekend movie marathon of Clint Eastwood and *Police Academy* films had kept them up all night, and they had just gone to bed after their morning prayers.

"Is your son home, sir?"

Baba looked at me.

I grabbed Maman's scarf and joined him. "I have many brothers, sir. Which one are you speaking of?"

"Your family owns the white Toyota Tercel that's parked outside, right? The Tercel with the tinted windows and chrome wheels? I need to talk to the boy who drives that car."

They were not here for Hadi and his unpaid speeding tickets, or for Zain for driving under the influence. They were looking for Iman. Iman, the obedient and observant one who, at 16, never broke the rules, never called attention to himself, and was living the life Baba had wished for Abdollah.

I stepped forward. "Our car doesn't have tinted windows or chrome wheels; it's the basic model." A speed junkie like his brothers, Iman had been pulled over a few times for weaving in and out of traffic. I gathered that the Irvine police had already identified our white Toyota Tercel and its Middle Eastern-looking driver.

The first cop removed a notepad from his back pocket. "Do you know where your brother was last night at midnight?"

"Yes, he was with me and my other two brothers. We were watching a movie at home like we do every Friday night." I glanced toward the second floor. "What is the problem, sir?"

"Well, that's not what I think he did last night. Is he home?" As I translated, Baba and Maman grew alarmed. They had never been this close to American policemen.

"We just need to talk to him, ask him some questions. OK?" A second cop spoke softly as he took his hand off his gun. "Just for a few minutes."

It turned out that the officers wanted to question Iman about a crime the night before involving two teenagers who had attacked and robbed two Caucasian kids behind the Albertsons grocery store near our house. Because it was dark, the victims had not gotten a good look at the attackers, but had identified them as Hispanic teenagers and the getaway car as a white Toyota Tercel with chrome wheels and tinted windows. It didn't matter that our car did not match the description, that Iman was Iranian not Hispanic. The officers seemed sure they had come to the right place.

When Maman walked down the stairs with Iman, I explained that it must be a case of mistaken identity. Besides, Iman had an alibi: He had been with us. When the cop saw Iman walking toward him, he put the notepad away.

Smoothing his hair and rubbing his stubble on his face, Iman looked from the policemen to me, confused. He had never been in trouble before.

As the cop pulled out handcuffs, Maman screamed. "You can't do this! Leave our son alone." Baba cried out in Persian. The policeman, undeterred, began reading Iman his rights.

Hadi, wearing only his underwear, ran down the stairs, getting dangerously close to the officers.

The cops pulled Iman by his handcuffed wrists and shoved him in the squad car. When Iman turned to face us in the rear window, his welled-up eyes took in the scene: Maman collapsed on her knees, emitting earsplitting screams as Hadi and I, yelling, chased the squad car. Baba, eyes closed, head cast downward, sat down; he was some-where else entirely.

Later that day, I held the glass of sugar crystals and hot rose water in one hand as I applied yet another cool cloth to Maman's forehead and watched her face for signs of waking.

For every hour of the next two months, we relived the helplessness and horror of Abdollah's arrest and imprisonment at the same age as Iman. Hadi refused food and wouldn't shave until Iman was freed. Zain disappeared and drank, and Zahra's first birthday passed without a party—only a small cake with a candle.

Every night my parents stayed awake conducting midnight prayers, and Baba spent the days struggling to learn the system and find legal help. Constantly weeping and praying, without eating or sleeping, Maman suffered exhausting emotional attacks. Missing classes for the first time, I stayed by her side and refused all my friends' phone calls. I couldn't believe that God would let this happen again. I was ashamed, though I wasn't exactly sure why.

Even though Iman had little memory of Abdollah, he now felt, more than ever, the impact of his brother's death. When he placed tissue paper on the floor of his cell to prostrate himself in morning prayers, his gangbanger roommate kicked him in the kidneys and slammed him against the wall, calling him "camel jockey." After a guard removed the bully and Iman returned to his prayers, his words were soft. Iman found himself talking to Abdollah, whom he had last seen in a cold cell like the one in which he was now imprisoned.

"When I put my forehead on the ground, I can feel you here with me, Brother. It's been so long, I hardly remember your face anymore. I was two when you died, but I know of you. I know some of your stories, and I know you must have felt so much more terror than I feel right now. Brother Abdollah, I'm sorry you went through this. I'm grateful you're here with me now. I wish I could have been there for you then."

Although we all drove to the juvenile detention center, only two visitors were allowed at a time. My parents always told Iman we were all there, sitting in the visitors' area, giving up our turn so our parents had more time.

The next time I saw Iman, it was in a courtroom nearly three months later, where the judge dismissed the charges against him as wrongful incarceration. The only reason Iman had been arrested was because the cops had shown the boys only Iman's picture, asking them if he had been their attacker. In the lineup, the victims couldn't identify Iman. They had been drunk; it had been dark; they never did get a good look. Iman wasn't Hispanic, and the car didn't match. Iman was free. But he wasn't really. In public he no longer made easy eye contact. And despite the fact that he was the victim of profiling, he relived the trauma in his nightmares for years.

I sued Orange County on Iman's behalf six months later. We had a great case. But a year later, the county filed for bankruptcy, and all cases were discharged.

A few weeks after Iman returned home, I awakened him from a nap and convinced him to go out to dinner with me, Hadi, Shanna, and the baby. My parents preferred to remain at home, since Zain was unaccounted for. On the ride home after a casual dinner at a café, Hadi drove the car with increasing recklessness, swerving sharply on the turns. The wipers couldn't keep up as raindrops pounded the windshield like bullets, making it hard to see as we sped across lanes of traffic. "Will you please slow down, Hadi? We have the baby in the car," I said.

Shanna and I locked eyes over Zahra as she dozed between us in the backseat; we each held one of her tiny hands. I began to relive another dangerous car ride, years ago, in Mashhad.

"Hadi?" Shanna suddenly leaned over closer to the front seat. "Is that Zain's car?"

Hadi was gripping the steering wheel, his mouth clenched tight, and his eyes fixed on the white convertible ahead. I was thrown to the side, landing on Shanna's shoulder as he changed lanes again. Then I saw it, too. We were chasing Zain's Mustang. This was déjà vu. I flashed back to Mashhad, to Baba pursuing Abdollah, racing ahead in his Camaro . . .

When Hadi caught up, Zain's license plate clearly in view, he slid alongside, maintaining a speed above 80, and motioned to Zain to pull over.

I leaned forward. This couldn't be happening. There was a blonde woman, scarfless, beside Zain in the passenger seat.

When Zain saw Shanna and me, he sped up.

Rain slammed into my face. Hadi lowered the passenger window and yelled, "Get back here."

But the Mustang was gone.

"Let him go, Hadi," Shanna said as she squeezed Zahra's hand. Zahra was now wide-awake. "The baby's in the car. Just let him go."

The next week, after Zain didn't come home two nights in a row and Shanna banished him to the couch, he announced that he and Shanna were taking Zahra to Fiji. They were off to dive, snorkel, and take pictures in the pristine waters of the Pacific. They had no budget or planning; it was an impulsive decision made to save their marriage. They planned to use their student loan money to cover the basics. We didn't ask too many questions, because Zain and Shanna were holding hands and flirting with each other again. Usually the fighting between them was intolerable, then reverted, for a few moments, to bliss. As usual, we hoped that these episodes might build together to improve their marriage.

For the two weeks they were in Fiji, things improved. Zain fed Shanna fresh strawberries and papayas and pineapples. Each morning he told Zahra a new joke and jumped with her into the clear blue water from their glass-bottomed bungalow. He told his daughter how much he loved her and how she completed his world. And he meant it. But then, home again after a week of good behavior, Zain began sneaking into the house at dawn, sending his marriage down another twisting alley.

didn't ask too many questions, because Zain and Shatha were hold-ing hands and flirting with each other again. Usually the fighting between them was intolerable, then reversed, for a few moments, to bliss. As usual, we hoped that these episodes might build together to improve their marriage.

For the two weeks they were in Fiji, things improved. Zain fed Shatha fresh strawberries and papayas and pineapples. Each morn-ing he told Zahra a new joke and jumped with her into the clear blue water from their glass-bottomed bungalow. He told his daugh-ter how much he loved her and how she completed his world. And he meant it, but then, home again after a week of good behavior, Zain began sneaking into the house at dawn, scuttling his marriage down another crushing alley.

THROUGH THE
GREEN DOOR

❧✸❧

1993
California and Mashhad

MAMAN KISSED BABA'S CHEEKS and forehead and smoothed his hair. She was smiling—something I hadn't seen often in the last ten years. "*Gerefteem!* We got the green cards," Baba said, his voice cracking. We could finally go home.

Wrapping my arms around his neck, I kissed him again and again. To secure green cards for a family of six in America was no small task. It had cost tens of thousands of dollars, all from the hotel proceeds, lots of angst, and eight long years. Of course, this was a bittersweet victory, as my brothers couldn't accompany us. Because they had not served in the Iran-Iraq war, they would be immediately conscripted into the Iranian army if they returned. Although I was sad we had to leave them, I was overjoyed at the prospect of seeing Iran after nearly a decade away. Maman had already called her sisters, her mother, and all her friends.

The next day, I heard Baba's voice coming from the kitchen. "Why don't you understand, *azizam?* We just don't have the money."

For the last ten years, Maman had been trapped in London, and then, in the United States. For her, the American dream meant the freedom to return home.

I heard a pot clatter in the kitchen. "How come we have the money to rent a ceremony hall and cater it for religious ceremonies? How come we have money to help the community, your friends? But now that it's my chance to go home, I can't?"

Waving her arms in the air, she paced the room.

"After watching you sell everything we owned, lose everything we worked for, this is what you say to me? You know that I walked away from my life, my family, my home with a suitcase for a 12-day trip to London." Maman took a breath and patted her chest, the first sign that a panic attack was starting. "I didn't get to go back and pack anything or say a single goodbye. My heart stopped beating every time you went back and I couldn't. You realize that?" Her voice cracked, and she opened a window.

I had never seen Maman confront Baba about his spending—and certainly not about spending money on religious ceremonies.

Baba was calm. "I'm just starting our Mecca business. Wait a few months, *zan.* We'll take the tour together and then we'll go to Mashhad from Saudi Arabia. You can stay there and be with your mother, sisters, and visit the Haram of Imam Reza as many times as you like."

Combining his unwavering commitment to serve God with his strong entrepreneurial instincts, Baba had put the last of his resources into a new business leading religious pilgrimage tours to the holy cities of Mecca and Medina in Saudi Arabia. It was thrilling for Baba to help make the dream of a hajj—a once-in-a-lifetime journey to Mecca, and one of the Seven Pillars of Islam—a reality for so many Iranian Muslims in his community.

"You can't ask me to wait—not anymore. I can't wait a day, Haji. The way you do things, it could be another year before we are ready to go." Maman bumped a large pot with her elbow; it slammed against the drain board and crashed into the sink. "I can't count on a promise. I've waited ten years for this moment. Ten years! And now you want me to wait longer still?" She closed her eyes.

Baba lowered his head. "We just don't have it now. We don't have the money."

I stood in the doorway watching the two of them. All my life, it seemed I had watched them fight in the kitchen. Maman started tossing pans into the sink; Baba sat at the dining room table looking out at the yard. I could hear Zahra's rabbit, Dodi, chewing on a carrot while waiting for Baba to let him loose from his cage. At the end of the day, Baba would spend an hour running after him, catch him, and put him back again. He hated that he had to confine the rabbit, even for its own safety.

At that moment, looking at Maman, I understood why she had supported my decision to start working as a teenager. She never wanted me to be financially dependent. She didn't like the feeling of being trapped; she hated feeling helpless.

Maman was determined. "My mother is ill, and I must see my son's grave. I'll find a way. I'll conduct ceremonies myself and borrow the money if I have to." Her steely tone was new.

Baba kept his eyes on the rabbit cage. He had disappointed Maman once again. He remembered how he had taken a third of the revenue from the Rose Hotel sale and donated it to a rebel ayatollah who would use it to run a prestigious school. Now, in addition to multiple unsound business ventures and having put a significant portion of his resources into the Iranian Muslim community in America, Baba had also lost his investments and the house. After placing others ahead of his family for years, he had invested in a new business—one that would serve the community, revive him emotionally, and increase his significance. But he had nothing left to help the one person he cared about the most: his wife.

A few weeks later, I found Maman in the yard watering her potted plants. I handed her a white envelope. "Are you ready to go to Iran, Mamani?"

She opened the envelope with her wet hands. Although she couldn't read English, she recognized what was inside: two plane tickets. Our 45-day trip would give us the chance to visit Maman's family, see Abdollah's grave, reconnect with our home, and still return in time for my fall classes.

In my mind, it was a simple plan. Because I still lived at home, I could drop out of my summer college classes, use my student loan money for the trip, and take 26 units in the fall while working full-time. I began to coil the water hose around my arm. "Let's go see Grandma. But first, we have a lot of shopping to do."

Ten days later we packed our oversized suitcases with the Iranian "wish list"—Neosporin, Tylenol, Advil, antibiotics, Valium, Xanax, Band-Aids, Saran Wrap, sugar-free gum, Ziploc bags, paper toilet seat covers, used cell phones, perfumes, designer clothes, brand-name makeup, and boxes of Kit Kat bars—and headed to the airport. When we landed in Tehran, the female passengers reached for their folded scarves one by one and lined up for the bathroom to remove their makeup. Hearing so much Persian on the plane made me feel at home.

Tehran's Mehrabad International Airport, which seemed so enormous when I left Iran at the age of nine, now seemed incredibly small compared to the Los Angeles Airport I had departed from .17 hours earlier. As we taxied to the terminal, we passed broken-down cars, plane parts, and containers of trash along the runway. Planes were haphazardly parked on the grounds, some far away from the single entrance to the building. As a tinge of orange lit up the morning sky, I took a deep breath and finally set foot again in what was once my sacred home.

Tehran now made London and the United States seem like distant dreams. But everything seemed odd and out of kilter, diminished in every way. The cars were old, covered with dents and scratches; they had broken taillights, and fenders were held on with duct tape. The city was much smaller than I remembered, and posters of Khomeini and Khamenei were plastered on every wall next to pictures of dead men "martyred" in the Iran-Iraq war. On the streets, the people looked tired and worn by decades of despair, loss, heartbreak, and economic paralysis. I had returned, but to a dirtied, wilted Iran. It was as if a heavy layer of dust had buried everything I remembered.

During the 72-hour layover in Tehran en route to Mashhad, where most of her family lived, Maman had time to take care of some business—including an unresolved dispute between Baba and the buyer of our mansion on Parvaneh Street. She was determined to collect the rest of the money owed to our family—money that Madressi hadn't had a chance to steal. Maman was going to make the owner pay us for the five Persian rugs and all the furniture we had left behind on our abrupt departure from Iran.

The 20-foot, long green metal door opened, and we were greeted by the dark-haired, unshaven man who now owned our mansion. I was already predisposed to disliking him: He lived in my home and I did not. I was grateful for the chador that hid my eyes, helping me conceal my disdain.

Almost immediately, I was flooded by memories: *Where were the chickens? Where were the willow trees where we played hide-and-seek, the path where I learned to ride a bike, the orchard of walnut and cherry trees?* The yard had been rendered lifeless. The garden and playground that surrounded our home and had given our family refuge against that stormy time was unrecognizable. All was dust.

As we entered the house, the clamor of children screaming filled the rooms. One child entered and began smacking a broomstick against the carved wooden headrests of the once elegant upholstered European couch. Maman and I were aghast as we noticed that much of the furniture and antiques were in disrepair; the paintings in their frames were scratched and dusty. Maman's blue antique Venetian vase was chipped, the hand-carved wooden frames gracing her pictures of Mecca were damaged, and her large Persian rug was missing its fringe.

I wanted to scream at the man, but when I looked at Maman, I knew we had more important business to take care of. She had come to settle an old score, and she knew how to play the game artfully. After two hours of discussing the weather, politics, family, and the life expectancy of chickens—everything but the disputed debt— Maman finally broached the topic.

"You're a man of respect. You are also a man of God. I'm coming to you to offer a compromise to end this long-standing dispute between our respected families." Maman slowly placed her teacup on the table. In the background a door slammed, followed by the rattle of furniture and floorboards as eight little children pounded down a distant hallway.

"I have no problem with the sale price of the home. I come here asking that you settle the debt for the price of the furnishings and belongings that were left here. I'm confident that we can part ways in agreement and close this chapter for both of us." She was making her first business deal ever, and she sounded firm and self-assured.

The new owner nodded, but averted his eyes from Maman's direct gaze. "You are a respectable woman and a mother of five children. I bought this home, including the furniture and rugs, but if you dispute the deal I made with your husband, I'll have to settle this with you." He wasn't just complying out of kindness. He knew that since Maman was in the country, she could pursue a financial settlement in the courts.

Four little girls with colorful scarves that barely covered their heads approached me and tugged on my chador. They wanted me to play with them. Even though I let them pull me into the hallway and I loved children, I was in no mood to play. The sound of a basketball thumping against the floor jarred my memory. It was the ball Baba had bought for Iman in Kuwait, shiny orange with black-and-white stitching. Now, it was blackened by filth.

I let go of my chador for a split second, and as it rolled off my head, revealing my head scarf, I grabbed the ball with one hand. Backing away from me, the boy's eyes never left the grimy ball. At the time we left Iran, I had been hiding it on the top shelf of my closet, checking on it during weekend visits to Parvaneh Street, waiting for the day when Iman would be bigger and would return from London to play with it.

Still staring at the ball, the boy shrugged. "You can have it. It's not mine, really."

As I held the dirty ball, my eyes stinging, I saw myself in the boy. I felt ashamed and guilty for the accusing look I had given him. I wasn't angry with him, but with my father for selling the house without telling Maman, for not saving our keepsakes, and for not securing us another home in Iran to return to one day. All my feelings flooded in. I hated Maman for being dependent on Baba, hated Abdollah for dying, and hated Khomeini for allowing this to happen to Iran. And I hated Iran—everyone and everything connected to it. Tears rolled down my face.

"I'm sorry. Take it. Really, it's not mine either, little guy," I said, tossing the basketball back to the boy. "Nothing here is mine anymore."

The boy grabbed the ball, fixing his eyes on me.

I dried my eyes and winked at him. "When spring comes and the trees blossom, don't forget to play hide-and-seek with your sisters. And make sure you give them a chance to bounce the ball around, too. All right?" I could see my face reflected in the little boy's big brown eyes. He nodded.

When I said goodbye to the eight little kids that now had lined up near the door, witnesses to my return home, I put to rest the memories of my own childhood. I had finally said goodbye to the little girl in me. But that didn't mean I had given up on wanting my mother. And at last, in Iran, I had her.

The moment Maman stepped off the plane, she became animated and alive. She commanded the attention of others as she bargained in the stores, talked to friends in the streets, coordinated our outings, and translated difficult phrases from formal Persian so I could understand them. We were mother and daughter again. And after she opened an account in her name for the first time in her life—a savings account to deposit the money we received from the disputed estate dealing—we walked out of the bank chador to chador, shoulder to shoulder.

⚜

Almost immediately after arriving by plane in Mashhad, we hailed a cab to my uncle's residence, where my grandmother, now 88, was living. As we were greeted, my uncle's wife told us that my grandmother had been in a car accident and was recovering from hip surgery.

"Why didn't any of you tell me sooner?" Maman didn't wait for an answer. Dropping her chador, she ran upstairs. I trailed behind her but couldn't keep up. When I entered the bedroom, Maman was kneeling by her mother's bed, their faces wet. "*Dokhtaram,* I knew you would come back for me before I died. I just knew it."

The next day, we headed to the Haram of Imam Reza to visit Abdollah's grave. After we were searched at the Haram's entrance, Maman kissed the 50-foot door. The reflection of light on the gold dome winked at me, and I squinted; the dome was the only part of Iran that had stayed exactly the same. The pigeons circled in the clear air. The decorative blue tiles and gold Arabic writing engraved on the entrance doors reflected the sunlight. I had forgotten how beautiful the Haram was and how light I felt when inside. The smell of incense transported me back in time to something ancient and familiar.

As we descended the dark staircase to the lower basement, a thin layer of dust tickled my throat. When Maman pulled her black chador to cover more of her face, I knew she was beginning to cry. I moved closer to her, dreading what seemed inevitable: her uncontrollable sobbing.

The dark walls of the underground cemetery held hundreds of photos in frames. The faces of young boys, martyrs of the war—*shaheeds*—were all around us. The walls echoed and magnified the sounds of women crying for their beloved sons and brothers, repeating their names, and beseeching God to return them to their families. The air was thick with dust and heat and human suffering, dark and oppressive. I wanted to flee.

Out of nowhere, an old man appeared. Clothed in a white shirt with two buttons missing, dark blue pants rolled up to his knees, and heavily worn plastic sandals, he had worked here for ages, cleaning the cement tombstones of the young men and boys who had died too young. His soft beard was peppered with dust. "Come, my dearest girl," he said, gesturing me toward the frame that held my brother's photo.

Maman immediately began to thank him profusely. Hired by my parents when we left Mashhad, this man had been cleaning Abdollah's grave for ten years now, making sure the photo that hung over the grave was straight, that the headstone was washed every day, that flowers adorned it. When the ink on the tombstone faded, he dutifully reapplied it, making sure that the letters of Abdollah's name were legible and dark.

"He's been waiting for you," he said quietly.

As we stood at the headstone, Maman took my hand and began to cry softly.

"He *has* been waiting for us for a long time, *azizam*," she whispered. As I squeezed her hand, I felt pressure in my chest, and the heat made my cheeks flush. This time, it was me who needed rose water and sugar crystals. Suddenly my pain turned into anger—I hated Abdollah for leaving, for causing us this enormous pain. I couldn't watch Maman cry again.

Maman reached out her hand from her chador and softly ran her five fingertips along the cement tombstone, following the grooves of the letters of his name. "*Salaam pesaram.* I've missed you, son."

As Maman prayed aloud, she looked toward me twice. She was calmer than I had ever seen her in the ten years we had been away from Iran. "I never told anyone this, but after he died, he visited me whenever I prayed," she said, checking my face. "One day he told me to accept, to let go and focus on the children. That day, I made a decision to live again."

"What was he wearing?" I asked innocently.

Maman cocked her eye at me. "Why? What do you mean?"

"I saw him too, Maman. In Grandma's cellar. He waved goodbye, and when I finally got the courage to run down the steps, he was gone. I didn't know then that he had died."

Maman took my hand. She, too, had seen Abdollah in his navy blue suit, a white light around his body. "He told me he had to leave, and that he needed to be in heaven. He had a wife and children, and was now with my father. Then, he told me goodbye. He never came again."

My anger began to fade. I spoke to Abdollah without thinking: *I'm sorry I've been so angry. I'm sorry this happened to you. I'm sorry I stopped talking to you a few years ago. I'm sorry I couldn't help you, Brother.*" I looked at his name on the tombstone and finally acknowledged years of mourning. *Brother. I love you. I miss you, Dadashi.*

Weeks later, before catching our flight back to America, Maman and I made a special stop. We went to the Rose Hotel. As we stood in front of it, it seemed to stare back at us, its windows empty-socketed eyes. No one stayed there; the school had shut it down years ago, its operational budget too high to maintain. The hotel seemed to be in mourning, waiting, as we had been, for the past to return. Only ghosts walked the echoing empty halls, including the shadow of fates that once occupied Room 314.

We returned to the taxi dry-eyed, accepting that the Rose Hotel had been a dream place. That dream had died with Abdollah.

We had now been away 45 days, and the smell of exhaust filled the air as we sat at the gate of the airport waiting for our return flight. From the taxi driver to the steel factory owner, everyone had complained about the "changed" Iran and the existence of a new reality: the extremes in living, the contradictions in society. Having visited cousins who lived in fancy mansions with gold knobs and imported Italian marble while seeing that the majority of the Iranian people now had to live hand to mouth, I was filled with sadness: for those who didn't have enough and were hungry, and for the ones who did and felt guilty. I was grateful to have gone home to visit—and though it felt strange, I was also relieved to realize that it wasn't home anymore. In many ways, going to Iran and visiting Abdollah's grave had finally brought him back to us, and freed me.

Maman smiled at me and took my hand as we walked toward the plane, side by side. We would be returning home different people. It was finally our turn—the women's turn—to shine.

THE CLIFF

❦

THE TRIP TO IRAN HAD PROVIDED much-needed healing, especially for Maman who had experienced success as a negotiator. Her visit with the rest of her family had also reminded her of her old self, when she was more like her mother—always supportive of her husband, but quietly challenging his authority. Maman was determined to change things. After our return to the United States, she began to engage in the tour activities with Baba and soon became his business partner.

Although Maman and I had addressed our past in Iran, at home in America, Zain had not. In every family that is traumatized, it seems that there is always one member who is most vulnerable—one who absorbs more than others, as if giving voice to everyone's pain. In our family, this person was Zain. And without meaning to inflict so much hurt, he hurt everyone who loved him.

One night, I heard a heavy thud from the shower next door to my bedroom. The sound was so loud that my heart began to pound and the hair on the back of my neck stood on end. It was dark; the only light in the cold room was the digital clock, its blue numbers reading 4:15 a.m. I gritted my teeth, got up, and walked toward the bathroom. A dim strip of light came from below the bathroom door;

as I got closer, I was met with an unfamiliar odor. Assuming Zain had come home late again, I asked, "Zain, is that you? Are you OK?"

The water was gushing full volume, making it impossible to hear or be heard. "Zain. Open up." I raised my voice and jiggled the doorknob. My parents, Shanna, and Zahra were asleep across the hallway. This was no time to be taking a bath. *Why was he so thoughtless? What was wrong with him?*

At the sound of an even louder thud, I tugged at the doorknob. "Zain, open up! I mean it." The water was trickling beneath the door. My feet were getting wet. "Zain, open up!"

I threw my shoulder against the door and finally pushed it open. Zain was submerged in the overflowing tub, his hair floating on the surface and his eyes closed. I grabbed his head and pulled him up. When he finally took a breath, the stench of alcohol filled the air. "Breathe," I said. "Breathe."

Even though the scorching water burned my feet, I held steady and dragged his body out of the tub, trying to prop him up against the towel rack. In a panic, I slapped his face a few times. Eventually, his eyes popped open and rolled back in his head. I hit him again, "Wake up Zain. Wake up!"

His eyes still closed, Zain flapped his limp arms and then tried to push me away. "Don't look at me, sister. Don't look at me," he said. His voice slurred.

I drained the water and struggled to wedge my hands under his armpits. "Zain, for God's sake! You could have drowned here if you hit your head any harder." Pulling him up, I wrapped him in a towel. The stench of alcohol burned my eyes. His skin had pruned and peeled off around his cuticles where he chewed his nails.

"Just breathe and open your eyes. I'll help you to bed."

"I was right there at the edge . . ." His words trailed off. "I wish I'd have the guts to drive off that cliff."

I stared at him. He was drunk and incoherent, but I could hear the desperation in his voice.

Finally in bed, he blinked at me with his bloodshot eyes as if to say "thank you" and drifted off to sleep. Although now I was beginning to understand that Zain's problem was alcohol, I also knew something else was eating away at him.

After cleaning the bathroom and drying the floor quietly so no one else would wake up, I knew it was time to force the family to get help. Since we had been transplanted in the States, we had become lost in a new country, and to ourselves. We needed an intervention. And the whole family needed to participate.

❊

Only weeks later, I found myself with Zain, passed out, again. My best guess was that it was a cocktail of methamphetamine, cocaine, ecstasy, and vodka that caused Zain to snore, sprawled in the front passenger seat of Hadi's latest financed car, a Lotus Elite. Drool slid from the corner of his mouth.

Sitting in the backseat for the drive to Irvine, I rechecked my seat belt and tried to ignore Hadi's impulse to send text messages while he weaved in and out of traffic at 110 miles an hour, the seat belt light still blinking. *And we thought Zain was the problem?*

After the bathtub incident, Zain's drunken late-night antics were the subject of frequent family fights. Finally, I convinced Iman, Hadi, my parents, and Shanna to meet with a substance abuse interventionist. To prepare, we met with the doctor in advance; Baba needed the most help understanding what alcoholism was. True to his nature, he believed that a conversation with God and a religious path would be more effective than any of this Western-style mumbo-jumbo talk therapy we were suggesting. But although he didn't understand it, he still agreed to come.

As I dragged Zain from the passenger seat, he put his hand on my shoulder, and in his fog asked, "Why are we here, Sis? I'm really tired."

"I told you, we are going to have a family discussion. This is not just about you," I reassured him.

When we entered the office, Baba, Maman, Iman, and Shanna were waiting for us as planned. Four-year-old Zahra played in a corner, wearing a headset and coloring with her markers. Zain opened his eyes wider and abruptly adjusted his posture. "What's going on here?" he asked. Even drunk, he couldn't be fooled. "I need my sunglasses," he said, holding a hand out toward Hadi. "Car keys, please?"

"I'll get them for you, Bro." I stood up.

When I returned with Zain's sunglasses, he put them on and sat on the edge of a chair, indicating he wasn't planning to cooperate.

As instructed by the psychologist, we had each written letters to Zain, which we read aloud. Iman went first, expressing his concern for Zahra and his observations about the impact of Zain's absences on everyone, particularly his wife and parents. Zain kept readjusting his sunglasses up and down his nose. When Shanna spoke about her drunken, abusive father, how this was a repeat of her past, and how she wanted something very different for her daughter, Zain's leg began to shake.

When it was Baba's turn, he looked directly at Zain while I translated for the doctor. "This doctor tells me that what you have is a disease. I'm just learning these things because, as you know, no one in our family drinks." He continued, explaining the damage alcohol does to the body. I was sure he was quoting sections from the pamphlet "Why Alcohol is Forbidden in Islam" that he placed at the entrance of the Rose Hotel all those years ago. "You have to quit putting this poison in your body," he said. "I cannot bear to see this happen to you." Baba's shoulders drooped as he pushed his glasses back up on his nose. His tone was somber.

After we all had spoken, the room fell silent. Zahra looked up, and then returned to placing stickers in her coloring book. I placed a cup of coffee in front of Zain. Finally, he adjusted his glasses and sat forward, his leg shaking faster now.

"Doctor, I was brought here under false pretenses," he said. "I'm listening to all of my family members, and I love them. I respect what they're saying, but I don't have a problem." He took off his sunglasses and looked the psychologist in the eye. "You see, my father is a religious man——too religious, if you ask me. And my parents lost their kid in Iran. That's the real problem here." He didn't take a breath. "I don't drink any more than any other guy my age. I want to live my life. They want to control me. That's just not going to work out, for me or for them." He looked spent; he had used every ounce of energy he had. Through half-open eyes, he added, slurring, "Did I mention my brother died?"

No one spoke, but the room seemed to relax as the psychologist let the past go as quickly as it had appeared. Instead, he redirected the conversation to the impact of Zain's drinking on the family.

Zain slid his sunglasses back on and let him finish. Then he went for the jugular. "You see that guy right there?" He gestured at Hadi.

"His name is Todd, but his real name is Hadi." Zain smiled. "Now I can't even call him by his real name or he flips out. He'll even refuse to answer us if we speak to him in Persian. He's not OK with who he is. I am. I am exactly this guy you see—the good, the bad, and the ugly." Zain took a sip of his coffee, put his cup down, and glared at Hadi. "My family is hurt; we're not OK. But I'm not the problem here." His leg stopped shaking as he looked over at me.

I knew he was right to a certain degree—except for the fact that he didn't seem to be including himself in any of the indictments.

"I like to have fun, and these guys are just way too uptight about it," Zain continued. "This isn't Iran, you know. This is America. I like to dance. I like to drink and be free." He stood, zipping his yellow ski jacket, never looking at Zahra. "You know, guys, I love you. Thank you for coming here for me, but you're asking for too much. I'm fine. I'm happy. Leave me be." He cupped his hand on my shoulder for balance, pretending it was to reassure me, and left.

"He needs to be ready to accept his problem," the psychologist said.

I felt light-headed. I had worked so many weeks to set up this meeting. "You mean there isn't anything you can do?" I asked.

"He needs to hit rock bottom." The psychologist locked eyes with Maman. "Maybe even face death."

Clearly, this doctor had no idea what he was asking of us. My parents would never knowingly risk Zain's life. I could see Maman's determination. Pulling her scarf tighter, she grabbed her purse and headed for the door. Now I knew we were in real trouble.

On the drive back, a ray of sunlight slid through the gray puffy clouds and shone on Zain, who was in the backseat of Hadi's car, passed out.

ENTRY INTO THE PAST

⸎

1995
Mashhad, Iran

I COULD FEEL THE SWEAT DRIP DOWN my belly as I placed my hand on Hadi's shoulder. "Hadi, aren't you coming inside?" I spoke in English so Maman wouldn't understand us. She had been dreaming of this day for so long, and I didn't want anything to spoil it. It was now possible for all of us to return to Mashhad together—and to visit Abdollah's grave. New laws were now in place, and Baba had been able to buy his sons exit visas that allowed them to return to Iran while he stayed in the States to keep the business running.

It had been two years since the intervention with Zain, and this time, it was Hadi who paced back and forth, his hand on his leather bag, sunglasses covering his eyes. Each time he circled the decorated tiles of the Haram's outer yard, he avoided the entrance where the old men were sweeping dust and dirt into the air. He wore a summery white cotton shirt, Calvin Klein pants, and white Kenneth Cole shoes; smartly dressed though he was, he was ill prepared for the dusty Haram cemetery in the basement.

"You go with Mom," Hadi waved his hand in the air. Calling Maman "Mom" was something he never did. "I can't take the smell," he said, anticipating my disapproval. Although I knew the place would be suffocatingly hot and crowded with perspiring, grieving family members, I couldn't contain my reaction.

"What do you mean? We've been waiting more than ten years for this!"

"Really? *You've* been waiting to visit this miserable place for years?" Hadi snapped. Even through his designer sunglasses, I could see the rage in his eyes. I left him alone, facing the alluring golden dome.

Hadi lay on the dusty ground, faceup, so that he could see Abdollah looking down at him from the framed picture hanging above. A few hours after Maman and I had left the Haram, he had gone down to the cemetery to have his moment with his older brother, alone.

Hadi placed his head on Abdollah's tombstone. "I wish we could switch places," he said as he moved his hand across the letters. He took a deep breath and closed his eyes. "I've never forgotten my promise to you."

Almost unaware, he continued talking aloud: "I'm sorry you're not here to see Zain—he would make you laugh. Rahimeh—she's brave, —and Iman—so gentle." Tears pooled in the corners of his eyes.

The old man with the broom who cleaned and guarded Abdollah's grave whispered a prayer for the two brothers.

Hours later, at closing time, Hadi walked backward, never taking his eyes off the headstone, and saying again, "Goodbye, *Dadashi,*" in a way that connected him to his brother forever.

Zain and Iman had also visited the cemetery, and that night there wasn't enough *shish kebab*, jasmine rice, and Persian stew to fill the void. Zain ate uncontrollably. Later, while the rest of us were sending prayers to Abdollah, Zain drove to the east side of Mashhad. He spent the rest of the night at an underground party where champagne corks popped and plates of Ecstasy were passed around like offerings of sugar cubes.

The old man with the broom who cleaned and guarded Abdollah's grave whispered a prayer for the two brothers.

Hours later, at closing time, Hadi walked backward, never taking his eyes off the headstone, and saying again, "Goodbye, Dadashi," in a way that connected him to his brother forever.

Zain and Iman had also visited the cemetery, and that night there wasn't enough shish kebab, jasmine rice, and Persian stew to fill the void. Zain ate uncontrollably. Later, while the rest of us were sending prayers to Abdollah, Zain drove to the east side of Mashhad. He spent the rest of the night at an underground party where champagne corks popped and plates of Ecstasy were passed around like offerings of sugar cubes.

MECCA

1996

A YEAR LATER—THIS TIME IN MECCA, the holiest place in the Muslim world—our family faced another dilemma. It began in Orange County, California, when Baba was hospitalized.

"I won't discharge you from this hospital, sir," the doctor said. For the past ten days, he had been treating Baba for a dangerous infection, and was now suggesting that he cancel his next trip from America to Mecca.

Adjusting his bruised and IV-injected arm, Baba pushed himself up on the bed. "Doctor, I'm grateful for all your help." With his free hand, he pulled on his hospital gown. "But let me be clear: I will not, under any circumstances, miss this trip to Mecca. I take my orders from God, not from medicine." He pointed a wavering finger at the doctor and spoke freely in Persian. "Look, I have pilgrims who are packed and ready to go. I've worked night and day for weeks to get them their visas. More than six months of preparation has gone into this." He paused, catching his breath. "My wife and I will take these pilgrims on the hajj. I will not disappoint them."

The doctor turned toward me, switching from Persian to English. "I will not discharge him. He would be leaving against medical advice. With his diabetes, this infection could turn ugly fast. It's cellulitis now, but it can turn into sepsis or worse; it could shut down his organs. Are you willing to take him against medical advice?"

The doctor didn't know Baba. The choice wasn't mine.

I had left college once to take Maman to Iran—and this time, at 23, I would leave my fourth year of my doctoral program in clinical psychology to take Baba to Mecca. I packed a large cooler with bags of IV antibiotics, and accompanied my parents, Iman, and Zain there as Baba's traveling nurse. Zain and Iman, who ran the tours with Baba, would ensure 75 happy pilgrims; I would try to keep Baba healthy and alive.

In our suite at the Mecca Hilton, I wrapped a blanket under my chin and huddled on the couch. I had just unhooked Baba from the last of his IV treatments for the day. I was not a real nurse, but things seemed to be going well, despite the fact that his leg was infected with cellulitis. Baba was limping, but in the first three days of our trip, he hadn't felt the need to use the wheelchair I had arranged. When he rose two hours early each morning and headed for the Haram to reserve the best seats for his pilgrims, Maman woke, too, despite Baba's protests. She would straighten his collar, caution him to drink plenty of water, kiss his cheek, and finally, promise that she would go back to sleep. Tonight, standing over Maman, who had fallen asleep on her prayer rug, Baba was backlit against the 17-foot windows facing the bright grand lights of the great mosque. Lighting up the sky, it was the home of the *Ka'ba:* the cube-shaped building that all Muslims around the world face during prayer. Baba was at home here, peaceful.

I had watched as Baba laid a blanket over Maman, tucking it under her chin and lifting her feet just enough to wedge the blanket under her toes. "You're an angel, *zan*—my angel," he whispered. He pushed back her bangs from her forehead, leaned over slowly, and kissed her. These were the parents of my early childhood.

A few hours later, from my bed on the hotel couch, Baba's uneven footsteps woke me, and then I heard a clinking sound. He had rolled his wheelchair out from the corner and was heading toward the door.

"Are you kidding me?" I jumped up, throwing the blankets to the floor, and tried to grab the room keys from his hand.

"I'm taking a group to the Haram for the special midnight prayers. Just hand me a bottle of water, *azizam*. I'll be fine."

"Your leg's still infected, Baba. You need to rest. You've been up for two days; this is insane."

"I'll be all right. Don't worry." Baba pushed open the door and rolled himself out.

I was used to being ignored by Baba, especially if God's duty called.

When he returned two hours later, Baba's face was yellow, the pink around his eyes unusual, even for a man who hadn't slept for a few days. "You're so stubborn," I whispered, but he was disoriented and couldn't hear me. As I had been directed, I gave him an extra shot of antibiotics and monitored him throughout the night. Within a few hours, it was clear we had to go to the hospital. His leg was as swollen as a watermelon, and the flesh was just as red.

Zain, Iman, and Maman wanted to come with me, but they had to stay with the pilgrims. I waited with Baba in the busy, crowded emergency room as he lay, unresponsive, on the gurney. I rubbed his cold hands in mine and put my *hejab* jacket on him. Three hours later, we were still waiting to be seen.

In a silent moment, I looked at Baba, who had neglected his health for years. Anger welled up. But then I reminded myself of what was important to him. He would die for what he believed in; he would sacrifice himself and his family in the service of others. I knew that his schedule, his agenda, his needs or those of his family would always come second to his need to contribute and be significant. For the first time, I wasn't taking it personally anymore, and the rage in me dissolved.

After four hours of treatment, Baba slowly awoke and began speaking in Arabic, a language I did not speak well. Without acknowledging me or translating, he spoke at length with the nurse and doctor as he began to pull himself up on the gurney.

I understood immediately from his tone that Baba was telling the doctor that he was leaving against medical advice—again. Another wave of anger flashed inside me, but I pushed it aside. I had injected his medication, checked his IV every hour for nights on end, and had just spent seven hours in a foreign hospital advocating for his care. The new feelings of empathy gave way to the more familiar ones of being dismissed, ignored, and insignificant.

"I think I missed my prayer," Baba said after he was discharged with several bags of antibiotics. By the time I rolled him out of the emergency room and hailed us a cab, he was wide-awake.

As the driver headed back to the hotel, I sat in the backseat, reflecting. This latest crisis with Baba had made me afraid: first, that we would lose Baba, and second, that we would lose our last chance to learn the truth about Abdollah. When would I get the courage to ask Baba?

From the front seat, Baba turned his head to look at me. "What's the matter?" His glasses were crooked on his face.

I hesitated. Over the past three years of graduate school as I studied to become a therapist, I had become more conscious of the dynamics in my family, acknowledging the role of mood disorders and finally understanding the unique ways that we deal with secrecy, loss, and trauma. But it was one of my professors who pointed out one of the most meaningful patterns between my parents: my father the aggressor, and my mother the saint.

As a part of my graduate requirement, I began my own therapy, making a real investment in my own mental health and becoming who I wanted to be. I had realized how secrecy had been a part of our family for generations. All of the young dead—my parents' lost sisters and brothers—had also been covered over; acknowledging and discussing it was too frightening.

I thought about this all in the moment Baba asked me what was wrong, but I kept quiet. I knew that once we returned to the hotel, I would lose him to the crowds, the pilgrims, the hotel managers, the cook, and the waiters who loved to shake the hand of Haji from America and offer their appreciation for his return through their enthusiastic "*Salaams.*"

"*Begoo digeh,*" he said, insisting I tell him what I was thinking.

I felt my cheeks throb. Finally, I blurted it. "Baba, *what happened to Abdollah?*"

"Drive slower, please," he said in Arabic to the cab driver. He looked back at me. I'm sure he saw the desperation in my eyes, but he didn't blink, or seem too surprised.

"Where do you want me to begin? At the beginning?"

"Yes, please, Daddy." I had never called him "Daddy" before.

For the next 40 minutes, as we drove through the dusty streets of Mecca, Baba kept his head turned toward me from the front seat, only looking away once. Every few minutes, he would stretch his neck and ask, "You follow? Got it so far?" continuing as he saw me nodding.

As he told the story of the days of the revolution—the lawlessness, the violence, the smell of freedom that mesmerized millions—it seemed as if a movie were playing in front of me. Back then, I knew about the chaos; even as a child, I had felt the energy of it. But now, I had the context. Baba told me about the rape of the old woman, how he was called to act, and why he couldn't say no.

"Your mother was opposed to keeping the boys at the hotel. She worried about Abdollah. And about you, since you were a girl. But I reassured her, over and over, that it would be OK. At least we knew where they were, instead of loose on the streets, I told her. It was supposed to be for two weeks." Baba looked at me, but he was clearly elsewhere.

He grew quiet for the first time during our ride. "I told her we would all be safe. I promised her."

I kept silent. I knew he had been carrying this burden for many years, and that he, as much as I, needed some relief. But given the fragile state of his health, I didn't want to press him too hard. "Baba, you all right? Do you want to stop?"

three

Baba readjusted his right leg, which rested on top of the dashboard, next to the IV hanging from a hook above the door. "Sometimes it feels like yesterday. I can smell it. Taste it. Still," he said.

"What?" I leaned forward.

"The past." His gaze faded again.

A few minutes passed as we both stared out the window into the space of our memories. Then, Baba's voice grew louder despite his palpable sadness.

"I gave the best speech of my life there in that courtroom. After that, everyone was certain he would be freed." His voice dropped again. "I mean, *everyone*."

I sat, silent.

"At first, I thought it was a mistake. I thought I could fix it because he couldn't be . . . But when I got close, I saw . . . I knew it was over."

"You saw . . . ?" I couldn't complete my thought.

The cab pulled up to the Hilton. Baba turned back to look at me and pounded his index finger in his chest. "Three bullets."

LOVE AND WAR

❧

1997
California

IN MY NEXT BATTLE WITH MY FATHER, the territory in dispute was the human heart: mine. I faced this predicament on a camping trip with the man I was falling in love with. I knew that Baba would oppose me, although I was 22 and finally living on my own. Everything he cherished was about to be tested.

Here, under the sapphire California sky in a national park where I felt at peace, I questioned everything. *Would I really go to hell if I didn't wear the scarf? Or if I dated? Was I even a good Muslim anymore? What did I believe?* Although I had covered my hair since I was six years old, I began to ask whether I was doing it out of habit or true religious belief.

I sat with the cascade of a waterfall whispering behind me, seeking relief from the August sun in the shade of colossal redwoods. With one bold gesture, I untied the scarf under my chin and let my hair fall free. Dipping my head in the icy Kings River, I shivered as the water chilled my scalp and dripped down my neck and back. When I lifted my face to the sky, the sun's scorching heat felt wonderful.

I arranged my scarf over my wet hair and checked to see if Yarek was still sitting on a rock near the trail. This was his first outing with a girl wearing a head scarf. Fourteen years my senior, he was my colleague at the psychiatric hospital where I worked on the weekends to pay for my graduate courses. When I called his name, he smiled and looked away again, giving me my privacy. Looking into the sun again, I shut my eyes and took a deep breath. I had embarked on my two most profound challenges yet: questioning my religion and falling in love.

꧁꧂

A year had passed. Rather than keep another dark secret, and in the hope of integrating Yarek into the family, I asked Baba to invite him on one of our family's upcoming pilgrimage trips to Mecca. The plan was that Baba would come to like Yarek, just as Maman had on a secret day trip to Mexico. Only then would I tell him we were dating.

Maman, always the mediator, arranged the meeting, hoping for the best. Before sitting down to tea and fresh cut watermelon, Baba kissed Yarek on each cheek and shook his hand, pleased to have a foreigner express interest in Islam and a trip to Mecca. He did not know that Yarek was a Polish atheist.

"So, tell this nice gentleman that he is very welcome in our home. And that I am very curious about his quest of—*Mosalmuni*—becoming a Muslim." Baba pushed the teacup close to me as he passed me three large sugar cubes.

I translated for Yarek as my heart pounded against my chest. At 23, I was apprehensive about Baba's reaction to the fact that I had a boyfriend. But I believed I was truly in love.

Baba asked Yarek dozens of questions about his age, his parents, his upbringing, his extended family, his work, and his family's religious beliefs. He asked how Yarek had come to America and met me. Finally, he got to the most important question of all: How did Yarek feel about God?

The discussion began not with a question, but with a sermon. Baba began with Adam and Eve, then Jesus, Abraham, Mohammad, Jerusalem, Mecca, and ended at the Ka'ba. True to his nature, Yarek was quiet, making Baba feel that he had a captive audience.

Three and a half hours and four cups of tea later, I felt a sense of relief. Perhaps I had underestimated Baba after all. Perhaps the years in America had softened him. Perhaps Baba would come to embrace Yarek's tender spirit and calm soul while we traveled together on the trip to Mecca. On the trip, I, too, could feel things out and consider a more serious relationship—maybe even marriage. I had watched my parents act like newlyweds on the Mecca trips, and it had inspired me to believe in the possibility of deep, spiritual love.

At the end of his lecture, Baba asked Yarek in broken English, "You understand?"

Yarek nodded. "Yes. Your daughter did a great job translating." He looked away from Baba for the first time and smiled at me. By the time the second dimple appeared, his eyes on me, Baba's smile had faded. He had seen the love in Yarek's eyes.

"Rahimeh, what is the nature of your relationship with this man?"

"I told you, Baba, I met him at the psych hospital where I work. He's a nurse there."

I looked over at Maman, who had been coming and going from the room in her unobtrusive way with fresh tea and pastries.

"I wasn't born yesterday, Rahimeh. I ask you again: What is the nature of your relationship with this man?" Baba pushed Yarek's visa application out of his reach and yelled in Persian. "I am a man, and I know about the look in his eyes."

Now Yarek's smile was gone, too. The furrowing of his eyebrows told me how confused he was.

"Baba, we met at work. He's a friend." I felt my shoulders tighten. "I thought that on the Mecca trip, I would get to know him better and see what happens."

Yarek and I both jumped as Baba slammed his fist on the table, rattling the teacups. "What do you mean 'see what happens'? What has already happened?" He pressed his palms on the table and stood facing Yarek. "You tell me what his intentions are—tell me that now before I kick him out of my house!"

Yarek didn't move, appearing both surprised and cautious.

Baba suddenly began to shout in his broken English. "Are you planning to marry my daughter?" He turned to me. "Tell him I want the truth. Right now, Rahimeh."

Yarek's voice was calm. He had dealt with angry patients in the hospital before.

"I'm interested in Islam, sir. I genuinely am. But I'm mostly interested in Islam because of your daughter." Yarek's innocence was endearing, but, as I translated his response, I realized it was a mistake.

Coming around the table, Baba reached behind him and, without looking, picked up a crystal bowl and raised it above Yarek's head. "Get him out of my house before I kill him!" The veins in Baba's neck were pulsing as he yelled at Yarek in Persian. "You're 14 years older than my daughter—you child predator, you atheist!"

I had stopped translating.

Baba raised the crystal bowl higher; his birthmark was the color of beets. "How dare you come to my home under false pretenses? Get out of my house!"

Swinging my purse over my shoulder, I headed for the door. "If he's leaving, so am I." I grabbed my shoes, Yarek following behind me.

"If you go, don't come back." Baba was holding the bowl above his head as if it were his Qur'an.

I yanked the door shut with a slam.

December 1998

At Maman's request, my cousin had managed to get Baba dressed in a suit, but on their way to my wedding ceremony, Baba reversed his acquiescence.

"Turn the car around."

Since the crystal bowl incident more than a year earlier, Baba would leave every family function as soon as I arrived. He hadn't realized that his rage that night would drive me to buy a condo with Yarek. Since then, not only had he stopped speaking to me, he threatened other family members who did. This continued, even on my wedding day. He went home to fume.

I was crestfallen that Baba had not come to my wedding. Despite his attempts to prevent her, Maman not only attended, but also officiated our wedding vows. Yarek and I sat together, circled by Maman and my brothers. Even without Baba, I was hopeful we could break the cycle of misfortune that had befallen our family.

Neither of my brothers was faring well in their marriages. Although Hadi and his half-Persian wife of two years attended my ceremony together, their impending divorce was taking its toll. Zain seemed happier with Shanna than I had ever seen him—but, as usual, his happiness was cause for alarm.

Raising his glass of sparkling apple cider in Yarek's direction, Zain declared, "If you hurt my sister, I'll kill you." He laughed aloud into the silence that followed. "But seriously, I know you're a great guy. That's why my sister loves you . . . I think anyway!" He shrugged his shoulders and, despite the palpable discomfort of the guests, continued. "Actually, I'm not sure what she sees in you," he said and laughed again. The room grew tense. "I'm kidding, come on! I know you're a good man. And I want to welcome you to the family." Zain's eyes darted and his words became more slurred. How did I miss it? Somehow, my brother had managed to sneak alcohol into my alcohol-free wedding.

As we all raised our glasses, Zain continued to mumble parts of an impromptu speech that seemed to mock Martin Luther King, Jr.: "I have a dream that someday my sister and Yarek . . ." My heart sank, and I could feel the flush of embarrassment on my face. Except for the final cheers of our guests when he finished speaking, I tuned him out. I knew others wondered where they, too, could find some alcohol.

I knew then that I had been foolish to imagine this could be a happier time for my family.

Months later, Shanna came running into my parents' bedroom, her hair uncombed, wearing only a thin robe that flapped loosely around her. Outside a thunderstorm was shaking the trees in the yard; Zahra's pet rabbit had to be brought inside because he was thumping at his cage in fright. Shanna was trembling as Maman wrapped her arms around her and called me into the room to translate. I had just arrived to visit Maman, and was telling Baba through his closed office door that I loved him and missed him. Even ten months after my wedding, he still refused to speak to or see me.

"What's happened?" Maman tucked a strand of Shanna's hair behind one ear.

"Zain is screaming that I've cheated on him. He's so angry. I'm afraid." Shanna buried her head in Maman's shoulder.

In unison, our heads swiveled toward Shanna's room. Zain usually slept in the living room with the television blasting through the door.

Shanna's hands were shaking as she accepted a tissue from Maman. "It's OK. He's gone. Zahra's fine. But he's never yelled like this before with Zahra in the room. I'm afraid for both of us."

For the first time since my wedding, Baba didn't leave the room when I entered. He did not look at me and expect me to translate; instead, he spoke in English. "I will fix, Shanna." He looked angry. "I will fix. You go sleep. OK, Zahra. I will fix."

Trembling as Maman rubbed her back, Shanna dabbed at her eyes and blew her nose. "He was drunk. I didn't want to tell you. He told you he stopped drinking, but he hasn't. I stopped going places with him. It's embarrassing. I'm sorry to tell you."

When Maman returned from walking Shanna back to her room, Baba stood waiting for her. He pointed a finger at Maman. "You encouraged these two to get married. Look at this mess now." The window shook in its frame. "He ignores his wife and child and doesn't come home at night." Baba began to wave his arms in circles, speaking more loudly. "He promised that if I took him to Mecca, he would stop putting that poison in his body. He's broken his promise again." Baba looked at the empty rabbit cage. "He's missing work, he's staying out, and now he's out of control, his wife afraid of him? I will not tolerate this in my house." The veins in his neck throbbed as he headed toward the door. "I will not."

Maman followed. "Where're you going, Haji? Please calm down before you do anything foolish."

"I'm going to find him and set this straight. Of all the things that I've been forced to endure in this country, this will not be one of them. I would rather see him dead than a drunk." The door slammed behind him.

I knew we would need more than sugar crystals and a cool towel to calm Maman. She sat on the edge of the bed, her face red and wet. Wadding the tissues in her hand, she began tearing them up, pounding her chest and crying like a wounded animal.

"Maman?" I reached for her hand.

She was screaming over and over, "*Ey Khoda*—What's happening to us, dear God?" Her breathing became shallow, and her eyes rolled back in their sockets. I knew the signals. She was back in Mashhad.

"Breathe, Mamani, breathe with me." When she began to gasp, I was now the one screaming. "Maman—breathe!"

"I can't." One arm went limp, her fist opening, while with her other hand she tried to rub her chest before the hand slid to the bed.

"Maman, can you hear me?"

When the ambulance arrived, Maman didn't argue; she didn't even motion for her scarf. She was mumbling nonsense. When the paramedic told me it could be her heart, I was glad she couldn't understand English. I helped her on with her scarf and, with the paramedic, moved her to the door. As we left, the microwave alarm signaled that the cup of hot water and sugar crystals were ready.

I whispered, "You're going to be OK, Maman."

Maman's cell phone rang. It was Baba. Maybe he hadn't spoken to me since I had left him holding the crystal bowl, but now he had no choice.

"I'll meet you at the hospital," Baba said after hearing what had happened. But Zain's shouts were drowning him out. "Shanna's crazy!" he screamed. "I hate her. She's imprisoning me. You're imprisoning me. This is not the life I want." There was the sound of fumbling and static, then Zain's voice on the phone. "She's cheating on me, Maman. She's cheating on me."

I didn't respond.

"Maman, where are you? I need you." Zain began weeping. "Mamani?"

"It's me, Rahimeh. Zain, you need to stay away from Maman. For a few hours at least—until she's better."

"Let me talk to her! What's happened?"

I hung up and turned to Maman. Her face was swollen and red like bruised tomatoes. The injections the paramedic had administered had left her numb and semiconscious.

An hour later, from the window of Maman's hospital room, I could see Zain and Baba pacing the parking lot below. Zain pounded his fist on the hood of our car; Baba's pose was defensive, as if trying to contain a charging animal.

When I phoned Baba, I could hear Zain's voice: "This isn't fair. This can't be my life. You did this to me. I didn't want to be married. I would be rich now if it wasn't for her. Where's my Maman?"

"Baba, take him home," I said. "I made sure Shanna and Zahra are gone. He's losing his mind. Take him home, Baba."

"I'll wait until he calms down, I can't drive with him like this." Baba's voice was surprisingly relaxed until Zain came charging toward him, screaming so loudly that I pulled the phone away from my ear.

"She's trying to trap me for the rest of my life. She's after my money—my wealth. You hear me?" He kicked the car door, denting it.

"My life is crap. I'm crap." He began to slam his head against the windshield.

"Baba, I'm calling the police," I yelled into the phone.

"No police. You hear me, Rahimeh?" Baba yelled. He would never call the police on one of his sons again. "He'll stop. Just *no* police."

In fact, Baba had a point: This wasn't the first time we had seen Zain cycle back and forth from infantile sobbing to uncontrollable rage to remorse and back again in a span of minutes.

The phone went dead as at last, Baba pushed Zain's tired, bruised body into the car. Yarek was right that we should have gotten Zain into a psychiatric hospital. But my parents weren't ready for any of that yet. In their minds, Zain's issues were only marital problems.

For the next nine hours, until Maman woke up, I had no news of Zain. He, no doubt, was in a drugged sleep, too.

When the doctors couldn't find anything physically wrong with Maman, they offered her a bottle of Xanax. They didn't understand that they were dealing with something untreatable. She was a *Dagh*

Dideh, a burnt mother, who had lost one son and was in the midst of losing another. None of them could see the depth of her pain or the physical danger it posed.

Maman returned from the hospital counting on God and Baba to save Zain. But because Baba couldn't understand Zain's mood issues, the severity of his alcoholism, and the demons that tortured him, he focused on what he did recognize: irresponsible and lazy behavior inspired by Western decadence. After each round of fighting, Zain would float from job to job—sometimes even leaving the state—drinking, seeing other women, and leaving the responsibility for his wife and child to his parents and siblings. In the end, he would return broke, hung over, and demoralized. This would lead to more confrontations with Baba, apologizing to Zahra, sleeping on the couch, and eventually repenting and making up with Shanna for a night. Then the whole cycle would start all over again. I wondered, *Wasn't this rock bottom?*

Of course, Zain wasn't the only one failing at love. Hadi was still depressed about his recent divorce. And, in my second year of marriage to Yarek, I knew in my heart that our relationship was struggling.

COMING OUT

❦

2001

THE LIGHT AROUND THE HOUSE WAS BRIGHT, the sun beating down on the asphalt so harshly that I could feel the heat through my shoes as I arrived.

Baba stared at the loose part of the scarf under my chin, but quickly met my eyes, smiling. When we moved our fruit plates to the couch after lunch, Maman kept busy washing the dishes and clearing the table. She knew what was coming.

"So, your mother tells me you'll be a doctor in a few months— and you're only 24 years old! I'll never forget how proud I was watching you get your bachelor's degree four years ago. You were wearing your scarf and were the youngest in the entire class." He paused, and with a strange, sad look on his face, leaned back into the couch.

"What is it, Baba?"

"I want you to tell me the truth. No matter what. OK?" Baba put his fruit plate on the coffee table.

"OK, Baba, sure I will."

"Do you still wear a scarf in public?"

I took a deep breath, set my plate next to his, and looked out the window. I watched two little birds flirting as they sat on the three-level fountain next to a palm tree.

"I wear my scarf when I come here and also around your friends out of respect for you and Maman," I said. "But, no. At my internship and school, I've taken it off. I wear it at work, but that won't be for long . . . I'm slowing coming out to everybody."

Maman shut off the water and started to walk toward the couch, standing directly behind me. Her quiet support gave me strength, as it had so many times before. Choosing Yarek had felt like a betrayal to Baba, but now I was rejecting him, Islam, and God himself.

Baba's calm was disconcerting. "Why?" he asked.

"I've worn it since I was six and I don't think I believe in it anymore."

Baba's eyes narrowed. "I don't understand. This is your future. Your afterlife. You're telling me you don't believe in God?" His voice rose a little. Maman moved behind Baba.

"I'm saying that I don't believe in wearing the scarf, and I don't think I'll go to hell if I don't." I gathered my hair in a bun and fastened it with my clip. "I live my life with integrity, character, respect for people, and I contribute like you. Whether I wear a scarf is not relevant to me anymore. I know it is for you, but not for me. I'm sorry, Baba." I was starting to move closer to him on the couch, still surprised at how well he was taking it.

"You're wrong." Baba stood and faced me. "You understand what this means?" His voice went from calm to hysterical in a nanosecond; I held my ears. I heard something like "hell" and "embarrassing" and "shamed me" and "that husband of yours." Soon, it was not about religion at all; it was about Baba's reputation and my failure to be an extension of him and his life.

With my eyes, I told Maman I was leaving. But this time, I didn't slam the door. Since grad school, I had been working with a therapist, Dr. Caffaro, and had decided that if Baba was going to cut me off again, I would make this time different. I would not join Baba in his anger or reciprocate his coldness. Before the door clicked shut, I heard Maman's sweet voice. "I'm upset about this too, but she's an incredible young woman. I'm proud of who she has become. She is choosing her path, and we *will* love her regardless."

A half hour later, I returned to the house, my eyes red from crying. I knocked at the familiar place on Baba's office door. "I love you, Baba. And I'm sorry you're hurting again. But I'm the same daughter, with the same heart. Nothing else is different. Please don't do this again." I ached with his silence.

Regardless of their transgressions, Baba never stopped talking to Hadi or Zain for more than a few months at a time. But I had been punished for almost two years for my decision to marry—and I feared that my banishment for a sin of this magnitude would last at least that long. So I visited Baba every week, wrote him letters, and told him how much I loved him through the closed office door. I couldn't believe he would leave me fatherless again, but I refused to let him sever our relationship. I would change this destructive family pattern by changing the only thing I could control: my reaction.

A few months later, I invited Baba to my graduation ceremony from my doctoral program. Though I knew he desperately wanted to come, since I was the first in my family to earn this degree, he simply couldn't.

I kept up my work in my therapy, and began to accept the depth of Baba's pain and the roots of his emotional patterns. Unknowingly, he taught me a powerful lesson, one that his upbringing had failed to teach him. The world is comprised of opposites: day and night, light and darkness, pleasure and pain. I would learn to embrace those opposites—even if they occurred in the same moment, even though it was painful. Graduation was the best day of my life, and my whole family, minus Baba, showed up for me.

The best day . . . until my divorce.

January 2002

When I walked into my parents' house, Baba was sitting on the couch, watching Iranian satellite television.

Maman hugged me. "*Dokhtaram,* how are you?" From the dark circles under her eyes, I knew she had been worried about me. I didn't want to tell her that after three years of marriage, my divorce papers were filed. And I didn't have the heart to tell her how painful it had been. I had changed so much in the four years since Yarek and I got together. And though Baba and Yarek were opposites, I had learned that they were different sides of the same coin: both emotionally unavailable to me. I wished I'd had the family support to have simply dated Yarek when we started out, instead of feeling pressured to get married to justify my choice.

Baba didn't look at me, but he rubbed his hand over his half-balding head and said to Maman, "Don't forget to bring out the bowl of pomegranate kernels." Baba knew what I loved. Now I was sure he knew my news.

"I'll be just fine so there is no need to worry, OK?"

Baba stared at the television.

"Ask her what happened?" Baba looked at Maman.

I picked up the bowl of pomegranate kernels and held it in my hand.

"Yarek's a great guy, but we grew apart. I'm an entirely different person now. And he is who he was then; he refused to change or to meet my needs. I tried and tried, but I just couldn't stay married."

I settled back on the couch. This was the closest Baba had come to talking to me since I had told him about the scarf.

"I'm divorced now, but you don't need to worry for me, Baba. I'm going to be just fine." I didn't want to tell him how the family pressures had added to our marriage problems, or that I had moved out of our condo in Long Beach and was now sleeping in a friend's extra room until I started over somewhere.

"I knew he would do this to her!" Baba said, looking at Maman.

"It wasn't his fault, Dad. I left him. He didn't do anything to me. He's a good man." I took a spoonful of pomegranate kernels. "These are great. And sweet." After about three bowls, I stood and straightened my jacket, getting ready to leave.

Maman ran to the kitchen for the bags of oranges, baby apples, and large pomegranates she had prepared for me. "At least have another bowl before you go."

"I've had plenty, Maman. Really, don't worry. I'll be fine." I hugged her as we walked to the door.

"I'm sorry, *azizam*," Maman kissed me.

When we let go of each other, I was surprised to see Baba standing there. He locked eyes with me for the first time in years. His shoulders drooped more than I remembered; his hair was thinner and more streaked with silver. Then he looked away from me, and stared down at the rug.

I kept my gaze on him. "Bye for now, Baba jaan."

Baba stepped around Maman and, with his eyes on the ground, softly kissed my cheek. I wrapped my arms around him, kissed him back, and whispered, "I love you, Baba. Always and forever, no matter what."

I walked outside and got into my car. When I looked back, for the first time in more than four years I saw Maman and Baba, side by side, standing in the front yard, waving. I started the car, and Baba stepped toward me. "When are you coming back?"

I rolled down the window and smiled at him. "Soon, Baba jaan. Very soon."

⁂

By the end of 2003, we'd had five marriages and four divorces in our family. Hadi had married and divorced twice; I had divorced; Zain had divorced and remarried, and was on the verge of another divorce. It was time for some good news. The next marriage—Iman's to a woman with whom he had fallen in love during his travels to Iran—was what my parents had been waiting for: a proper Iranian Muslim wedding.

On the big day, the broken-up cement streets of Tehran cooked in the heat; not even a slight breeze stirred to cool our sweating bodies. Baba was glowing. After so many years of offering his religious leadership to many Iranians in America, he finally had the chance to officiate at a traditional Iranian ceremony for his own son in his homeland.

At the ceremony, the scent of jasmine, Casablanca lilies, dahlias, and gardenias at the sofreh mingled with the odor of *esfand* seeds, burned to ward off the evil eye. When Iman's fiancée answered "I do," the claps and shouts of the guests startled the little girl in the front row. Baba closed his green folder. He walked toward the only child he had married in public and kissed his forehead. "I'm so proud of you, son."

As Baba and Iman's new bride embraced, the smile on Baba's face grew wider. "Daughter," Baba whispered in her ear as he kissed her cheeks.

Later, when Baba had left to the men's ballroom and the women were enjoying the lavish meals, Iman and I were summoned to the hallway. The rhythmic beats and exotic sounds of Shahram Shabpareh's song "Vaveyla" emanated from the speakers.

Baba glared at me. "Who did this?"

I stepped in front of Iman. "I gave the CD to the hall manager to play. It's a wedding, Baba, not a funeral."

"As if what you're wearing isn't enough to embarrass me?" he said, gesturing toward my backless dress. "And now this? In my own country?" he said, waving toward to the music-filled room and the blaring speakers. Guests were clapping to the beat of a *tombak* drum, flute, and 72-string *santoor*.

"Baba, please stop." Iman put his hand on Baba's arm. "Rahimeh's in a room with all women. Come on. Let them dance."

Baba's eyes didn't leave me. "Turn the music off now," he said.

Iman removed his hand from Baba's sleeve. "Baba jaan, it's a wedding. It's our plan, not Rahimeh's doing. My wife wants music."

"Son, you're doing this to me in front of all these people? These men have known me for 40 years. I'm known for being the man who wouldn't allow music, alcohol, or uncovered women into the Rose Hotel."

Iman and I exchanged looks. Here was his son's wedding in Iran with a woman Baba approved of, a ceremony the likes of which he had seen only in his dreams, and he was still spoiling it. I was reminded that no matter what we did, whom we married, or how hard we worked, we would never fulfill Baba's old wishes and dreams. And Baba would never let himself be happy.

I took Iman's hand. "Baba, I don't care about your reputation or the people here. You're spoiling Iman's wedding. Most of the women aren't wearing scarves, and they want to dance. At their weddings, they have music, and they have kids who drink, and go on dates before marriage." I threw my free hand in the air. "You're naïve to think they don't. The world is changing, Baba. You need to adjust. I'm going in. And the music stays on." I looked at Iman.

"Baba jaan, it's my wedding, and I want to make my wife happy. This is the wife you approved of, remember?" Iman's tone was soft. "We'll turn off the music on the men's side. OK?"

Baba hesitated, and then turned his back and headed for the men's ballroom.

Iman walked me to the entrance of the women's side and squeezed my hand. "You ready to go dance, Sis?"

Squeezing his hand back, I whispered, "It's your wedding, darling. I was born ready."

It was the beginning of a beautiful marriage. Iman, who was two and half when Abdollah was killed and had little memory of him, was able to sustain the longest loving relationship of his siblings.

For my older brothers and me, still trying to outrun old demons, marriage wasn't the answer. Marriage wasn't even Baba's answer anymore.

FILTHY RICH
AND BANKRUPT

❧❧

2003

PERHAPS I WAS MORE LIKE BABA and my brothers than I knew. Two
years after earning my doctorate and becoming a licensed psychologist working for the county, I, too, became an entrepreneur. I had
witnessed the soaring rises and plummeting crashes that had marked
Baba's business life and the real estate ventures of my brother Hadi,
so I was more careful—at first. I invested in my first condo and
flipped it for a profit, which allowed me to pay off my student loans,
invest in another property, and buy into a cognitive training center
franchise that helped adults and children with learning issues.

But on the day I showed the family my new house, perched on
a hilltop overlooking Laguna Beach, I did not see any parallel—or
foresee the peril. As many people did before the 2007 crash, I rose
too far, too fast. For immigrants familiar with the experience of losing
everything, the quick ascent was particularly heady. I had bought—
mostly on credit, of course—a house facing the Pacific with three

levels. The decks, stacked on top of one another, had breathtaking sunset and Catalina views.

I couldn't wait to invite my family over to my intimate heaven. On that first sunset visit, I heard the screeching of the brakes and looked out the window to see Maman and Baba parking their car in front of my new home. Thirteen-year-old Zahra came bouncing out of the passenger door, wanting to be the first person inside. Her long brown hair danced in the air as she ran up and down the different levels, yelling her approvals. Just as I had been at Hadi's last mansion—one in a series of homes he had bought and lost—Zahra was openmouthed as I gave her the tour. Three bedrooms, marble baths, double living rooms, an ocean-view dining room. I could hardly believe it was mine.

We walked out to greet my parents. Maman was holding a pocket-size Qur'an and a little mirror on the silver Rose Hotel tray. We crossed through the wooden front door into the living room toward the deck, Maman holding my hand. The immense sun was disappearing. With still hearts, we took in the canvas of the sea before us. As the brick-orange glow colored the sky's maroon backdrop, Maman went back inside the house and placed a blossoming orchid she had brought on the kitchen island.

"So, tell me." Baba settled on the couch near the stack of unopened boxes. It was time to talk business.

I explained that I had bought into a four-month-old enterprise, a learning center franchise. Baba bombarded me with questions: "Why buy into one and not open your own?" and "How much did you spend?" and "When will you make money?" and "Can you manage this huge mortgage at 30 years old?" and "What do you do there again?"

"It's a center for training the brain, Baba. We improve how people learn," I said, smiling. "And I still have my private practice as a psychologist. Baba, like you, I wanted to run a business. I'm a social entrepreneur: I want to help people overcome their learning problems. It's what I wish we had in Iran when we were struggling in school. You know, something I think would have helped Zain and Hadi and me if it had been available back then."

My center soon involved many members of our family: Iman, who had always been an incredible support, became my business manager. He had grown beyond being the baby of the family into a businessman. I employed Shanna as my receptionist. I knew the success of my business would be measured in the lives we changed, and not the money we made.

Part of the joy of the business was being able to include Baba; I told him about my amazing students, and how we were helping them. I told Baba how I thought Zain—who was still searching for jobs between drunken, manic episodes and living with various girlfriends—was never the same in school after Abdollah died. How I wished somebody had helped him in the same way that I was trying help these students now.

The day my second center opened, Maman and Baba arrived with a mirror and Qur'an on a tray. They found more than a dozen people waiting for me: two families, four children, and three trainers awaiting instruction. Shanna kept reminding me of my three calls on hold. I barely had time to talk to my parents. Baba didn't blink an eye; as an entrepreneur who built a hotel at the age of 21, he understood. He leaned over to kiss my cheek, and whispered, "You run your business; I've got the rest."

Within six days, Baba had two men working for him. They finished a vast office expansion for a quarter of the cost, in half the time. Baba and I had grown very close since we had overcome the head scarf episode. Now we shared a mutual language: business. I was learning to speak it well. By 2007, my centers were respected and successful in every way. I knew Baba was proud of me.

By the next year, I was bankrupt.

BABA'S DREAM

I WAS NOT THE ONLY ONE in the family to open a center dedicated to serving the community. Since we had arrived in Orange County in 1986, Baba had led religious ceremonies out of dedication—first in his own living room, and later in rental community centers. Over the years, with unwavering perseverance, one knock on the door after another, he had managed to gather enough funds to build a community religious center, the *Elahieh*. Now, he was about to conduct his first ceremony in a center that he founded and built.

The smell of rose water sweetened the air as Baba removed his shoes on the marble floor and placed them in the shoe rack that held over 150 pairs. He picked up a Qur'an from the bookshelves for his prayer later and sat at a podium under the inverted dome, where dividers separated men and women in the 2000-square-foot prayer room. The scent of turmeric and saffron floated in from the lamb stew brewing in the kitchen's 25-gallon cooking pots.

For this larger-than-life project, Baba was only an "Abdollah"—a servant of God. Here the Muslim congregation would be connecting to the higher power and the prophets through prayers, poetry, and celebrations. My father used his conviction, his contacts, and his reputation as a man of contribution and faith to share this vision with the community.

Two years would pass between the day Maman and Baba received the keys to the building that would house the center and the grand opening. During that time, Baba worked 15-hour days as the building was gutted and rebuilt. With his broken English, Baba became an expert on permit issues, design, contractors, and plumbing. Feeding the workers Persian stews for lunch before eating himself, he was with them at every step, nail by nail, hour by hour. He supervised the installation of every fixture, the laying and grouting of each tile, until the job was perfect. Iman was the only child by his side.

Maybe Baba couldn't control Zain's substance abuse, Hadi's spending, or my renunciation of a head scarf. Yet his creating the Elahieh—a charitable and religious enterprise—was both a worldly contribution and security toward his children's safe voyage after death. Finally, Baba would have a mosque-like center, bringing the community together, serving people, and fulfilling his purpose in a life of service.

At the Elahieh, Baba and Maman stood together with one goal, one mission. Their losses—their lost son, lost homes, lost homeland, and lost hopes—were of this earth. In the Elahieh, they found themselves again. They were with God, they were home, and they had peace.

MAMAN'S DREAM

MAMAN HAD HER OWN MISSION: saving the lives of her endangered sons. Both young men had spun out of control. Hadi was a wreck— financially, emotionally, and physically—and still driving over a hundred miles an hour toward an inevitable collision. Zain, too, was in desperate need as he staggered forth, drunk and drugged, his blood alcohol hovering at toxic levels. It was only a matter of time before a fatal overdose. The question: Which son was in more immediate danger, and whom should we try to save first?

"*Koja rafti?*" Maman tapped her finger on the back of my hand. "Can you hear me?"

I noticed that her fingernails had gotten long. She started to tap her other hand on the table until my eyes met hers.

"I know you've been out of touch with Zain for two years now. I know you don't want to interfere or fund him anymore." Maman looked out toward the yard. "I've respected your wishes and haven't pressured you to talk to him." She turned her eyes back to the table, staring at the empty plate she'd pushed in front of me. "I know I've made a lot of mistakes and helped him when I shouldn't have. Baba and I didn't listen to you eight years ago, after that intervention, but now I understand the mistakes we made. This time it's different. We need help. We really do." Maman continued without blinking or taking a break. "I called an Iranian substance abuse counselor today."

"What?" I looked at her, my eyebrows raised. I had given up long ago, telling my parents if they were not willing to face Zain's addictions and mood disorder, I would not support them in any way.

"An Iranian counselor?" This was hard to fathom—Maman with a substance abuse counselor?

"Yes. I've talked to them. I even talked to Zain about going. He refused, but your father is willing to go now. We are going to the group on Friday night." She paused. "It's called Ala-noon or Allahnoon."

I almost laughed at her Iranian inflection. But this was no laughing matter. It was life and death. I had been half expecting that any night, my phone would ring with the dire news: Another brother was dead.

"A group? You mean Al-Anon?"

Maman nodded. "It's an Iranian substance abuse group. I found them by talking to a friend. I promise you this time I'll do exactly as you say. He's in real danger. I can feel it." Maman clasped her hands on the table, clutching them tight, gazing at the plate. "Please, *azizam,* we need your help."

I walked to the garbage can and threw away my uneaten soup. As I began to rinse the bowl, I watched the water spill out and fill the sink. It had been raining for a few days; dark clouds mostly obscured the sun, but streams of light were making their way into the living room, cutting through to illuminate Maman. Suddenly, she lifted her hands to the ceiling. "*Khoda,* this time, you either help my son, heal him, or take him from me. I would rather he die than live a dead man's life." A single tear rolled slowly down the side of her face, sliding into her ear. "Are you listening, God? I would rather die myself or grieve another son than watch him like this!"

Maman grabbed my purse. "Whatever you think is best, do it. Call the police, take him away. Please, honey, help me. I understand what this disease is now. I wasted so much time doing wrong things." She met my eyes. "Go. Take him to a hospital. At least that way I know he's being watched." She took a deep breath. Her drooping shoulders and fully grayed hair were surprising. I hadn't really "seen" Maman in so long.

Maybe this time would be the end. Maybe this was the bottom of rock bottom?

Maman put the strap of my purse over my shoulder. As I reached the door, she kissed my cheek, whispering in my ear: "I'm afraid he'll kill himself."

⊰⊱

I planned a rescue strategy for Zain with my other endangered brother, Hadi. It was an ongoing irony that other people's crises brought out the best in him.

"I'll go in with the police, Hadi. You meet me at the door when you get there." From the time I had left Maman's until I arrived at Zain's girlfriend's apartment that afternoon, I had made more than 40 calls, recruiting the police, a specialist in bipolar disorder, and a psychiatric emergency team equipped to take Zain against his will in case he wouldn't be admitted voluntarily.

I wanted the plan to be airtight, and made sure to be clear with Hadi. "If he becomes belligerent and wants to run out, the two of us can talk him down. I want to avoid the psychiatric emergency team. It will traumatize him." I explained that there was also a county therapist coming to evaluate Zain and place him on an involuntary 5150: a three-day psychiatric hold.

For the first time in the 13 years since I had dragged Zain's body out of a boiling-hot bathtub, I now felt a faint hope that things might change.

I called Hadi again. "No matter what he says, we have to tell the police what he told Maman, that he threatened to hurt himself. He'll deny it, but if he's not a danger to himself or others, they won't take him to the hospital. There are requirements for an involuntary hold. You understand that, yes?"

Hadi's voice was hoarse. "Can we make sure he'll go to the hospital and not jail? I can't see him in handcuffs." He was already having flashbacks of Abdollah and Iman.

"He's not being arrested. No handcuffs." My heart started to pound faster. "That is, unless he becomes belligerent. If he does, just leave. I've got this." I had no idea if I could really pull it off, but Hadi couldn't see any weakness in me or he would back out. "Zain might die of an overdose if we don't do this. We don't have much time, and I don't want him to run away. This is it. Are you with me?"

Two squad cars screeched up to Zain's apartment building. I watched the officers step out, the outline of their Kevlar vests visible through their crisply pressed street blues.

"Listen, Hadi, the police are here. I have to go. Don't worry. He's not in trouble with the law, but he's in trouble. Text me when you're here. Stand by the door. If you can't do it, don't come."

"I'll be right behind you," Hadi said.

It had taken more than 15 minutes to get Zain's girlfriend to open the door. Now in the living room, police officers stood guard over Zain, who had sunk deep into the couch cushions. He was at least 50 pounds heavier than when I'd last seen him two years earlier; his bald spot more pronounced. He was clean-shaven, but his face was unusually pink, lost in rolls of fat. His Hawaiian shirt had crept up above his belly button, the curly hair on his stomach visible. I barely recognized him as the brother I knew. I couldn't meet his eyes.

"There is nothing wrong, officers," he said. "My family just really worries about me. You can see that I'm fine. Really. Thank you for coming. I'm not hurt, and I'm not hurting anyone, right, honey?" He gestured for his girlfriend and tapped the couch cushion next to him. She began to take a step toward him, but a tall, stocky officer motioned for her to stay back.

"Please, officers, can't she just sit next to me?" He wrung his hands. "It's scary having the two of you there with guns."

I was aware of Hadi listening near the hall's entrance. But Zain didn't know he was there.

The blond officer moved two feet closer to Zain, his arm by his side over the pistol. "Sir, the only reason we are here is because your sister and brother are worried about you."

"My brother?" Zain gasped. "Iman's here?" He tugged at his shirt, covering his hairy belly.

I took a step closer. "Honey, Iman isn't here. It's Hadi. He's by the door. We're here because we want to help and we want you to come with me to a hospital. We want to get you better."

When Zain's bloodshot eyes finally met mine, I realized something was different. He wasn't drunk. He pushed his back farther into the couch. "Officer, my sister is a doctor, and my brother over there is rich and thinks he can boss me around. He would be a nobody if it wasn't for me, you know?" He looked over at the other policeman to his left.

In some ways Zain was right; he lived in the shadow of his siblings: Hadi, who had become the business manager of his girlfriend's plastic surgery clinic while dabbling in commercial and residential real estate, was wildly successful. I had my job as a psychologist and my learning center venture. And Iman had a thriving career buying and selling food franchises.

"I just want you to know that I drink sometimes." Zain continued. "They think it's too much. I don't ever drink and drive, and today, I haven't even had a drink; I'm just relaxing at home." The uncontrollable shaking of his leg began to move the coffee table. Suddenly, he stood and began to yell as he pointed his index finger at me and toward the wall that hid Hadi. "I said I was fine. You can take them out with you when you leave."

The officer walked a step closer to him, bending toward Zain. "You need to calm down, sir. Just take a deep breath. OK?" He softened his voice as he watched Zain's eyes. "I'm told you have threatened to hurt yourself, even end your life. Is that true, sir?" The officer put his hand down as Zain fell back into the couch. Hadi stepped into the room, one hand in his pocket, still wearing his sunglasses.

"No! No! No! I never said I wanted to do that, officer." Zain took a breath before lowering his voice. "I told my mom I was unhappy. I never told her I was going to kill myself." He began tapping his leg with his hand. "I really want to be left alone, sir. Please. I don't want to be disrespectful. Please, please, please, leave." His hands were waving in the air, his voice quivering. Just as quickly as he'd gone from calm to yelling, he now started to whimper. His face turned the color of beets, his eyes flooded with tears, and he began sobbing uncontrollably.

I kept telling myself that he was a grown man, but he looked like the little boy back in Iran who refused to go to school after Abdollah was gone. In Mashhad, after we fought, he would bring me Kit Kats: "It's your favorite, Rahimeh, and it's all yours." Then he would tell a joke and laugh, whether or not I laughed. We would go back to playing, offering each other our toys. I missed that brother.

"I just don't know what to do anymore." Zain reached out a hand to me. "Please help me, sister. Please get them out of here. I'll be fine. Please. I beg you."

For the next hour, I tried to convince Zain to enroll in the hospital voluntarily, but it was no use. He was now struggling for air, weeping, his body lightly convulsing. As the light that was left in the living room faded, he got on his knees, begging me to let him stay home. Hadi's attempts to convince him were also unsuccessful.

"Hadi, please go wait for us outside." I knew it was going to get ugly.

I released my hand from Zain's. "I'm taking you to the hospital. I won't ask you again, Zain. I won't argue with you, and I certainly won't negotiate with you."

"But why?"

"Your mood is spiraling up and down. I don't know what's in your system, and you told Maman you want to die." I passed him a tissue and broke eye contact.

His girlfriend was silent, her eyes glued to the carpet. I looked over at the officers. "Let's do this." I almost tripped on the carpet as I made my way out of the room.

When the psychologist walked in, Zain curled himself into a ball and started to shake. At first, he answered her questions, but soon his words became mumbles, nothing making sense. He then went back to bargaining, and, when she didn't ease up, he fell into weeping and yelling.

Five hours had passed when we finally left the apartment and the psychologist agreed that Zain could be admitted on the involuntary hold. Driving him to the psychiatric hospital, I had no idea if this would help. In fact, I knew it was likely not to work. I had worked in a psych hospital for years. I knew how to get him there and that he needed to be safe. But I also knew he was a smart negotiator, and within 24 hours would have the system figured out and convince the staff he was good to go home. The fact that he didn't have private insurance would support the psychiatrist's probable decision to cut him loose.

Maybe I was putting us through hell for nothing. But I was trying to plant a seed for his health, and for the family's. Losing one brother had tormented us. Watching another one die was not an option. This was better than nothing. And, at the very least, he would dry out for a few days until we figured out something else.

Two days and five visits later, Zain was power walking barefoot on the hospital's cold tile floor, his gown half open as he bummed cigarettes off other patients. He laughed and cried seconds apart; he had made some new friends. He loved it. He hated it. He was refusing the medications offered. When I left, I wept.

The next day, Shanna drove to the hospital with Zahra and picked up Zain as he stood, dressed in his hospital gown and holding his bag of clothes, in the street.

Maman didn't call me for 24 hours after Zain was discharged, and I knew we were back to Russian roulette. When she did finally phone, she reported the ordeal had been a success. "He has quit drinking, honey. Nothing since you hospitalized him." I could hear the hope in her voice.

⹌

The sound of car horns filled the air. Zain was in the middle of three traffic lanes. He walked haphazardly in circles, yelling at the drivers, and came dangerously close to hitting the hood of a Mercedes that was changing lanes. He leaned into the driver's window of a slowing car. "Yo, man, you got a cigarette?" Honking, the car sped off. Under the 80-degree heat of the California sun, Zain was wearing a black wool hat pulled down over his eyes. His Matrix-style long black jacket covered his barely buttoned shirt; his navel peeked out as he walked. Playing with a half-smoked, unlit cigarette, he reached out to the next car speeding past him. "No cigarettes, huh? OK. How about a light, then?"

I followed Hadi and Iman into the traffic. In the weeks since his release, Zain had been cycling between belligerence, ecstatic happiness, extreme crying spells, and deep paranoia. Now he was going to die in traffic before we got a chance to visit the Iranian psychologist we had arranged to see.

I sidestepped the fender of a Hummer that Zain was about to pound with his fist. Together, we pulled him to the curb and into the building that held the doctor's office.

Talking nonsense, Zain didn't know where he was or what day it was. As a practicing clinical psychologist, I tried to assess what I was seeing. *Mania? Drugs? Both? Psychosis? Schizophrenia? Drug-induced mood disorder? Was he always bipolar and we hadn't noticed, or was this alcohol?* I didn't know. What I knew was that only weeks after being released from the psychiatric hospital, Zain was worse than I had ever seen him—and in some ways I was glad. I knew that we were getting close to the end, and that, having finally scraped rock bottom, things would finally look up after this.

The session focused on Zain's drug abuse. His self-medicating patterns for his potential bipolar disorder did not come up, nor did his trauma history. We ended by discussing alternate ways that the family could help him, since previous efforts had not been successful.

We didn't hospitalize Zain again; without insurance, we knew he would be out in a day, more traumatized than the last time. The day after the session, Zain's girlfriend kicked him out. As a family, we decided to be united in not giving him shelter, a job, or a car. Maman, his most reliable ally, refused to let Zain sleep on her couch, asserting that if he wanted her in his life, he had to check in to a sober living facility.

The intervention that day was the beginning of thousands of dollars spent on Iranian psychologists and psychiatrists. And, with Maman and Baba attending groups that educated them about bipolar disorder and alcoholism, the Save Zain Club embarked on a new chapter. My parents finally understood that Zain was not the only one who needed professional help. Or so I thought.

Within a month of Zain's enrollment in a sober living center run by Iranian clinicians, Baba picked him up and took him home. Whenever Maman reached a place of strength in her dealings with Zain, Baba would falter, and vice versa. It was a vicious cycle, and I reached a new and bitter place in my dealings with my brother and my father.

ACCIDENTS

❧

2005

SPEEDING AT 80 MILES AN HOUR, the Porsche scraped against the freeway rail, shooting sparks of gold into the brick-colored sky. A 12-wheeler truck, unable to maneuver around Zain's wild driving, crashed into him at a high speed that brought the bumper within inches of the headrest. The right front tire of Zain's car popped, deploying the airbags and knocking the girl in the passenger seat unconscious.

Zain didn't remember leaving the dance club or driving the car. He didn't remember being blinded by the truck's headlights in his rearview mirror. What he did remember was the pounding of techno music, his blood drowning in a rush of cocaine, vodka, and lithium.

Ten hours later, when Zain tried to pull himself up, wanting to vomit, a stab of pain collapsed his arm.

"Don't get up, sir. There's nothing in your stomach that you can throw up now."

"What happened?" Zain managed to mumble, staring at the nurse's blue scrubs.

"What happened, sir, is that you survived death." The nurse put away the scissors as she finished taping his arm with fresh bandages.

"What?" Zain blinked. Pain gripped his stomach again.

"We've pumped your stomach. It's going to hurt for a while." She tucked his arm—being pumped with IV liquid—under the blanket. Leaning toward him, she whispered, as if she knew his ears hurt. "You are very lucky to be alive."

"Where am I?"

"ICU. You've been in a coma for ten hours."

"What?"

"You were in a car accident. A really, really bad one." The nurse shook her head. "That accident saved your life. It was your miracle."

"Miracle?" Zain squinted as the pain ran down his spine.

Putting her hand on the sheet over his hand, she sighed. "You passed out while you were driving, my dear." Her voice was louder now. "If you had been passed out for more than 20 minutes and the truck hadn't plowed into you, you would have died of a drug overdose."

"Overdose?" Zain tried to open his eyes, but everything was spinning.

Before the nurse slid the curtain closed, she looked back at Zain. "You have an angel looking out for you. You're a lucky man." She opened the door to leave. "Make this count."

⬧⬧

Hadi wouldn't tell me who was going to be at his party, but I hoped Zain wouldn't be among the guests. Since Baba had caved and gotten him out of the sober living home more than six months ago, I had refused to see my brother or help my father with any dealing with him. It was too painful, and I did not want to be roped into enabling him anymore.

I wasn't the only one who was angry at Baba. Maman was furious, too. She had pleaded with him not to rescue Zain. "What? After I saved $2,500 for him to be there?" she'd said. "I told your father that I can't go through this again."

Though a decade had passed since the first intervention with Zain, and it was clear that Baba was still not open to involving outsiders in his problems. "He begged me, *zan*. He had been crying to me for days. He said people there were doing drugs and he wanted to stay clean. So I got him out."

Zain had indeed been crying. Since sobriety had begun to kick in, he saw the mess he had created: his credit, his finances, his relationships, and his estrangement from his most prized gift—his daughter. Everyone was wrong. Life without liquor was harsher than he had feared. It was easier to drink. He had to get out.

According to my mother, my father had tried to justify his actions. "I had to make the choice. He was killing me with his crying. And, *zan*, we have a reputation. Those places are filled with Iranians that know us. I couldn't see him imprisoned like that. You understand?"

Maman was aghast. "Your reputation? He's going to die, Haji. I don't care about our reputation. You hear me?"

Zain had finally found the right approach with Baba. Actually, it was an easy sell. Baba had almost no resistance to Zain's claims that he now understood his illness—that he had, at last, truly repented and turned to God for his sobriety.

Maman tried to reason with Baba, but he wouldn't listen. From then on, it had only been a matter of time.

During this period, I felt angry and frightened. I tensed every time the phone rang, knowing Zain was out there, untreated, driving under multiple influences. I expected to get the news any moment that he was dead of an overdose or had killed someone on the road.

So only two weeks later, when I walked into the party at Hadi's house, I was somehow not surprised to see Zain in the living room, sprawled out on the couch with two pillows under his legs. His arm was in a cast connected to a chest brace. His head was wrapped in bandages edged with dried blood. He was swollen, and the fat in his face was unrecognizable under all the bruising. I ran toward him and knelt on the carpet. "Zain. Oh, dear God. What happened to you?"

"He can't hear you, honey." I jumped as Baba put his hand on my shoulder. "But he'll be all right. He was in a car accident." He pulled me to my feet. "He's OK now. No one died."

I leaned over and gently put my hand on Zain's swollen hand. Even his fingers were bruised. Vicodin and other painkillers cluttered the coffee table. The ground beneath me began to spin.

"I'm going to tell Maman you've arrived." Baba made a quick exit.

I wanted to scream. I wanted the world to know how crazy this was. How crazy I felt being there. This last attempt to save my brother's life had come to nothing? He was a bloody mess lying on the couch in front of me and I could do nothing. I hated being so helpless.

And most of all, I hated being right. It seemed inevitable that Zain would suffer a terrible injury, and ultimately death. Until we dealt with the root of our problems, they weren't going to go away.

Despite the thousands of dollars Maman and I had paid for the therapy and treatment, there had been no real discussion of Abdollah or the demons that haunted Zain. The focus had been on pathology and substance abuse, not complex trauma. And now he had almost died.

While Zain slept on the couch in the other room, Maman could no longer contain her anger and grief. Her voice shaking, she stood up to Baba. "You're killing him like you killed Abdollah."

The house stopped breathing. Finally, she had said it aloud.

Baba slowly moved to his recliner and began a prayer. He had things to say, to God.

THE FALL

ZAIN'S ROCK BOTTOM had come at a deep cost. He was lucky that the girl he driving only had minor injuries, but the police had given him his second DUI. Without his family willing to support him, he saw a glimpse of his future: unsuccessful marriages, lost jobs, debt, legal problems, homelessness. He was out of ideas. After months of physical recovery, and with the financial help of Baba and the reluctant Maman, he fled to the land of opportunity: Dubai, a city on the rise. He left the family, including his daughter, with little explanation. Soon afterward, he met a woman from Tajikistan and won her over in typical Zain fashion: with irresistible charisma and boyish charm. They married a year and half later, and she was soon pregnant with their first child. Rather than face the present, Zain's solution—just as it had been when he was a kid—was to start over and imagine he was creating a better future.

And soon, without any choice, the rest of us had to start over, as well.

I entered the office, now empty. Practically tasting the sweet coffee Shanna used to prepare for me every day, I switched on the lights in the conference room. In my mind, I could still hear the laughter of children roaming the facility, the ticktock of the metronome that was used in cognitive training procedures, the voices of trainers spurring people on. But today the phone didn't ring; there were no fresh flowers on the reception table. It was all gone.

My steep rise to the top had been followed by a precipitous fall. In the last quarter of 2007, the housing bubble burst and shook the economy and my business, dragging me and the Golden State into a deep recession.

I brushed away my tears when a loud knock at the office door shook me from my thoughts. I already knew who it was. Baba walked in, soaked from the rain, bringing with him the comfort of home. He was holding a blue trash bag over his head. Shaking a spray of water from it, he smiled. "Salaam, *azizam*."

A stack of books slid off the table, slamming against the floor. I tried to meet his smile; I didn't want Baba to see how upset I was. He glanced at the thousands of files on the desk, the psychological testing kits on the chair, and the books on marketing and small business.

"You shouldn't be here, Baba. That's a doctor's order." Baba's health was in jeopardy. The previous week, he'd been hospitalized for two days with a severe infection and blood poisoning. The whole family had finally left the emergency room with Baba and an IV drip. As I'd helped him into the car, Baba had squeezed my shoulder and whispered, "Thank you for being at the hospital, *dokhtaram*. I'm sorry I've become a burden to you."

After Baba's crisis with cellulitis and sepsis before our Mecca trip, I had taken over as his medical care coordinator. With all the stress in our family, it was no surprise that our parents would become ill. Years ago in Iran, it had been Maman who had suffered serious physical manifestations of her emotional distress. But now, in his sixties, Baba was the one showing his stress with regular bouts of illness. He had become older, weaker, more vulnerable. That year alone, he had been hospitalized 11 times.

Baba had the comfort of his children by his side. Around the clock in the ICU, we were busy translating and coordinating treatment with nurses and medical personnel. We slept on a chair beside him through the night, never leaving him alone for one moment. Far too many times, Baba had credited me with saving his life; I'd overseen his care as his diabetes was brought under control, his heart blockage was caught and treated, and his bouts with cellulitis and sepsis became less frequent. He had also seen me return to him in the face of his anger, his rejection, and his severing of all ties with me. He now held a more expansive view of me: that I, like him, was contributing to the community with my work—and that I was relentless in my love for him. After more than five years, Baba had grown to trust me entirely. And he no longer yelled at me or dismissed me. He didn't question my choices, even when it came to dating.

In my view, Baba had morphed from an unreasonable dictator to a flawed but great man. Had he been born in another era, before the cultural and religious revolution took hold of Iran, perhaps he would not have been caught on the wrong side of a regime that turned out to be brutal and corrupt. In the chaos of a punishing war and changing times, his devout Muslim faith failed to save his son and led him to make grievous errors. He had alienated the very children he tried to protect, but there was never any doubt about the love between Baba and his children.

Like Baba, I had failed in business. But also like him, I would recover and rise even higher in the future. I had not anticipated that he would be here to help dismantle my office.

"You should be home resting, Baba."

Baba wiped the raindrops off his lapel. "Where am I starting?" he asked, ignoring me. He looked around and picked up the black trash cans piled inside one another. "I'll start here. The new ones I can return and get the money for you."

"We can't return them, Daddy. I've used them for over three years. Plus I want you to take everything you need to the Elahieh." I grabbed the trash bag from his hand.

He paused near the packages of copy paper and smiled. "I'll take those. I always need more copy paper."

Baba knew how to make me feel better. He didn't need the paper, but I needed him to take it. Since his tour business had slowed down after 9/11 and his health issues increased, he hadn't been using his copier to print trip itineraries and prayer time schedules as frequently as he had.

Holding a package of paper, Baba circled the furniture now haphazardly stacked in the middle of the waiting room. "You can sell these."

I spoke to him over my shoulder as I placed a box by the door. "No. The conference room, all the training tables, chairs, and all of the other supplies will go to the Elahieh, Baba."

Baba ran his hand over a leather chair. "You sell it."

"I'm delivering it all to you tomorrow. This is not a negotiation."
I began to empty my desk's overhead compartment. "Maman and
you can decide who gets which desk." I knew Baba loved my red oak
office desk, and Maman had always eyed my desk at the other center.
I also knew Baba would give the bigger, nicer one to Maman.

Baba didn't move as he searched for the right words to refuse.
When we were kids and he traveled to Kuwait or Lebanon, he would
buy everyone in the family three sets of gifts and never bought himself anything—not even a shirt.

"It's my donation, Baba. It's not for you, I'm doing it for God." I
knew my Baba too well. He wouldn't take for himself, but he couldn't
stand in the way of my contributing to a higher purpose.

"God bless you, *dokhtaram*."

Six hours later, Baba had taken out the lightbulbs from every fixture, folded and packed the lamps, unscrewed each table and chair
attachment, packed the papers in boxes, took the unused kitchen
supplies and labeled the box "Return to Costco." He made over two
dozen trips down 20 flights of stairs to throw out trash and pack the
van before going home. He was starting to limp.

Two days later, as he sat on the couch looking at the boxes still filling the room, he lifted his foot up and positioned a decorative pillow
under it. "We're making good progress."

I nodded and sat next to him. Shoulder to shoulder, we sat resting
our heads on the back cushion. We stared up at the ceiling, in silence.

When he stood to kiss me goodbye, he said, "I'll see you tomorrow at 6:00 a.m. sharp. I'll be here until it's all done. All of it. You
understand?"

It was pointless to argue with him about not coming back.

A week later, the wind blew softly as I stood in front of the 20-foot-wide double glass doors of my office. The light still shone on the sign above it; Maman and Iman stood behind me. I could sense their hearts' palpitations. We had all seen something like this before, all those years ago in Iran. I closed my eyes, remembering the nightingale that had perched on the Rose Hotel sign when Mr. Gaffari had switched off the light. As I felt Baba's hand on my shoulder, I thought I saw the same bird fly by.

HADI'S CRASH

IN 2008, AFTER THE MARKET CRASHED, Hadi's world began to fall apart. As his plastic surgery clinic and real estate transactions went sour in Orange County, he watched as one property foreclosed after another. Stacks of lawsuits weighed heavily on him, and his mornings began with wake-up calls from creditors and lawyers. Of course, he told no one of his troubles. Instead, he had begun isolating himself from his family—separating from his second wife, refusing invitations and phone calls for his 40th birthday, and avoiding all meaningful contact. As the final gesture of his inner turmoil, he shaved his head early one morning.

Unlike Zain, Hadi was never going to live in Dubai or run back to Iran. While the rest of us worried about him, he thumbed his nose at looming bankruptcy with a credit card spending spree that included a $90,000 Range Rover and two fully loaded—and very dangerous—BMW motorcycles.

In a horrific parallel to Zain's accident three years earlier, Hadi took one of his prize bikes around a curve at 120 miles an hour while on a joyride through the hills of Oregon. Crashing into the single boulder that separated the road from a 500-foot drop off a cliff, he was left lying injured under the silver light of the moon. But just as his brother had "cheated death," so did Hadi. A rock pierced his back and snapped his ribs; they in turn stabbed his lungs and collapsed them. But Hadi, too, was rescued in time: A couple, both nurses, had found him.

Three weeks after his accident, Hadi lowered his bruised body into a seat at a softly lit Thai restaurant and told me the story of the "wonderful peace" he had felt as he had been "floating in the air." My reaction to his reckless behavior had always been anger and sadness, but now I felt a new emotion. I was curious.

"Truly, Rahimeh, when I thought I was dead, I felt the deepest calm I've ever felt in my life." He moved his plate closer and took a sip of water. "I know this will worry you, but please don't be upset. It was a gift to me. I know now that I'll be a biker forever." He wet his lips, avoiding my eyes.

Fear overtook me. I finally realized that Hadi wasn't preparing for death; he was hoping for it. Just as Hadi had made his decision to remain a biker, I made my decision, too.

I had one brother in exile who had been killing himself slowly with alcohol, and another hoping to die with the aid of hundreds of pounds of hurtling metal.

Had I also acted out in extremes in behavior? On the one hand, mastering a profession dedicated to healing pain and loss, aiding recovery from trauma. But also on the other hand, overextending in my own way? We all seemed to have chosen to love the particular people we did at least in part as a rebellion against Baba. Even Iman, who was a baby during the revolution, was not fully exempt from the impact of trauma. He, too, was running from our past, working overtime and running himself ragged for his family at the cost of his own well-being. To be still meant feeling decades of emotion.

Were we reckless in various ways with our own lives? Were we perhaps, on some hidden level, challenging our own survival? Could we even be ambivalent about living when our oldest brother had met such a terrible end?

Would the shroud of mystery that had veiled Abdollah's disappearance for so long now threaten us all?

I wouldn't wait any longer for my family to be ready to uncover the past.

BABA'S FINAL CONFESSION

❧

2008

ON A SUNNY AFTERNOON, when I was alone with Baba in the garden of my parents' home, I finally asked him to finish the story he had begun in the taxi ride in Mecca. He must have sensed my need to know the truth about what happened to Abdollah after seeing Hadi's bruised body a few weeks earlier. Perhaps, he, too, was ready to unshackle the burdens of what happened that night in September 1979. Eyes steady, he recounted his memory:

Hours before the wailing women appeared at our home next door to the Rose Hotel and we children were rushed to our grandparents' home, Baba's dear friend Mr. Gaffari had driven him through the lit streets of Mashhad to a gray cement compound on the outskirts of the city, near the cemetery.

"What is this place? Tell me what has really happened!" Baba begged.

Mr. Gaffari drove Baba into the newly constructed courtyard. In the distance, illuminated in one of the windows, was a group of men in uniform, gathered around a desk.

"There has been an accident." Mr. Gaffari told him.

As they drew closer, Baba could see that the men were armed and there were tombstones leaning upright against the office wall. Even though the car was moving, Baba flung open the door. Mr. Gaffari slammed on the brakes as Baba jumped out.

"Haji, wait!" He ran after Baba. " Haji!"

As Baba was about to charge into the office, Mr. Gaffari grabbed his arm and pulled him aside. "Come with me, Haji. Come this way."

"Tell me what's happening!" Baba yelled. "Where is Abdollah? Where is my son?"

The men in the office stared through the window as Mr. Gaffari guided Baba to the back of the building. "Just come with me," he said again, his head down.

They entered a dark, concrete hallway filled with a series of doors. Mr. Gaffari stopped at one of them and dropped his hand from Baba's arm. Through the one-foot-wide window, a body, partially covered with a dirty, bloodstained sheet, lay on a raised cement pallet.

"What is happening? Why isn't somebody telling me the truth?"

Then Baba saw the Kuwaiti gold watch he'd bought for Abdollah on the body's limp arm. He grabbed the edge of the bloody sheet, pulling some of it with him as he collapsed to the floor.

Baba woke to his own screams. Mr. Gaffari was sitting next to him holding a cup to his lips. Knocking the water away, Baba grabbed the fabric of Mr. Gaffari's shirt. "Tell me what's happening."

Mr. Gaffari's eyes were puffy, his face streaked with sweat and tears. "I'm so sorry, Haji."

Gently releasing his shirt from Baba's grip, Mr. Gaffari offered him the water again. "I wish I could spare you this, but these bastards wouldn't release the body."

Suddenly remembering where he was, Baba rose, shoved Mr. Gaffari away and ripped the rest of the sheet aside.

Abdollah lay on the cold slab with three bullets in him, one in his forehead, and two in his heart. Throwing himself on the body, Baba touched his son's cheeks.

"You're not dead. You can't be dead." His cries echoed off the walls. "He wasn't supposed to be executed! He's not a murderer. He's only 16." Baba's wails grew louder. "He's my son! They promised me. Even Khomeini!"

Mr. Gaffari tried to pry Baba from Abdollah's body.

"I will kill them all. Take me to Qom so I can kill them all." He fell to the floor, pulling the bloody sheet with him and exposing the naked body of his eldest son. Everything went black.

When Baba awoke, he was on the grass, leaning against the outside wall of the compound. Mr. Gaffari's voice was shaking. "We have to act quickly. They plan to throw his body in a ditch with those thugs and the mujahedeen they've killed."

Baba rose to his feet, his hands clenching into fists. "They'll have to kill me before they throw him in the ground with those rapists." He paused. "I'll do the ritual bath myself and bury him properly."

Mr. Gaffari put an arm on Baba's shoulder. "Haji, there are secret police all around us. We can't have a funeral, Haji, I'm sorry."

"My son *is* having an Islamic burial," Baba retorted, making his way to the office. The guard behind the desk jumped when Baba slammed through the door.

"My son was a man of God, unlike you imposters who pretend to be good Muslims. We're taking him away for an Islamic funeral. Now, sign the papers. You understand me?"

The man behind the desk glanced at a colleague, then back at Baba. "You owe the government 7,000 tomans for each bullet that was shot—that's 21,000 total." His voice was flat.

Baba could not contain himself. He shook his arm free from Mr. Gaffari's grip and leaned across the desk, pushing the papers onto the floor. The veins in his neck throbbed, and he grabbed the guard's collar. "I'm taking my son. Try to stop me and I'll kill you."

The official tried to shake himself free of Baba's grip, cursing him. But Baba wouldn't let go: "Sign the papers, now!"

Mr. Gaffari moved between them. "You've killed the man's son. He wants to take the body to his wife. He wants a proper burial. Let the man have that, for God's sake."

The official stared at Baba and freed himself. Finally, he pulled papers from the drawer and signed the form. "Take it before I change my mind."

Baba wanted to conduct the religious washing of his son's body himself. But after seeing the holes on Abdollah's face and chest, he fell to the floor again. Mr. Gaffari dragged Baba outside, where they crouched together and offered instructions to the official body washer. Their prayers mingled with their tears.

When he saw the *kafan*—the shroud that Mr. Gaffari had brought to wrap Abdollah's body—Baba felt faint again. He put his hand on it, gripping it tightly before relinquishing it to Mr. Gaffari who whispered, "God will keep him safe."

Telling the manager to inform only a few family members of the burial, Baba gave him a check for a million tomans to buy a grave site at the Haram of Imam Reza and pay the local grave digger. It had to be done fast, in silence.

❧❧

When Baba walked through the doors of our home at the Rose Hotel, holding a plastic bag in each hand, Maman rose and pushed through the crowd of women, including her sisters. "What are these bags? Tell me what's happening." Her eyes were wild, looking everywhere but at Baba. "Where've you been? Get these people out of my house, and let's go see Abdollah, as we planned." Baba's gaze dropped to the Persian rug. Silence filled the room.

Maman dug into the bag and grabbed a wrinkled yellow Rose Hotel towel. "What is this?" It smelled of Abdollah. She pressed it to her face, taking deep gulps of air from the soft fabric. When she pulled the arm of Abdollah's jacket from the other bag, she screamed and scratched at Baba's hands.

Baba dropped the bags and pulled her to him. Abdollah's gold watch was still clenched tightly in his fist. "Please forgive me."

"Haji, tell me you saved him? Tell me." Maman was choking for air.

Baba buried his head into her shoulder. "I am to blame. I am responsible." He began to weep. "I'm so sorry, we've lost our son."

Maman gripped Baba's hair in one hand as they embraced; their cries were like a chorus. Maman pounded her fists on Baba's chest as they dropped to the floor.

The hotel workers, clerics, and the ayatollahs in the yard grew silent. As Baba remained on the floor, his face in his hands, Maman raised her fist high in the air. "I hope all of you burn like me someday. Death to all of you!"

Khaleh pulled Maman close. "You can't say things like that out loud," she whispered. "Don't curse them; they'll arrest you or Haji." Standing outside the gate to our yard was a man wearing a white shirt buttoned at the collar with a carefully groomed short beard— all telltale signs of the undercover police of the new Islamic Republic.

Pushing Khaleh aside, Maman faced the yard, bracing herself against the door frame. "I want them to hear me. He was my child. Nothing else matters now. I want the same bullet. Kill me, too!"

My grandmother pulled Maman away from Baba and handed her a folded paper. When she recognized Abdollah's handwriting in red ink, her screams grew louder. Her sisters tried to take the letter back and lead her to the bedroom, but she pushed their hands away. She unfolded the paper and began to read Abdollah's final letter, written just moments before his execution. She kissed the pages, pressed it against her forehead, and wailed.

"Drink all of it," my grandmother pushed a glass of watermelon juice toward Maman's mouth. Small white pieces of crushed Valium floated in the glass. Maman did not notice.

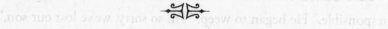

At the Haram of Imam Reza, Baba fought dizziness as he, Mr. Gaffari, and several hotel workers carried the wooden box suspended above their heads and circled the shrine three times in their bare feet. Thirty men followed behind. As the sun's light dimmed, they descended into the Haram's catacombs, which smelled of fresh turned earth; particles of dust caught in their throats.

Baba and Mr. Gaffari gently lifted the white *kafan*-wrapped body from the coffin. The voice of the imam recited prayers that echoed off the walls as Baba held both hands under Abdollah's head and the other men gently lowered him into the earth.

Baba had not uttered a word in hours; Mr. Gaffari had done the talking. Now, above the soil that covered his son's body, he prayed. The dirt was fresh and wet—the same smell that filled the air minutes after Maman watered the yard: the scent of home. When Baba finally lifted his head from prostrating, Mr. Gaffari helped him stand up. They stood side by side, hands folded in front of them. The color drained from Baba's face as he stared at the raised mound. "My wife mustn't see this," he told Mr. Gaffari.

In the Haram's outer yard, Maman banged her head and fists against the wall. "Take me to my son. Take me to see him now!"

As the women descended the cement stairs into the underground cemetery, men with pickaxes were ripping new graves into the earth. Maman's breathing was labored. Across the muddy dirt floor, her sisters held her arms as they walked toward Baba and Mr. Gaffari. "You cannot scream here," they whispered. "You must stay quiet, sister."

As she stared at the fresh mound of dirt—the resting place of her eldest son—she faced Baba, meeting his eyes. "I want to see his face. I need to talk to him." She began to wheeze. Baba tried to steady her, but she pushed him away.

Maman dug her fingers into the earth, not caring that everyone was watching, listening. "Let me be. Let me be with my son," she said, laying her body onto the mound of wet soil.

❦

After the burial, a man with a salt-and-pepper beard wearing the stiffly buttoned white shirt of the new regime was waiting for Baba at the hotel. He spoke in a lowered voice. "I need to warn you: There won't be a reception or mourning ceremonies." His tone was arrogant. "We won't tolerate any commotion. Your wife certainly made a scene at the Haram. That won't continue."

"Are you threatening me?" Baba's swollen eyes were magnified by his glasses as he stood nose to nose with the man.

The lobby grew quiet. Somewhere a teacup rattled on a saucer as the wind shook a window. Baba's anger filled the room. "What are you going to do, shoot me? You've already killed me," he yelled. "Tell your superiors that if any of you come near me or my family from now on, I will do to you what you've done to my son. Keep your secret police away from me and my home. You hear me? Now get off my property, and take your fake faith with you!"

Instead, the man followed Baba into his office.

"Listen, we're offering you a Paykan. You could put your son's picture in the back window of the car so passersby can send prayers for his soul. We would also like to name this street after him, in his honor, *Shaheed* Abdollah, the martyr."

"You executed my son! Now you want to buy me off?" Baba took a big step toward the man. "You put an ayatollah with no experience in charge of a courtroom and my son's life and then called it Islamic? Nothing about how you are running this country is Islamic. Nothing." Baba was shaking now, and the blood vessels around his temples were pumping wilder. "My family will never be free of this, you ruthless bastards!"

"We realize you feel you've been wronged," the man insisted calmly. Without letting Baba's anger sink in, he added, "How much would be sufficient?" The man began to reach for his checkbook.

Holding a pen and impervious to Baba's rage, he said, "how about 300,000 tomans? That's 45,000 U.S. dollars. Should I make it out to your wife?"

"Go to hell!" Baba swung his briefcase at the official's head. "Get out before I claw out your eyes." The man opened his mouth, but Baba took another swing at him. "*Get out.*"

Baba stopped, drained by his story. The truth of that night was now out, there in the garden with Baba and me. I felt hollowed out, but also renewed.

I never saw my father the same way again.

a big step toward the man. "You put an ayatollah with no experience in charge of a courtroom and my son's life and then called it Islamic? Nothing about how you are running this country is Islamic. Nothing." Baba was shaking now, and the blood vessels around his temples were pumping wilder. "My family will never be free of this, you ruthless bastard!"

"We realize you feel you've been wronged," the man insisted calmly. Without letting Baba's anger sink in, he added, "How much would be sufficient?" The man began to reach for his checkbook.

Holding a pen and impervious to Baba's rage, he said, "how about 300,000 tomans? That's 45,000 U.S. dollars, should I make it out to your wife?"

"Go to hell!" Baba swung his briefcase at the official's head. "Get out before I claw our your eyes." The man opened his mouth, but Baba took another swing at him. "Get out."

Baba stopped, drained by his story. The truth of that night was now out, there in the garden with Baba and me. I felt hollowed out, but also renewed.

I never saw my father the same way again.

THE EMPTY CHAIRS

❦

2009
Thanksgiving

WHEN WE ARRIVED IN MY DOCTOR'S OFFICE for a family therapy session, Hadi sat on a chair next to Dr. Caffaro, facing Iman and me on the couch, his body set as rigidly as his lips. It was obvious that he could not open up about his secrets; the only way he knew how to acknowledge his emotions was to floor the gas pedal or spend $100,000 on a single purchase. To my now trained eye, Hadi exhibited the classic traits of a traumatized person—ambivalent about his own survival, and only able to raise his adrenaline with self-destructive actions.

Across from Hadi, a wooden chair sat empty where Zain would have been had he been living in this country. His absence reminded us of the other missing part of ourselves: Abdollah.

The doctor began speaking.

"I think one result of not talking about things is that you all feel powerless. There is a sense of helplessness about not being able to put the past behind you, even though each of you in your own way has tried to do so."

Hadi finally looked me in the eye, "What do you want from me?"

"I want to know what you know, what you remember," I said calmly. "I want to know how you feel. I want to talk about the past as part of our memory—not as if it's happening to us all over again, every day."

I told my brothers about my breakthrough conversations with Baba and Maman, my talks with our cousins and friends about what had happened in Iran so many years ago—the rape, the boys, Room 314.

Hadi looked away, exasperated. We sat in silence.

Dr. Caffaro spoke up. "The fact that your brother died isn't as much the issue here as the memories are. That's how we all understand ourselves. But if you can feel curious about them instead of powerless, I think you can free yourselves from the guilt that, by proxy, you all experience with your dad. He probably feels tremendously guilty, even if he had nothing to do with his son's death. Your mom, too. That's a guilt parents never generally get over."

I looked at Iman and thought of his secondary trauma: the pain of watching his older brothers and me struggle with the past, his own work pressure, and the enormous responsibility of caring for our immigrant parents who were dependent on us. I worried about the cost of Iman's excessive caretaking to himself—the martyring, the sainthood. But I was never concerned about Iman the way I was for Hadi or Zain. Iman was not impulsive; he was grounded and consistent. He thought things through, he planned, and he seemed to be at peace. So I was shocked when Iman, and not Hadi, suddenly spoke—as if at last given permission to ask the question that frightened him all his life.

"Did Abdollah kill someone?"

Abdollah had not shot anyone, I reassured him. He had been guilty of transgressions typical of a 15-year-old boy: rebelling against his father's traditional ways.

"You know, when somebody dies and you could do nothing to save him, you carry that burden for the rest of your life," Dr. Caffaro observed. "The guilt prevents you from living. When Abdollah died, Iman was two or so. He had nothing to do with his death, but to this day, he also feels guilty."

Hadi focused on Iman before turning his attention to Dr. Caffaro. "There wasn't a single thing that he could have done to save him. Nothing."

I looked at Hadi. "Do you think there is something you could have done to save him? Do you feel guilty?"

"I do," Hadi said without hesitation.

"How old were you?" Dr. Caffaro's voice was soft.

"I was 11."

"What could you have done to save your brother at 11 years old, Hadi?"

"It's a long story," Hadi answered, his feet fidgeting.

Looking at his watch, Dr. Caffaro quipped, "Well, we have time." Everyone laughed nervously.

Hadi remained silent. His eyes caught mine, and I smiled encouragingly.

"There was something I saw . . . something that maybe I could have done something about. But it's between me and Abdollah. So don't ask me about it, Rahimeh."

Tears trailed down my cheeks. "Please, Hadi, no more secrets."

"Listen, I knew what he was doing. Like when he listened to music, or when he snuck out the window late at night. You know? Things like that, I kept secret. I covered for him."

"Misbehaviors? Acting like the teenager that he was? Is that what you're talking about?" I asked.

Hadi spoke slowly. "Yeah. Maybe if I hadn't covered for him . . ." His voice collapsed as he shook his head.

"Do you think you could have prevented him from hanging out with those boys?"

"You know, it happened so quickly. Just two weeks. What if I had ratted him out? Baba would have confiscated his car, and those thugs would have found someone else to give them a ride."

"Was there anything else that you saw or that he told you?" I asked gingerly.

"That's between me and my older brother. There may be things he shared with me, but that's private."

"So there's something we don't know?"

"I'm just saying if there was something, and he made me promise, I want you to respect that. That's between him and me."

"I don't get you. He's dead and we are alive. What are you doing this for?" I asked. I felt close to breaking down myself.

Hadi started to get up, and then sat down again. "I'm doing it so you understand what the hell I'm going through."

Silence filled the space between us, and I took a deep breath. I knew I couldn't push Hadi anymore. But Dr. Caffaro was not going to stop now.

"Saying something like that, Hadi—that it's between your older brother and you—is keeping a 'secret' in the company of your siblings.

It basically excludes them. What you're saying to them is that you have a special relationship with Abdollah that they will never have because he shared something with you that you won't share with them." Dr. Caffaro watched Hadi lean back, crossing his legs again. "Even if that is not your intention, that's the effect it has. Even if what you're holding back won't change the narrative of what happened with Abdollah, by not sharing it, you're creating a separation between you and them. They're here, and your older brother is gone."

The image of Hadi was becoming a blur as my eyes filled with tears.

"I love you very much, Sis. You know that? And I'm sorry." Hadi put his head down, and for the first time, I saw tears roll down his face. "I'm sorry you lost him."

I leaped across the room to him, knelt on the floor before him, and held him in my arms. "I'm sorry you lost him, too." Hadi tried to push me away.

Dr. Caffaro spoke up. "Let yourself be comforted by your sister, Hadi, instead of having to be the one to do the comforting." And with that, Hadi leaned down and rested his head on my shoulder. For the first time, we wept together.

A few minutes later, Hadi let me go. "I'll be fine," he whispered. For the first time in 30 years, I believed him.

Then Dr. Caffaro made his final descent into our past. "Hadi, do you remember the last time you saw Abdollah?"

Hadi looked out the window, lost in memory. The sound of a distant train whistle brought him back into the room.

"I went there with my parents. I didn't want to be there. The prison. It was painful."

"You didn't want to see him in jail?"

"I had no idea he was going to die. If someone had told me, I would have . . ." Hadi's voice faltered. "I saw him for a few minutes, but I looked away. I didn't want him to . . ." He stopped talking and started to cry again—the kind of weeping that boys and men hold back.

"I was embarrassed to be there. I didn't want to look at him."

"You were only 11, weren't you?"

"Yes, and it was the last time." Hadi's tears wet his blue shirt.

"Do you remember being afraid for him?"

"No. He was strong." Hadi stuttered. "You know, this family makes it through somehow. We're tough."

"Yes, you are all real survivors." Dr. Caffaro looked around the room at each of us. "None of you could have saved him."

Hadi kept crying.

"So you never got to say goodbye to him because you had no idea you weren't going to see him again. No one told you the grave nature of his situation. No one, not even your parents, could possibly have believed it."

"I just remember what he said to me when he pulled me toward him with his hands between the bars." Hadi stopped to catch his breath. After several minutes, he began to speak, almost in a whisper.

"Abdollah was on his knees in his orange jumpsuit. He said, 'You take care of these little guys now, little brother. You are the eldest now.'"

Hadi's agonized cry filled the room. It was the cry he needed. The cry we all needed to witness.

"I've lived by those words all my life," he said. "That's it. That's all of it. There is no other secret." He looked out the window for a moment and then at me.

"So after Abdollah was gone, I lied to my siblings and pretended, like my parents did, that he was studying abroad."

Dr. Caffaro nodded. "How could you bear to tell them the truth? It's hardly bearable now, 30 years later."

"I just don't want to lose another brother." He looked over at the empty chair. Zain's absence was now as profound as a presence. "We need to see him. We need to see Zain."

We stood in the middle of the room as the session came to a close. I hugged my brothers for a long time.

"You are lucky to have each other," Dr. Caffaro observed.

We walked toward the door, nodding.

"Where is Zain now?" Dr. Caffaro asked.

I opened the door.

"In Tajikistan."

"So after Abdollah was gone, I lied to my siblings and pretended, like my parents did, that he was studying abroad."

Dr. Cattaro nodded. "How could you bear to tell them the truth? It's hardly bearable now, 30 years later."

"I just don't want to lose another brother." He looked over at the empty chair. Zain's absence was now as profound as a presence. "We need to see him. We need to see Zain."

We stood in the middle of the room as the session came to a close.

I hugged my brother for a long time.

"You are lucky to have each other," Dr. Cattaro observed.

We walked toward the door, nodding.

"Where is Zain now?" Dr. Cattaro asked.

I opened the door.

"In Tajikistan."

FROM TAJIKISTAN

❦

JANUARY 2010

Sis,

I know it's been a few years since I left and we really connected. And I know that behind the scenes, you and the family have been the support in my life and Zahra's, too. Thank
you for everything you've done and always do for Zahra and
her mother, all these years that they've lived with Maman
and Baba.

I'm coming to America to deal with my DUI issues. I'm
scared shitless but I'm coming to face up to my past. I hope
to see you when I'm there. And, if you don't mind helping, I
would like to improve my relationship with Zahra and could
really use your guidance.

I'm sorry. For everything.

Zain

Only a week later, Zain held the door open for me as I entered
the courthouse. It had been more than three years since I had seen

him. He was much heavier than I remembered, but he also seemed clearheaded, sober in the best way. Baba had been transporting him back and forth to court, but on the day of the hearing, I offered to be there with him.

We couldn't help having a few laughs at the expense of his lawyer, with his slicked-back hair and ancient briefcase overflowing with creased papers.

"He's old and half deaf, but he's a nice guy," Zain said. "You know, I think he's still drunk. He told me he has been in recovery for 20 years. He said he only deals with DUIs now."

Waiting on the bench in front of Room 19, I asked my brother about his adventures over the last three years in Dubai, Syria, and now Tajikistan.

"After the car accident, I went to Dubai. But before that, I stopped in Mecca. It's the only place I have ever been free of drinking, out of respect for God. I begged God to free me from my addictions. And it was there that the miracle happened. I stopped. I mean, I really stopped. The temptation to drink and use left me. I went to Dubai to find some kind of work, and there, I met my wife." The sweat glistening off of his forehead began to roll down his face. Zain had been married for almost two years.

"I'm so grateful to be free of drugs. When my son was born, I had a new addiction: him." He wiped his face with the tissue I held out to him. "Lithium makes me sweat. You see how much weight I've put on?" This was the first time Zain had acknowledged his mental condition.

I nodded. I had so many questions. "I'm so grateful you are alive and better, Brother. Tell me about . . . ."

Zain cut me off. "You know, you always talk over me. You need to just listen. Stop worrying so much, Sis. It's controlling." This was the first time Zain had confronted me.

"You're right. You tell me what you want. I'm shutting up for the next hour," I said.

Zain looked surprised. "I have nothing else to say. I said it all already. Ask me a question." We burst into laughter—loud enough that the Hispanic man next to me who had just been sentenced to three years in prison stopped crying and stared.

"Promise you'll stop worrying about me so much," Zain said, standing up. "OK, Sis?" Zain reached for my hand. "Thanks for coming to court with me for this DUI mess. I'm less scared shitless."

I stood up with him. "Don't worry, Bro. I hear prison has filtered water."

Zain laughed as he caught my wink. "And outstanding law libraries. Maybe I'll finally become a lawyer." He hugged me back, and we walked inside the courtroom together.

When we walked out, Zain gave his lawyer Persian sweets Maman had packed in a plastic bag. The two shook hands, and we headed for the car. Zain had been sentenced to two months of house arrest and some fees. But he would not have to go to prison.

Zain cut me off. "You know, you always talk over me. You need to just listen. Stop worrying so much, Sis. It's controlling." This was the first time Zain had confronted me.

"You're right. You tell me what you want. I'm shutting up for the next hour," I said.

Zain looked surprised. "I have nothing else to say. I said it all already. Ask me a question." We burst into laughter—loud enough that the Hispanic man next to me who had just been sentenced to three years in prison stopped crying and stared.

"Promise you'll stop worrying about me so much," Zain said, standing up. "OK, Sis." Zain reached for my hand. "Thanks for coming to court with me for this DUI mess. I'm less scared shitless." I stood up with him. "Don't worry, Bro. I hear prison has filtered water."

Zain laughed as he caught my wink. "And outstanding law libraries. Maybe I'll finally become a lawyer." He hugged me back, and we walked inside the courtroom together.

When we walked out, Zain gave his lawyer Persian sweets Maman had packed in a plastic bag. The two shook hands, and we headed for the car. Zain had been sentenced to two months of house arrest and some fees. But he would not have to go to prison.

HOUSE ARREST

◆◆◆

ZAIN WAS SURROUNDED BY CARNATIONS in my parents' living room. Maman offered everyone sweets and tea. She was delighted to have all her children, almost her entire brood, back together again. When Iman walked into the room, Zain stood to embrace him.

"Hello, my little brother!" Iman wrapped his arms around Zain.

"Sorry for the roller-coaster ride, man," Zain said.

"I'm glad you're back." Like Zain, Iman never hung on to old feelings for long.

For an hour we gathered, swapping stories, laughing, and sharing our favorite treats. As Baba pulled out the bowl of pomegranate kernels, Zahra knocked on the door. I went to greet her. Maman glanced at Baba. *How would Zahra respond to her long absent father?*

When Zahra walked into the room, her cheeks turned red and she reached for my hand. She had not seen her father since he had fled the country three years earlier, and had been so hurt that she'd refused to reply to his emails or answer his calls. I had spent hours talking with her and her mother about this reunion, and how important it would be to end the estrangement and to connect again. After seeing Zahra struggle with her father's ups and down, my only hope was that I had not made a mistake bringing her close to him again.

When Zain saw Zahra walk into the room, he jumped up off the couch and ran to her. The little girl he had left had become a dark-haired, beautiful 18-year-old young woman. He pulled Zahra in his arms, and she held onto her father tight. "*Dokhtaram,*" he cried out, "My little girl." They cried together.

Maman stopped biting her lip as she cried—this time, happy tears.

LETTER IN RED

❦

SEPTEMBER 16, 2010

ALMOST A YEAR HAD PASSED since the therapy session with Dr. Caffaro, Hadi, and Iman. In the intervening time, my parents had not only shared their memories, but also offered the minutest details of their past: the smells in their kitchen, the expressions on people's faces. And after 30 years, we were able to speak openly about Abdollah.

One afternoon, Maman invited me to come over. I found her in the living room, clasping the Kuwaiti metal cookie container I had seen in her closet so many years ago. As she hugged me tight and leaned in to kiss my cheek, I could smell the jasmine on her skin. Smiling, she handed me the folded letter she had taken out of the tin. "Here you go, *azizam*. I'm glad you asked for it." The front door of the house shook from the heavy winds outside.

"You know, Abdollah was adamant in this letter that we should protect all of you from his story. That's part of the reason why we didn't . . ." I cut her off.

"It's all right, Mamani. I understand. I know you did what you thought was best. Nothing will make me love him—or you—any less."

Maman looked up at me and kissed my other cheek. "He really loved you. He always said you were so sensitive and strong." Her cheeks flushed. "I knew even then that he was right," she said, her voice breaking. "I think now he would want you to know him, to see this letter, to know the man he was."

I gripped the letter tight in my hand and reached for the door. Cool air touched my skin as I stepped out to the front yard, and I felt a bizarre sense of calm rush over me.

As I read Abdollah's letter, I was surprised I didn't struggle with the Persian, given my fourth-grade reading skill. Instead, it felt natural to me, as if I had read it many times before. As I turned the pages, written in red ink, I felt his turmoil in my body—as if I were sitting by his side on his pallet, watching him write in that small jail cell in Mashhad.

Mashhad 1979
Bismillah-e-Rahman-e-Rahim
—In the name of Allah, the Beneficent, the Merciful—
It's just before midnight, I was asleep in the cell. A few guards came to take me so I asked why? "Karet tamoomeh" they yelled again—"you are finished." I explained what had happened, I argued with them. I told them I was not a criminal, that I had been used, exploited, set up—eghfal shodam— that this was a mistake. I told them the verdict was scheduled to be reviewed in Qom, I was not sentenced yet, but it was too late. I begged for some time to shower and pray. I sang the call to prayer—the Azan—as loudly as I could before I took to namaz.

I will not forgive them, Maman. I will not. But I know Baba, I know what he can do, I know he will want to fight them. Please don't engage with this government after I am gone. They have their eyes on us. They have neither conscience nor soul. Please let it go.

Maman, I beg you to listen to me and move on. I know it'll be very hard for you to find out this has happened to me but please know in your heart that I did not know of this crime, I did not know their plans. This punishment is not just, not mine to bear. I should have listened to Baba and never talked to them. For that fateful decision, I am forever sorry.

No matter what people tell you, please promise me these commitments:

Don't battle with the government on my behalf. There will be no resolving this or bringing me back. You will just endanger yourselves more. I will be gone then, I will meet them all on judgment day—and there in Mahshar, I will hold them accountable. I will take my revenge with them there for the agony they imposed on us.

Don't worry for me, please. Khoda is compassionate—God knows what I did, what my wrongs were and what justifiable consequences should have been. I learned many lessons from this, Maman. I'm sorry I will not be there to show you what they are.

Maman, I beg you please—take real sacred care of my brothers and my only sister. Watch over them, I want their destiny to be better than mine. Please make sure this event will not ever be told to them so they are not burdened by it. I love them so much, and I don't want them to be hurt.

Maman, please forgive me for what this has done to you and our family, and our aberoo, your reputation. I'm sorry for the pain, for all the sleepless nights that will come.

Maman, my sister requires a lot of affection and love. I kept asking you for a sister, but now I am not going to be here to take care of her. She doesn't have a sister, and she's going to need you.

Maman, please forgive me.

Your son,
Abdollah

ANNIVERSARY BIRTHDAY

2010

FOR NEARLY 30 YEARS, getting together on the anniversary of Abdollah's passing, a few days from his birthday, felt like death. For days, I would strategically arrive at my parents' after prayers to avoid Maman's overwhelming sorrow. Each of us dreaded the anniversary for 364 days before. Every time, it felt like a wake. It was as if it had happened yesterday. But this time, it was different.

As the front door slid open, I was struck by the aroma of sautéed mint and parsley, saffron yogurt, and crispy rice *tahdig*.

"*Khoresht-e karafs*, Mamani? I love your celery lamb stew." I knew Maman would cook Abdollah's favorite.

"Of course, *azizam*." Maman kissed me and welcomed me into the house.

I followed her into the kitchen and watched as she began to stir the giant pot of stew on the stove. She looked content and beautiful doing what I knew she loved—feeding her children. She began to whisper, almost for my benefit.

"Slow simmer. Hot rice. Crisp *tahdig*." She knew I wanted to learn how to cook from her, and at that time, I had only learned the one dish: Abdollah's favorite.

Maman began to sing—something I hadn't heard her do in a long time. She added tomato paste and stirred it into the celery stew. This was beginning to feel like a birthday party.

I washed my hands and began helping her chop the cucumbers and tomatoes for the *shirazi* salad and the cucumber and mint for the *mast-o khiar* yogurt.

Over the Persian TV station blaring from the living room, Maman yelled, "Baba, go up and change. And wear something nice and light in color. You know how much Rahimeh hates black." She looked at me and winked.

Hadi walked in the kitchen as I heard Baba stumble up the stairs.

"Celery stew, huh?" Hadi smiled and came to hug me, even though my hands were messy and wet. We held onto each other for a long time. I was proud of him and the changes he was making: He had just sold his Range Rover and his two BMW motorcycles, and now drove with his seat belt on. I was grateful he was alive, and grateful for the new lightness that had settled in him.

After I wiped my hands on the dish towel, we held hands and walked into the living room. For the first time, Abdollah's black-and-white picture was center stage, the picture of Mecca moved to its right. It was the picture I had reproduced and enlarged for Maman in my high school photography class. At the time, his eyes were piercing and his face was sad. But today he seemed lighter and freer, too.

On the coffee table, Maman had another picture—one I hadn't seen before. It was Maman holding baby Hadi, with seven-year-old Abdollah standing next to her, his hand protectively on the baby. The black-and-white photo was curved at the edges, and I could see where Abdollah had been taped back into the picture. Maman had taped flowers to the frame and had lit a green candle next to it.

As Maman called for Baba again, I loosened my grip on Hadi's hand. Suddenly, I recalled that awful day when Abdollah stood in the dry field, staring down the barrel of the gun. I felt a sharp pain in my chest and head. Hadi squeezed my hand, and in that instant, I decided to let that image go forever. Instead, I tried to visualize my eldest brother there in the room with us, smiling.

After the rest of the family arrived—Khaleh and her husband and a few cousins who were also now living in America—we gathered at the table to enjoy Maman's feast.

To my surprise, there was no Qur'anic recitation, no sad commentary. Instead, we ate and laughed and felt the warmth of each other's company.

Baba passed the plates, insisting he go last, and directed us all to the serving table. He joked and gestured for Shanna to go ahead of him. She leaned into Baba, and in broken English, the way she knew he would understand, she whispered in his ear. "Baba. Do you remember the night you called me? It was before Zahra was born. You lied and said Zain wanted me to come over. When I got here, Zain wasn't here, but you and Maman were." Baba pulled back and looked into her eyes. "You gave me a new family then, Baba jaan. You became my father that night." She kissed his cheek. Wrapping his arm around her shoulder, he pulled her toward him and kissed her forehead as he said with his thick Persian accent, "You are my daughter. For all time, my daughter, OK, *dokhtaram?*"

"I love you, Baba." Shanna pulled him toward her and embraced him.

At the table, Hadi, Iman, and I looked at each other as Baba repeated the same joke about the bride and groom that we had heard a million times since we were children. Having lived in my parents' home for nearly 20 years with Zahra meant that Shanna also knew the joke by heart. She recognized the Farsi words, even though she never spoke the language, but Baba insisted I translate to make sure Shanna was included.

Maman leaned over the table and poured some celery stew on Baba's rice, catching his gaze this time. "May his soul be restful," she said.

The exchange of food and laughter continued until we finally adjourned to the living room. Through the large window, we could see that a few stars had already come out, and the air was crisp.

Baba pulled the lever of the recliner and put his feet up, resting his swollen left leg on a pillow. Before Maman brought out a pot of tea, she put a large bowl of deep red pomegranate kernels on his lap. Baba had spent five hours separating the kernels, and now he placed a spoonful of seeds into smaller bowls.

Hadi was fussing with the video camera. Like me, he wanted to document this occasion.

Zahra passed out the bowls of kernels, and I passed the salt. Maman finally stopped serving and sat down near Baba.

"I want to thank you all again for gathering together today," Baba said. "Let's all send our beloved ones a prayer or two as we think of them—especially, our elders."

After the recitation of a prayer, he raised his hand, waving it to get our attention.

"Zain is not here, and he is missed." Zain had gone back to Tajikistan to reunite with his new family, with the plan to return to serve his house arrest. "As you know, we have others who also are not here tonight, at least in body." Baba looked over at Maman, who was rubbing her hands together, her eyes glued to the sugar cubes on the coffee table.

I looked at Hadi as Baba's tone shifted and deepened.

"As you all know, I was in the hospital 11 times this year. It is a fact that we don't know when our time will come. I may or may not be here with you all next year." Hadi looked over at me.

"And as I age now, I have a desire to talk about my life, to make my wishes known, and connect with you."

We all stopped eating and gave him our full attention. Khaleh wrung her hands and bit her lips nervously. The room went silent.

"I've attempted to live a life of service," Baba said, looking up without focusing anywhere in particular. "All of my efforts have been based on my belief that these life choices and good deeds might fill my suitcase when I travel to the other side."

Maman looked up at Baba, a worried look on her face, her eyebrows knit together.

Baba gave tender gaze. "You all know I'm married to an angel. I owe her my life for the wealth of experiences we've had together."

Maman put her head down and looked up at Baba with a shy smile—the same one I imagine she gave him when they first met.

"And you all also know, we lost our son 30 years ago." The air went cold. No one had ever spoken so directly. Baba didn't pause.

"Of course, he is in a better place, away from worldly needs. He was unjustly taken from us, too suddenly and too early." He paused for a moment. "I made a fatal mistake all those years ago when he was here, and I've made many more since. I'm old now, and I don't have anything to give except my love and prayers—and to do good on your behalf so that you might travel well when you go to the afterlife."

Maman was silent, her hands neatly in her lap. She smiled and softly spoke the Arabic prayer for Abdollah as Baba recited it loudly.

Finally, everyone joined in. Hadi and I smiled and reached for each other's hands, and then moved toward Iman.

Maman got up and poured fresh tea in the small glasses that had traveled with us from Iran three decades ago. Zahra brought out the roulette cake and put it on the table. She walked over to Baba and stood behind him with her hand on his shoulder, winking at me. Baba reached up and pulled her hand toward him, gently planting a kiss on her forehead.

I looked up at Abdollah's picture, and this time, I met his gaze.

ABDOLLAH

❧❧

AUGUST 24, 2011

Dear Zain, Salaam,

The birth of your son is the single most significant event in my life. The realization came to me once I had a chance to visit you in Thailand. I'm glad you moved there with your wife. It's so beautiful, and I can see you are at peace there. I know that Maman and Baba will feel the same renewal and energy when they visit you. I trust it will help them move forward, and for that, I'm grateful. You have made a huge contribution to the family, and I hope this new challenging adventure fulfills you forever.

Thank you for naming your son "Abdollah."

Love you always,

Your brother,

Hadi—formerly known as Todd. Yeah, that's right. I've reclaimed myself, and my name.

Some months later, in Thailand, Maman and Baba were reveling in their visit with their two-year-old grandson. My parents wanted to connect him to all of us, at home in America.

"Stay still for one second, *azizam,*" Baba begged as he tried to take Abdollah's little shirt off. "*Aab-bazi*—bath time is coming," he said, offering up his grandson's latest favorite activity.

Maman held on tight to the iPhone as she repeatedly hit the icon for the Skype camera, magnifying her nose on our screen. "Can you guys see me? I can't see you yet," she yelled.

"Move the camera back a bit and give it a second. There's a delay," Hadi repeated. Soon, Iman, Hadi, and I popped up in her phone on her side of the world.

Zahra sat on the couch, not moving toward us, still ambivalent about meeting her half brother and recently born half sister, Zohre.

"It's taken us an hour to get him ready for the shower. He runs everywhere and opens every drawer. He finds the step stool and climbs to get to the freezer for ice; he loves to chew ice." Maman was talking so fast the phone connection kept cutting her off, but her smile was constant. "Zohre, she's a little angel, so quiet, so sweet. Just like Zahra when she was a baby." Maman's smile widened, as did Zahra's.

Abdollah looked over at the camera and reached for it.

"No, *azizam,* your hands are wet. After you're done with your bath, OK?" she said to little Abdollah.

I could read the curiosity on Zahra's face as she peeked at the Skype screen.

Zain had stumbled and fallen often in life, but he had made a remarkable contribution that none of the rest of us had—one that our parents had longed for: grandchildren.

Baba had not noticed the camera, having long since gotten used to Maman documenting each moment of their visit. He was singing a familiar song to Abdollah as he lowered the pull-down showerhead, pouring water on his grandson's head.

Maman looked at the three of us on her phone. Her happiness fed ours. Every time Abdollah appeared on the screen, Hadi and Iman smiled wider and Zahra's interest grew.

Little Abdollah grabbed Baba's left index finger as he stood, letting Baba wash him. Zain's laughter rang out in the background.

Baba's eyes didn't leave Abdollah's. The familiarity of the song he was singing sent us back to the tenderest moments in our childhood. Zain appeared on the screen, standing next to the tub, singing along with Baba and Maman.

"*Baroon barooneh*—it's raining, it's raining and the ground is getting wet. Don't worry my flower, everything will be set. We'll survive this storm, we'll survive this pain . . ."

Zahra moved closer to me, now openly looking at her half brother and half sister. Hadi, Iman, and I stared at the Skype screen, our shoulders pressed together. We joined in and sang along to the song being sung across the ocean.

EPILOGUE

❧

I WAS BORN JUST AS THE ROSE HOTEL OPENED. The two of us share a common—and poignant—history. My first five years, filled with love and security, were colored by the hotel's opulence: feasts, crystal chandeliers, Persian rugs. But then came monumental loss: the great hotel that sheltered my family; a transformed homeland; and most shattering, the life of my beloved brother.

Early memories are always powerful, and although mine will continue to stay with me, they no longer have that electrifying charge they once did. In recent years, we have finally begun to heal—but, like most families, our story is constantly being revised. We remain vulnerable; often, one person feels distant from or angry at someone else. But the years have taught me that whatever discord arises will end in feasts featuring Baba's beloved pomegranate kernels.

Maman and Baba are older now. Although they physically seem smaller, their spirits still loom large—even as the caregiving is gradually being reversed. Hadi is in a serious relationship; Zain, clean and sober for many years now, is raising his two young children with his wife. Iman is divorcing; sadly, his more traditional Iranian marriage proved no stronger than that of his siblings. In the end, neither his goodness nor aptitude for self-sacrifice could shelter him from heartbreak. Maybe the four of us are products of our time—or, perhaps, we are especially vulnerable because of the loss we experienced.

My family showed tremendous courage and trust by sharing their darkest moments with me as I wrote this book. In reading our story, perhaps you may find that you recognize in us characters from your own life. It is my hope that you have come to see my family as I do: imperfect, brave, resilient, and beautiful.

In the time since we left Iran, our homeland has become alien to us; historically, it was a tolerant and predominantly peaceful nation. In the last 35 years, Iran has weathered the hostage crisis in November 1979, the death of Ayatollah Khomeini, the Iran-Iraq war, and the Green Movement. As I write, I am hopeful about the possibility of a reconnection with the wider world. But the true spirit of Iran has, in a sense, been lost since the revolution—lost but not forgotten, like my brother Abdollah.

Since writing this book, I have moved to New York City, where I am in a private practice as a family and couples psychologist specializing in trauma. My work has taught me how crucial autobiographical storytelling can be to healing, and it has inspired me to branch out. My first effort, *Glass Houses*—an interactive hybrid of theater and therapy—helps audiences to transcend the barriers of experience, identity, and culture to foster growth and connection.

Starting a new life in a city I love has given me new hope and joy. The past is still powerful, but I have emerged from its shadows. I was once a little girl who played hide-and-seek in a great hotel. Now, I no longer hide.

ACKNOWLEDGMENTS

My deepest love and gratitude to my Maman and Baba, whose love and dedication gave me the heart to know compassion and commitment: Baba, who taught me to fight for life with unwavering determination, and Maman, whose courage and selflessness astonish me daily.

Much love to my four brothers whose resilience and adherence to their unique paths have taught me generosity and acceptance. To my eldest brother, my first Dadashi: *The Rose Hotel* is your story; it is written in your honor. To Hadi, thank you for encouraging me, for the surprises, and for wearing your seat belt. To Zain, who always makes me laugh and shares his Kit Kats, thank you for surviving your journey, and for finding your home. To Iman, thank you for encouraging me, even when that burden added to your already heavily laden shoulders. You have been so consistent in your love and support, and I could never have written this book without you.

To my mentor, friend, and fellow writer, Laura Shaine Cunningham, thank you for believing in my book and coaching me to become a better writer—and for being there, day and night, until the work was completed. Your generosity moves me. On behalf of my family and myself, thank you. I am fortunate to have you as my friend.

To my steadfast agent and marvelous friend, Melissa Flashman, thank you for commitment and enthusiasm, which made this publication a reality.

To my editors at National Geographic, being held in your loving hands has been a marvel. Special gratitude to Hilary Black for taking on *The Rose Hotel,* and to Anne Smyth for her tireless efforts.

I don't know how to thank Dr. John Caffaro, whose impact in my life goes beyond words. It is because of his support and guidance that I am living a fulfilled life with relief from past burdens, and the clarity and ability to contribute to the world. His generosity toward me over the last 16 years has been boundless, and his talent is admirable. The course of my life, and that of my family, has been forever changed by his contributions.

A bouquet of flowers to all my friends, supporters, and kindred spirits—old and new—who have made this ride spectacular. You have been critical to the makings of *The Rose Hotel.*

With gratitude,
Rahimeh Andalibian

New York City
May 2014

"All persons are caught in an inescapable network of mutuality, tied in a single garment of destiny. I can never be what I ought to be until you are what you ought to be."
Martin Luther King, Jr.

READING GUIDE

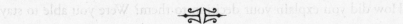

What did you learn from this account of the Iranian revolution? Have any of your perceptions of Iran or of Muslim life changed?

Among the challenges the Andalibians faced was adapting to British and then American culture. What insights did their journey give you into the immigrant experience?

Each family member grieved the loss of Abdollah in his or her own way. What were the impacts of the different coping styles?

Which family member most resonated with you and why?

To which scene did you have the strongest emotional reaction? What thoughts and feelings came up for you?

In times of tragedy, children are often "protected" from the truth. Do you think Baba and Maman's decision to hide Abdollah's death from his siblings was the right one at the time?

What were your impressions of Baba and Maman's relationship? What do you see as the strengths and the weaknesses?

What do you think of Rahimeh's decision to wear her head scarf at the age of six? Her decision to take it off in her 20s?

What do you think of Baba's reaction to Rahimeh's removal of her head scarf and decision to marry outside her culture and religion? Think of a choice you've made with which your loved ones disagreed. How did you explain your decision to them? Were you able to stay connected with them?

After suffering the loss of Abdollah, the Andalibians nearly lost their other sons to a different kind of revolution in California. How does the family begin to heal?

Have you experienced trauma or an especially difficult period in your life? What about a significant conflict with someone you love? If there was resolution, how was it achieved?

One of the themes in *The Rose Hotel* is family secrets and the shame and guilt that often accompany them. Think about your own family: What secrets do you share? Have they ever been addressed? What would happen if the secrets were brought out into the open?

The Rose Hotel is also about the impact of social and political events on the day-to-day life of one family. Consider your own history: What broader events have influenced you and your family on a personal level (for example, presidential policies, cultural traumas, recessions)?

What does this book say to you about religion, politics, and power?

What universal truths can you find in this book?

ABOUT THE
AUTHOR

RAHIMEH ANDALIBIAN WAS BORN IN TEH-
RAN and moved with her family to California
in 1979, at the onset of the Iranian revolution.
Raised and educated in Los Angeles, she is a
writer and clinical psychologist who since 2012
has been living and practicing in New York
City, where she specializes in intergenerational
family therapy. A dynamic speaker and a savvy, promotion-driven
author, she appears frequently at conferences and has promoted the
book on Martha Stewart Living Radio and BlogHer.